HIGH ACHIEVER

By the same author

HIGH ACHIEVER

The Life and Climbs
of Chris Bonington

JIM CURRAN

CONSTABLE · LONDON

First published in Great Britain 1999
by Constable and Company Limited
3 The Lanchesters, 162 Fulham Palace Road
London W6 9ER

Copyright © Jim Curran 1999
ISBN 00 94 79280 1

Typeset in Linotype Sabon 11pt by
Rowland Phototypesetting Ltd
Bury St Edmunds, Suffolk
Printed in Great Britain by
St Edmunsbury Press Ltd
Bury St Edmunds, Suffolk

A CIP catalogue record for this book
is available from the British Library

For Hugo

CONTENTS

LIST OF ILLUSTRATIONS

between pages 172 and 173

All photographs not otherwise credited come from the Chris Bonington photo library

ACKNOWLEDGEMENTS

It GOES WITHOUT saying that in order to write this book I have had to rely heavily on the co-operation and help of many people and I found tremendous enthusiasm from virtually everyone I spoke to. If they have not been quoted directly they may be assured that it was the combined views of dozens of willing climbers, friends and occasionally total outsiders who gave me the confidence to attempt to describe the life of Britain's most successful mountaineer.

First and foremost, of course, I must thank Chris Bonington for his backing and support for the book and for giving me access to anything I wanted from his own records. His wife, Wendy, two sons, Daniel and Rupert, and half-brother, Gerald were no less supportive, and I must particularly thank Helen Bonington, Chris's mother, for her unique descriptions of her son's childhood. I would also like to single out Lord Hunt who, only months before his death, made the time to spend a morning giving me the benefit of both his wisdom and his memories. My apologies must go to Lady Hunt for taking up so much of his time, but both John and Joy made my visit a special one. Thanks also to Reinhold Messner, who generously wrote the Foreword at very short notice, for which I am extremely grateful.

At home in Sheffield, my Luddite ignorance of new technology causes me to write everything longhand in ever more illegible scrawl. This has been salvaged by Serys O'Connor, who not only became quite brilliant at deciphering and typing it, but has also made many valuable suggestions and improvements. To her go my special thanks. Good friends have encouraged and supported me through all the various ups and downs of the book's gestation, particularly Geoff and Jackie Birtles, Hilary Nunn, Pam Beech, Pam Gleadall, Rita Davies, Joe Simpson, Gill Round and Terry Gifford. And, of course, now enjoying her new independence in the Gower Peninsula is my long-standing, long-suffering editor, Maggie Body, who for

xii ACKNOWLEDGEMENTS

the fourth time has given the book the benefits of all her hard-earned knowledge and expertise. My thanks also to Carol O'Brien at Constable for having the confidence in me to commission the book in the first place.

No less important are the many people I have interviewed or consulted or who have helped in a whole variety of ways: Martin and Maggie Boysen, Tut Braithwaite, Joe and Val Brown, Les Brown, Ginger Cain, Charlie and Ruth Clarke, Maria Coffey, Frances Daltrey, Dennis Davis, Vicki Elcoate, Carolyn Estcourt, Patrick Fagan, Bernard Farmer, Jim Fotheringham, Geoff Francis, Dennis Gallway, Peter Gillman, George Greenfield, Brian Hall, Sheila Harrison, Richard Haszko, David Hellings, Glynn Hughes, Allen Jewhurst, Ned Kelly, Robin Knox-Johnston, Alison Lancaster, Chris Lister, Graham Little, Jim Lowther, Hamish MacInnes, Ian McNaught-Davis, Tony Moulam, Victor Saunders, Doug Scott, Pertemba Sherpa, Mike Thompson, Margaret Trinder, Stephen Venables, Derek Walker, Ken Wilson, Louise Wilson.

Quotation from Chris Bonington's own books is made by permission of his agent, Curtis Brown. Individual publishers are acknowledged in the bibliography. Quotation from the prose and verse of Tom Patey is made by permission of the Orion Publishing Group.

To all the above, and to anyone I may have forgotten, my most sincere thanks.

Jim Curran
Sheffield, May 1999

FOREWORD

by REINHOLD MESSNER

THERE IS NO doubt that without Chris Bonington British mountaineering would have developed differently in the second half of this century. And it would have been less successful. Bonington has again and again been a determined innovator who has brought together the best in British mountaineering.

As it was the inspiration of Joe Brown and Don Whillans which linked the UK climbers of the 'fifties with leading exponents in the Alps, so it was above all thanks to the single-mindedness of Chris Bonington that the high standard of British mountaineering in Patagonia, the Himalaya and the Karakoram came to expression.

Too late for first ascents of Everest and Kangchenjunga, he devised and organised a series of remarkable ventures. Bonington made his international name as leader of the Annapurna South Face expedition which put the climbing legends Don Whillans and Dougal Haston on the top. With this pioneering feat and his style of leadership British mountaineering was in 1970 once again decisive in the future development of Himalayan climbing.

Bonington not only found methods of financing his expeditions and organising media coverage, he knew how to concentrate strengths so that the hitherto impossible became possible. He brought together the most capable mountaineers of the time from the English-speaking world and he led his operation, climbing at the front as often as possible, or ascended high with a heavy rucksack in order to take care of the lead rope. That he let Whillans and Haston go ahead on the Annapurna summit approach has nothing to do with weakness, all to do with wisdom. It belonged to his style of leadership. It is not for nothing that we call their line up the three-kilometre high Annapurna South Face the Bonington Route today.

Chris Bonington, who is also a photographer, journalist and

accomplished lecturer, has devoted his whole life to climbing. He still climbs to an extreme standard today. At least once a year he is off on an expedition. In the course of half a century he has made first ascents in England, the Alps, the Himalaya, the Karakoram, Greenland, Patagonia and the Antarctic. This creativity seems to recognise no limitations of age – he continues to climb further and further. Bonington has not only assimilated a rich tradition, he has built his own wisdom and his personal experience of fear and joy into it, creating a unity that makes him a personification of contemporary mountaineering.

Chris Bonington chases neither records not grades. He belongs to a rare group of people who lead the way and can walk by themselves – still maintaining the awe and inquisitiveness of a child. He has been an extreme mountaineer for fifty years and he still appears enviably young. Between the first ascent of the Frêney Pillar on Mont Blanc and summiting Everest at fifty he has diversified his role, as alpinist and expedition leader. After his successful Everest South-West Face expedition in 1975 he devoted himself to small expeditions and in so doing achieved great things.

What fascinates me personally about Bonington? Firstly, he has never been a grade fetishist, nor a pontificator. He has never been out for records. His personality is not to be measured by comparison with others. It is the sum total of knowledge, suffering, character. Bonington has stature. He has earned his title.

Reinhold Messner
Juval, April, 1999

HIGH ACHIEVER

Badger Hill

· 1 ·

Home Ground

THE EASIEST WAY to Chris and Wendy Bonington's Lakeland home is to turn off the M6 at exit 41 and follow the almost straight B5305 north-west for about five miles. The countryside is flat, and the distant views of the rounded Northern Fells, outposts of the Cumbrian hills, look more like the Pennines than the Lake District. Village names are brusque and grudging: Hutton, Skelton and Unthank. Near the last is a mass of radio masts. It is easy to imagine that they are Bonington's own private communication centre to the outside world. Past these a minor road leads to Hesket Newmarket, a small collection of rather twee cottages, set round a tiny village green. The pub, the Old Crown serves excellent home-cooked food, including the perennial Bonington favourite, 'a really good curry'. Over the years it has been the meeting place for many pre-expedition gatherings. Above the village it is best to drive slowly up the narrow lanes to avoid a sudden encounter with a tractor, or worse, a Bonington. Although the height gain is minimal, the landscape changes as the lane leads up to a cluster of farmhouses at Nether Row. The rolling hillside of High Pike is quite close and Badger Hill itself, just up a narrow track, is almost at its foot. More often than not a stiff breeze blows from the west. In winter it can be a bleak spot.

If it is a weekday there will be several cars scattered on the verges outside the house, including a large, fairly new estate car normally in urgent need of a car wash. It will probably be crammed with what at first glance looks like the sound equipment of a medium-sized pop group. This actually is the newest state-of-the-art digital projection and sound system for public lectures and business presentations. The high-tech theme continues in the offices occupying the upper floor of one side of the L-shaped converted farmhouse. Computers hum gently, keyboards click, international phone calls are fielded, slides are catalogued and, in the middle of all this, Chris Bonington himself presides over his domain.

'Hi there!' he will greet you, sounding uncannily like TV presenter Anneka Rice. He looks much younger than his sixty-four years. He is obviously extremely fit, yet his upper body is surprisingly slight (he was unimpressed when a journalist once unkindly described him as flabby). His legs and upper thighs are well developed and powerful. It is an ideal frame for a Himalayan climber, perhaps not so much so for a high standard rock climber. He will be dressed casually in T-shirt and jeans and a fibre-pile sweater. In a collar and tie or, even worse, a formal suit, his whole personality seems to change and the public face of Sir Chris Bonington is revealed. Serious, slightly wary, occasionally authoritarian, it is a transformation that takes some getting used to. Even his closest friends can get the same distant treatment when they least expect it. At ease in his study, and despite fielding the frequent interruptions of phone calls and queries from his secretaries Louise or Margaret, who work alternate days, Chris will ramble happily, eagerly catching up on climbing gossip. He is convinced he is out of touch in this far-flung corner of England, even though he is constantly travelling up and down the country.

Inevitably he will demonstrate some new bit of computer gadgetry, or describe the climb he did yesterday, or the Alpine Club meeting he chaired last night in London before catching the overnight sleeper back to Carlisle. Whatever it is, superlatives flow as you become immersed in the Bonington machine. 'Enthusiasm' is a word that this biographer will try not to overuse in the forthcoming pages but it is not easy: the man exudes it; it is the word most frequently employed to describe him in dozens of interviews. It was what Wendy noticed on the first day that she met him.

Often the purpose of one's visit is forgotten or put off, for if the weather is half-decent Chris will look round with a conspiratorial air and suggest a quick climb. Of course he has to be back in time to do a radio interview, catch a train, meet a journalist. There is always something pressing, but Chris works on the principle of fitting just a bit more into each day than it will actually hold.

If there is time he will drive into the heart of the Lake District – Borrowdale, Thirlmere or even further afield to Wasdale or Langdale. Conversation will continue non-stop with plenty of evidence of his legendary ability to think with his mouth open. Possible venues are considered and discarded, though often Chris will already have his own sports plan. With what he will probably consider to be gentle, even subtle, persuasion, you will be lured into attempting a climb that will invariably be significantly harder than you would normally choose. 'You can second an E1, I'm sure.' Chris will flatter and cajole and, unless his crafty advances are firmly spurned, it is all too easy to embark on a climb two or three grades higher than you hoped. If, of course, you are climbing better than Chris is, he will probably persuade you to take him up something too hard for him. Inevitably the proposed climb will be over-ambitious and take too long.

At the foot of his chosen climb he quickly sorts out his rack of slings, nuts and Friends, ties onto the double climbing ropes, and sets off into his own domain. He climbs purposefully and with little wasted effort. Suddenly he is completely focused. As the climb gets harder he talks to himself: 'Come on, Bonington, get a grip – you know you can do this.' His technique is direct and uncomplicated – reach up, pull, step up, repeat the process. Despite the range of gear he carries, Chris places protection only sparingly. Is his confidence misplaced? No; he climbs quickly and the difficult section is quickly behind him. Now on easier ground he revels in the fluid movement and is quite happy to run the rope out to the belay. It is an impressive sight. If he doesn't have the gymnastic ability of younger rock athletes, the languid effortlessness of a climber like Martin Boysen, or the technical cunning of Joe Brown, it is still a class performance. Here, in his element, it is hard to see him queuing for his pension next year.

Like many top climbers, Chris Bonington finds it difficult to understand why lesser mortals find it hard to follow him. His advice is encouraging but often slightly vague: 'You can do it – you're doing fine, just reach up with your left hand, no, your *left* hand, oh, sorry, I meant right hand; one more move and you've done it.

– I'm sure I put my foot higher up, perhaps not – gosh, just hang on there a minute and I'll take a photograph . . .'

The best thing about doing a climb with Chris Bonington is that it's just like climbing with anyone else. This is not a throwaway statement. He is perhaps what many ordinary climbers would like to be – bold, thrusting, committed, but still human, still in some ways vulnerable. Of course he's good, very good, but it is the sort of ability that's easy to understand. 'Mystique' is not a word that applies to Chris Bonington. By the time the climb is finished it will be later than Chris thinks and a rapid return will be made.

If time is really short, a visit to Chris's traversing wall is the only option. This is a low yellow limestone wall set just behind a farmyard about three miles away from Badger Hill. Chris thinks it is one of the world's great pieces of rock, and shows it off with proprietorial pride. To a newcomer it is an unimpressive little crag set above a sea of cow dung and often guarded by a bull. The purpose is simply to traverse the wall from end to end and to avoid falling into the mire. Chris, of course, knows every move and swings along in great style, feigning surprise when on a first visit you hesitate or fall off. After half an hour fingers and arms ache and Chris, who has won his little game hands down, is exultant. 'Never mind, you're climbing *really* well' he enthuses, rubbing the fact in that you are not. Then it's back to Badger Hill, where Wendy has returned from her work as a teacher of the Alexander Technique or, more likely these days, from her latest passion, a round of golf. They greet one other with uninhibited affection and each will give an account of their day as if they have only just met. It is a remarkable relationship and Chris knows full well that Wendy is the one in a million who can cope with the Bonington lifestyle. He is away for at least two or three months every year on expeditions and in between does a constant round of lectures, business presentations and charity work. He is a workaholic (though paradoxically he will describe himself as basically lazy).

At home Chris shares Wendy's long commitment to vegetarianism; though if a pub meal is decided on he is as likely to choose a steak. He drinks sparingly, claiming that alcohol gives him chronic pain in his neck and shoulder, though this could also be stress-related as it seems to occur when he has taken on too many commitments and indulged in a drink or two to unwind.

Chris and Wendy are not night owls and Chris is invariably the first to leave a gathering. But he is a ferociously early riser and, at home or on an expedition, will often have done a couple of hour's work before breakfast. He is also at his sharpest and most decisive in the early morning, which gives him a huge advantage in expedition-planning meetings often held at an unearthly hour of the morning before the average climber is more than semi-conscious.

Away from the office and its massed banks of high-tech equipment the rest of the house is unpretentious: paintings, musical instruments and mementoes are much in evidence. They are there for the Boningtons' own pleasure, not for show. True, there are rocks from the summits of Everest and Kongur inscribed and preserved in polished Perspex, but they are casually displayed, as is the ice axe Chris took to Everest in 1985. Overflowing bookcases line the open-plan kitchen and sitting room. The books are well thumbed for the Boningtons are avid readers. The house has a fair smattering of cats and dogs. The cats seem to change each time you visit, but the current are Sensi, inherited when their eldest son Daniel moved with his Australian wife Jude to Sydney, and Jessica, who replaces Bella and Bodie, for many years the Boningtons' treasured pets.

The overwhelming feeling of Badger Hill is that this is home. There is absolutely no chance of the Boningtons moving – it has played too large a part in both Chris and Wendy's lives. They belong there and the house belongs to them. And yet for the first forty years of his life Chris Bonington lived a strangely rootless, even nomadic existence. It was a lifestyle that had echoes of both his father and grandfather who were confirmed wanderers. Where you lived was not really important, it was what you did that mattered.

How then did Chris Bonington's journey unfold, from Hampstead to Caldbeck, from Harrisons Rocks to the Eiger and Everest, from High Pike to the endless Tibetan Plateau? It has not been an easy ride: for all the triumphs there have been many tragedies. What may seem like a ruthless progression of summits, books, films and lectures has been punctuated by setbacks, self-doubt and not a few controversies. Bonington ventures have sometimes been a target for critics and his very success has provoked jealousy, even scorn. His life has been a wonderfully complex medley of adventure, creativity, love, loss and, eventually, a rare fulfilment.

45 Downshire Hill

· 2 ·

An Only Child

ON 6TH AUGUST 1934 a young recently married secretary, Helen Anne Bonington, gave birth to a son in the Elizabeth Garrett Anderson Hospital in Hampstead, North London. The baby was baptised Christian John Storey Bonington in St Mary's Catholic church in Holly Place, Hampstead. Mother and baby returned to her husband in an unprepossessing bed-sitting room and kitchenette in Heath Hurst Road, a terrace of tall red brick gabled Victorian houses. Just around the corner is Keats' House where the Romantic poet had written 'Ode to a Nightingale' in 1819.

The arrival of the boy was received with unbounded joy by his grandmother, Winifride Storey, who had always longed for a son of her own, but there is little doubt that his birth pushed Helen Bonington's marriage to her husband Charles closer to the brink.

It had been an ill-suited match from the beginning. Helen Storey was born in 1910 in Wallasey on the Wirral Peninsula overlooking Liverpool sprawling on the other side of the River Mersey. She was the product of a middle-class Catholic family and duly went to Notre Dame High School in Liverpool. She won three scholarships and was accepted at Oxford University to read English at Somerville, the first girl from Notre Dame to go any further afield than Liverpool University. For her, the journey down to Oxford with her mother for her interview was the furthest south she had ever been.

In later life Helen Bonington outlined a possible book, to be called A *Mother and Son*, based on her notes, journals and diaries which she seems to have kept rather erratically from her Oxford days onwards. They give a curiously cool and dispassionate account of her relationship with her son.

At Oxford she was among the first wave of female state scholars, 'blue stockings', to penetrate the almost exclusive ranks of male public school privilege. She lived in St Austin's, a Catholic women's hostel with strict chaperone rules. Undergraduates were required to be in by 9 p.m. and a special late leave was valid only until 11. She dreaded 'the torture of dinner with its complex array of cutlery and variety of dishes'. Nevertheless she was 'taken up' by second- and third-year undergraduates who nicknamed her The Captain of the Fifth and introduced into 'the snobbish society of St Austin's and its often bizarre sexual life'.

At the annual St Austin's dance she met one Charles Bonington, also a fresher, from Brasenose College. He, judging from her enigmatic notes at the time, proceeded to lead her astray. Together with a friend Eleanor Martin she accompanied Charles and one of his friends to a dinner at Brimpton Grange, a forbidden hotel in the Oxfordshire countryside. Their car broke down and they were late back to St Austin's. At the Commem Ball Helen got drunk 'for the first and last time'. It all reads like a St Trinian's film script.

Because of these, and presumably other untold transgressions, Winifride Storey was asked to remove her daughter from St Austin's and the following academic year she took up new accommodation in a large blue-carpeted attic in a Victorian house in North Oxford, overlooking the Parks. It belonged to Mr Carr, a former don but now an invalid. His wife ran the house and was a confirmed social and intellectual snob. She had known Lewis Carroll as a child and her own daughter – named Alice – suffered from anorexia. Perhaps it is not too hard to guess why. The house was grubby and the food poor compared with St Austin's.

Helen's friendship with Charles Bonington continued amidst a typically undergraduate social life of parties, cinema, riding, rowing and punting. At the end of her second year Helen returned to Wallasey, by now finding it unbearably smug and provincial. Her father, Francis Storey, had been a doctor with the Colonial Medical Service in West Africa. He had been retired early, apparently with a drink problem, and was then urged by his wife to get a job as a ship's doctor and played little part in the family life. Helen persuaded her mother to move to London, a fairly radical decision and one that her father didn't appear to have anything to do with.

Before the move south Charles Bonington was invited up to Wallasey where he and Helen bathed daily in the River Mersey. This, in the early 'thirties with Liverpool Docks, then the largest port in Europe, in full swing just across the river, seems an extraordinarily risky thing to do to us environmentally-conscious softies, but they apparently suffered no ill effects. Back at Oxford Helen's work *did* suffer. She recalls attending only one lecture during her three years and frequently cut tutorials. She claimed an almost complete ignorance of Anglo-Saxon but somehow managed to scrape by, unlike Charles who was sent down.

Charles Bonington was the product of an extraordinary father and a mother who was so wrapped up in her husband's life that she had little love left for her children. Maximilian Christian Bonington was born in Germany in Schleswig-Holstein in 1874. His family name was originally Bonig (this explains the one 'n' in Bonington), and he claimed to be of Danish extraction, which seems quite reasonable, given that Denmark abuts the German border above Schleswig-Holstein and Christian is a common Danish name. With this knowledge it is tempting to see in his grandson Chris, the fair complexion, blue eyes and high cheekbones that point to Northern European origins.

The Bonig family owned a shipyard building sailing ships but young Maximilian, unhappy and unloved, ran away to sea and spent several years before the mast experiencing a wide variety of adventures. These included rounding the Horn, jumping ship in Nova Scotia, serving in the US Marines, deserting, and joining another ship which was wrecked off Cape Hatteras in North Carolina, Maximilian managing to swim ashore through the storm. Eventually he ended up in India. In Bombay he somehow secured a commission in the Royal Indian Marine. He was serving in the troopship *Warren Hastings* when it too was wrecked off Mauritius. With very little hope of survival he went below to secure the watertight doors. For his courage he was awarded a permanent billet in the dockyard in Bombay.

He became a British citizen and was offered a post in the then penal colony of the Andaman Islands in the Bay of Bengal, and it was there that Charles and his sister Marjorie were born. Initially Maximillian's brief was to establish a shipyard there but he later transferred to the Forestry Service and became officer in charge of the Aborigines. These tribes of pygmies were in danger of extinction from various punitive expeditions but Maximilian Bonington worked enormously hard on their behalf to save them. He also made a comprehensive survey of both the Andaman and the nearby Nicobar Islands. In 1947 he was awarded the Order of the British Empire and on his eventual retirement settled in Ireland with his wife.

None of this odd lifestyle left much time for his children who were packed off to England at an early age. Helen identified Charles's problems with his childhood: 'I suspect that the two elder Bonington children identified themselves in many ways with the aboriginal Andamanese, with whom they grew up. Marjorie and Charles were then wrenched from the primitive islands they knew and submitted to the strict and often unfeeling life of Catholic preparatory schools in this country . . . The results of this uprooting were clearly marked in Charles. His dependence on alcohol, his boasting, his evasiveness and the myths in which he lived are all suggestive of a virtual aborigine torn from his surroundings and forced into an alien civilisation.' Though it seems quite reasonable to assume a disturbed and fragmented childhood could lead to these problems, the analogy with the plight of the aborigines seems slightly far-fetched.

When Charles was sent down from Oxford his father managed to wangle him a job in Burma. Helen scraped 'an undeserved third' and moved to London with Winifride. Mother and daughter rented a flat in Frognal and Helen, bemoaning the fact that female graduates received absolutely no career advice from Oxford, took a secretarial course and found herself a job at *The Times* Book Club, from which she was soon dismissed. She quickly found another, this time at Ward's Book Shop in Baker Street, and set about the often bewildering task of finding her feet in London.

She had kept up 'a warm correspondence' with Charles who quickly became disillusioned with life in Burma and took the rather extreme measure of shooting himself through the shoulder in order to return home. Supported by his father with an allowance of £4 a week, he settled in Hampstead and resumed his romance with

Helen. In early November 1933, without telling their respective parents, they married in Kensington Registry Office. Within two months Helen was expecting a baby.

It was not an easy pregnancy. Helen developed an acute kidney complaint and was taken into Hampstead's Royal Free Hospital where she was put on something called a Ketogenic diet consisting mainly of 'meat and a great deal of fat'. Her mother who was a strict vegetarian persuaded her to discharge herself and stay with her for a time, living mainly on 'a huge intake of blackcurrant juice and a great deal of milk'. Despite these dietary extremes her pregnancy was unharmed and she moved into the bedsit with Charles in Heath Hurst Road. She wrote, 'in spite of our economic and other problems Charles and I are in love and very happy.' But Charles seemed reluctant or incapable of finding work. Helen listed his plusses and minuses: 'Physical courage; longing for travel and adventure; charm and gentleness, beautiful speaking voice.' But on the other hand there was: 'Immaturity, inability to distinguish day dreams from reality, laziness, heavy drinking.' She also quoted a limerick written about Pisces characters (Charles was born in February) which she felt summed him up pretty accurately.

> Compassionate, sensitive Pisces,
> May flinch from emotional crises.
> His personal chink
> Is a fondness for drink,
> And a longing to sail on the high seas.

By now worried and guilty about their registry office wedding, Helen insisted on having the marriage blessed in a Catholic church and this was performed at St Mary's, where the baby would later be baptised.

From the day of Christian's birth (Helen invariably calls him by his full name) Winifride became 'Nan', not just to the baby but the whole family. Helen seemed unprepared mentally and physically for her son's arrival and couldn't stop him crying day and night. They were given notice to leave the bedsit in Heath Hurst Road and found a small furnished basement flat in a cottage on the edge of Hampstead Heath. Charles still showed no inclination to work and stayed in bed all day. Helen, tired and fraught, had great difficulty getting baby and pram up and down the stone steps to the flat.

When he was only three weeks old Helen put Christian into a day nursery and managed to land a job working as a part-time secretary to Berta Ruck, the Welsh novelist.

Berta Ruck was at that time a well known and popular author. She probably epitomised the slightly Bohemian attractions of Hampstead life in the 1930s to which Helen had been drawn. She wrote two novels a year for, and about, young girls; had been to art college in London (the Slade) and Paris, and was a friend of Virginia Woolf. She swam every day in the Ladies' Pond on Hampstead Heath and worked standing up at a chest-high desk to keep her figure. Helen however had to sit on the floor with her typewriter balanced on her knees. Berta Ruck was often short of money and, despite the novelty of working for a minor celebrity, Helen's job didn't last long. She became increasingly tired and overwrought. By Christmas the rows with Charles had become unbearable:

> Charles and I quarrel over money and in the heat of the moment, I hit him on the head with a poker. He bleeds profusely and is unconscious. I drag him to the bathroom and let cold water from the old-fashioned geyser spout over his head. Convinced I have killed him, I rush to the nearest telephone box, my blouse and shirt red with blood. I tell Nan the situation and wait beside the kiosk until she arrives. We return to the cottage but our flat is empty. Charles has disappeared and does not come back for several days.

Not surprisingly the incident proved to be the last straw, and realising the impossibility of continuing a marriage in which she was the wage-earner, Helen returned to her mother, now living in a garden flat in Fitzjohns Avenue. While she looked for full-time work, Nan took more or less complete charge of Christian. Helen noticed: 'he cries much less in her expert hands but is still a hyperactive baby: he moves his cot from one side of the room to the other by vigorous movements and wrigglings. Mother tries him on Ideal Milk: this suits him and he becomes a smiling, equable child.' This experiment might raise a smile with those who know the adult Bonington who is able to eat and drink virtually everything *except* any form of processed milk for which he has an almost pathological loathing. Tea in India and Nepal is invariably made with powdered or condensed milk. Together with tea leaves and plentiful sugar, everything is boiled interminably. Expedition cooks often have a torrid time as they wrestle with a baffling notion that one of the members wants his tea black with no sugar.

In 1935 with her marriage over in all but name (they didn't actually divorce until after the war), Helen embarked on a series of full-time typing jobs, gradually increasing her pay. Charles meanwhile was once again bailed out by his father who paid for his passage to Australia, and Helen heard nothing from him for several years.

Popular myth has it that Chris Bonington was born with a silver spoon in his mouth, that he came from a privileged, if not actually upper-class, background and enjoyed a public school education, followed by officer training at Sandhurst. The truth was that he lived in rented accommodation throughout his childhood and money was always tight. Though he went to various prep schools and his secondary education was technically at a public school, it was in reality not much more than a good grammar school. Sandhurst, as we shall see, came only after a succession of setbacks and the social customs of the place were probably as unfamiliar to Bonington as those of Oxford had been to his mother.

It is tempting to look for signs of the future Chris Bonington, mountaineer and explorer, from the earliest days. It is as well to recall the words of warning from that master of mountaineering humour Tom Patey, who ridiculed the idea that the clues can be so obvious: 'Most climbers nurse secret ambitions to write a book. Invariably the story begins in the nursery where seemingly minor events are found to contain special significance: "from my earliest days I was aware of an irresistible urge to climb out of my cot. This clearly indicates that I was destined for mountaineering greatness."' With these words in mind perhaps one shouldn't take too seriously Helen's idea that the elaborate African-style cot that had been specially made for Christian provided him with his first climbing experience. Equally, it is no reflection on his future career as a writer that when, at the tender age of eighteen months, Helen bought him the *Children's Encyclopaedia*, she should be 'so surprised at how he misused it'.

But there is one recurring theme from the Bonington childhood that might just be a clue to the future. This was his fondness for running away, apparently for no other purpose than to see what it felt like. Most very young children are cautious about straying too far from home territory and only get really lost by accident. At the age of three, however, Chris Bonington took off, accompanied by an even younger girlfriend, to explore Hampstead Heath and the wide world. They were found three hours later and taken to the local police station where Bonington caused havoc by spilling milk over the Inspector's desk and tearing up the contents of his filing cabinets. 'I must have been a nightmare of a child,' he now admits, though there doesn't seem to be a great deal of evidence to support this. However, he does seem to have been highly strung. Helen described one incident at a pantomime where a four-year-old Bonington watched *Sleeping Beauty* at the Golders Green Hippodrome. 'He is excited, bewildered and charmed as the panto begins to unfold, but when the witch appears he gives an ear-piercing shriek and I carry him outside, still screaming and sobbing with terror.'

By the mid-1930s Helen seems to have abandoned Catholicism and become more and more politically aware, flirting with, and eventually joining the Communist Party. It is not too hard to see that she held much the same sort of views that left-wing idealistic, slightly alternative, middle-class intellectuals still espouse in Hampstead to this day. In 1936 Helen joined the huge crowds in Hyde Park to welcome the Jarrow Marchers and the same year threw herself into fund-raising and propaganda activities in support of the Republican Movement in the Spanish Civil War. Two years later she describes 'marching under Trade Union Labour and Communist Party banners. We are often out on the streets in massive demonstrations, Christian perched on some comrade's shoulders, joins vigorously in the cry "Chamberlain must go."'

Christian's education started early at a local 'Health Kindergarten' in Hampstead. It was run by a German lady, Mrs Kroemer, who was obsessed with healthy feet. The children spent most of the time running naked in the garden. But Helen began to disagree with Nan's progressive, and possessive, attitude to Christian, a rift that gradually widened over the next three years.

By August 1939 war seemed inevitable. Nan and Christian were on holiday in Wallasey. Helen came to visit and felt that the proximity to Liverpool Docks made it a vulnerable target for possible bombing raids. They travelled further north to Morecambe and in wet and cold weather found bleak accommodation in a boarding house on the sea front. On a country walk they stopped for tea and heard Chamberlain's declaration of war against Germany. Helen returned to London and, when nothing much seemed to be happening Nan and Christian also came back. The expected bombing raids failed to materialise.

During the Phoney War Helen and a workmate volunteered to join the Land Army and travelled to Nantwich in Cheshire to do training at an agricultural college. They found the work exhausting and, training completed, were despatched to a farm in East Anglia for potato-picking. This was little more than forced labour and they soon ran away and returned to London. Helen meanwhile had to face the problem of what to do with the five-year-old boy, whom she felt was in unnecessary danger living in the city. She decided that boarding school was the best solution and settled on Pinewood School in Goudhurst, Kent, bribing Christian with 6d to be polite at the interview. After a week as a day-boy staying with Nan in the village hotel, he began boarding on 18th January 1940. Though he initially seemed unhappy and homesick, by the end of term he had settled down and Helen noted few signs left of the spoilt child she felt he was becoming under his grandmother's care.

By spring Chamberlain had resigned and Churchill headed a coalition government which Helen rather primly noted 'assumes dictatorial powers'. France was on the verge of falling to the might of the German army and in Kent, Miss Reid, the headmistress at Pinewood, arranged to amalgamate the school with one in Kirkby Lonsdale – Moorlands, a wonderful mock-Gothic mansion on the southern fringes of the Lake District. Helen went to Euston station to see Christian on his way north. Newsreels have immortalised the scenes of bemused evacuees in school uniform caps and mackintoshes with name cards round their necks and gas masks in boxes being shepherded onto trains to be taken away from the cities and danger.

Despite Helen receiving a pathetic letter from Christian asking her to visit him, Bonington now remembers being quite happy with his enforced move which he seems to have coped with neither better nor worse than many other children in the same boat. In some ways his isolation as an only child of a single parent was now quite normal as fathers all over the country were called up to fight. He knew that his own father had become a founder member of the SAS and had been taken prisoner in Germany early in the war. Whether or not stories of escapes from POW camps influenced the young Bonington is unclear, but at Kirkby Lonsdale he plotted and executed his boldest break out yet. Together with five or six other children they stole food for the Great Escape, including a cake that had been made especially for visiting parents. Once again the escape had no particular purpose and certainly wasn't an attempt to go home. They wandered off and spent the day exploring the country-side around the school. As night fell they tried to sleep in trees because they were frightened of animals, but soon realised that they were extremely uncomfortable. Slowly and without any discussion they found themselves drifting back towards the school where they were caught in the beam of the headlights of a frantic headmistress combing the countryside to find them. Their punishment was to miss a visit to the theatre, and Bonington still has a memory of the miscreants sitting in dressing gowns in Matron's room sipping hot drinks in front of a flickering fire while she told them stories.

Eventually Helen managed to visit Christian and Nan in the holidays. They were staying at Windermere and she gave Christian a clockwork tank: 'Expressing his horror of machinery, he throws the key in the beck.' This did not bode well for a future Tank Commander and his mechanical dexterity has never been remark-able. At his sixth birthday party, attended by a group of evacuees, he cried because he didn't win any of the games they played.

In London the air raids started. Helen and her workmate Margo moved into a flat in Downshire Hill, Hampstead. Helen's accounts of life during the Blitz are compelling and detailed. Something simi-lar could have been written by many hundreds of thousands of people, but it is the personal minutiae which gives them their immediacy. Extracts from her diaries often reveal other conflicts:

I wake up with the sickly concussion of a bomb still shaking the bed, my bones and bowels. We go downstairs wearily and I open the back door. The clouds have vanished and the night is cold, clear and starry, with a single searchlight leaning across the sky like a luminous telegraph pole . . .

Christian writes asking for a glider and I send him one . . .

Margo and I join the [Communist] Party . . .

Home from work on 24 bus. Terminus destroyed by daytime
bomb . . .

I have half-decided that it was unwise to take out a party
card. It's hard to be honest. I get Christian's letters and absurd,
somehow touching reports on his progress in 'number', 'creative
arts' and other oddly named subjects. I feel I can't bear to inflict
further insecurity on him and that my inescapable duty is to pay
his fees, to keep him out of London and be available to see him
whenever I can.

Nan and Christian arrived unexpectedly at the flat in Downshire
Hill:

I come in to find their suitcases in the hall and a celluloid swan
in the bath. I go out, considerably disturbed, as I feel it dangerous
for him to spend a night in London. I spot him outside Dove's
[the newsagent]. He has grown very sturdy, with close-cropped,
pale flaxen hair and bright rosy cheeks. He runs to me and I kiss
him, lifting him in my arms. We go into Dove's and I buy him
a battleship . . . Nan decides to spend the night with a friend in
Hampstead . . . We fix up a bed for Christian in the shelter.

He knows all about night-raids from my letters and is delighted
to meet Maisky, the cat . . . I lie in the bunk beside Christian
and a candle burns on the ledge. The night is noisy, with guns
roaring and planes humming overhead, but he sleeps well, though
rather restlessly. The all clear sounds at dawn. I slip upstairs to
bed, leaving Christian sleeping . . . I wake to hear him sobbing
out there, in the shelter. I run out and stoop through the entrance
hole. He is sitting up in bed, crying quietly.

'What's the matter, Chris?' I ask.

He controls his tears. 'Nothing at all. I was crying for my
breakfast,' he says.

Since the outbreak of war Helen's health had not been good,
with frequent bouts of 'flu, bronchitis and chest pains. In 1941 she
was diagnosed as having TB in both lungs. She was admitted to
the King Edward VII Sanatorium near Midhurst in Sussex early in

1942. Nan took her down and left her. That night as she lay trying to sleep, 'I could feel tears rise behind my eye-lids. I was ashamed of my weaknesses and realised sadly how often Christian must have felt like this in the strange surroundings of boarding school.'

Several months later she was well enough to return to Hampstead and start part-time work again. Helen had steadily progressed from the inexperienced secretary with the typewriter balanced on her knees and was now a copywriter at the London Press Exchange, a major advertising agency. At this time it was a man's world but the men weren't there and Helen had risen quite rapidly through the ranks, handling accounts with major companies like Cadbury's and Bovril. Despite working part-time, she felt her work was going well and, more importantly, she was uplifted by the war news which, with the Battle of El Alamein and the rout of Rommell's army, heralded the turn of the tide.

Her only concern was for Christian still in remote Kirkby Lonsdale. At the beginning of the Easter term in 1943 she transferred him to St Christopher's in Hertfordshire, a progressive boarding school. At half term a letter from his housemistress said, 'He is settling down well, but inclined to be solitary.' At half term he came home: 'He looks well and heavier, but his eyes are sly and evasive. At night, his gallant pretence of happiness breaks down and he begs not to return to St Christopher's.' He had in fact been bullied quite badly and Helen decided to keep him at home for a while and engage a governess. He attended the Tavistock Clinic for a while. This was what was then known as a Child Guidance Clinic and dealt with problem children of all sorts. Helen was impressed to find that his IQ was 130 (average intelligence is measured at 100).

Helen's concern for her son brought her into head-on conflict with Nan, who resented his mother taking increasing responsibility for him. Helen still worried that his progressive education and lack of a father's control had given him many characteristics of a spoilt child.

One day she asked him, 'Are you ever invited to parties, or out to tea?'

'No, hardly ever.'

'Would you like to be?'

'You bet I would.'

'I can show you a way if you like. You just need good manners.'

'I'll give them a try.'

'OK, I'll give you a crash course and then you can check up on the results.'

This seems to have had a good effect and she decided to send him to Heysham Preparatory School in Hampstead. At his interview Miss Miles, the headmistress turned to him:

'Is there any question you would like to ask?'

'Yes, please. Do you have discipline in this school?'

'We do: a kindly but firm discipline.'

'Then I'll come,' says Christian, with decision.

He seems to have settled down happily at his new school but Helen couldn't help worrying about his future. Perhaps it was just the normal concern of an inexperienced single parent of a lonely child, or maybe there was some real cause for worry:

Chris comes in, his pale blue school cap on the back of his head, his face dirty, his fair fringe damp and streaky, giving me all the news of his day . . . I wonder often how he will develop. In these last months he has made the difficult journey back to reality, but he still dreams of a grand future in which he will be a king or a dictator and other people subservient to him. I ask flatly 'How?' and try to hammer home the adoption of working hard to achieve them . . .

Her conflict with Nan became irresolvable and she decided to end her son's relationship with his grandmother, which must have been a traumatic blow to the woman who had taken most of the day-to-day responsibilities for the first years of his life. The rift caused Helen much guilt and soul-searching. Bonington remembers 'being very confused about this. I think it was agonising in many ways. Nan had brought me up from very early on and suddenly I was told I couldn't go and see her. There was a huge gap. It was very painful but as a child you just accepted it. Nan was literally just round the corner but I never thought of going to see her. It must have really hurt her.' At the time, however, it seemed to Helen to be the right decision for them both:

As the weeks go by, Chris grows plump again. Now that the

over-close relationship with Nan has been ended, he seems to have sprung up, mentally and physically, like a retarded plant given new conditions. Instead of playing with the small children at school, he is accepted by and plays with the boys of his own age. He no longer seeks to dominate – the only emotional pattern he has ever known – but to co-operate.

Every night I dream of Nan. She stands in the dark room, rebuking me. But by day I feel an immense relief and an absurd sense that I, too, have grown and gained maturity.

Life in war-torn London struggled on with frequent bombing raids and disturbed nights spent in the Anderson shelter. Hampstead was, by comparison with the City and Docks, barely touched but in total nearly five hundred missiles and thousands of incendiary bombs fell on the area, damaging over thirteen thousand houses and causing over a thousand casualties. The worst night was in West Hampstead, when nineteen people were killed in the Mill Lane area.

Despite the war and Helen's poor health (she was still suffering frequent bouts of bronchitis and 'flu, not helped by damp cold nights in the shelter), Christmas 1943 was a happy one, chronicled in great detail in Helen's journal.

Christian goes to bed with the clock and a bicycle lamp on the floor beside him. He has instructions not to get up till six. The purple linen curtains are closed over the shutters and the Christmas tree stands before them. It is over five ft. tall and we have dressed it ceremonially, topping it with a gold bangle, as a crown, with crimson, yellow, silver and green streamers dependent from it, running round the dark tree like the ribbons on a maypole. Decorations are unobtainable, so we have stuck tiny candles into sugar cake-roses. The tree looks much prettier, we think, than a peacetime one.

When Christian is asleep, we lay out the gifts: two sets of Hornby trains – both second-hand, a frail but exquisite Arabian rifle which Margo found in an antique shop, a pile of books, a model aeroplane and a pair of fur gloves. We fill one of his skimpy utility socks with a shilling, an apple (providential find, for they are very scarce), a few battered second-hand soldiers and a magazine.

He wakes up every hour during the night, flashes his lamp on the clock and then settles back to sleep again. Just before six he gets up and I lie listening sleepily to his exclamations of pleasure, as one gift after another is examined. At seven, I go through the communicating door, put a light to the fire and admire the railway, now laid out in a pattern of great intricacy. I feel a profound happiness at this first Christmas that is wholly our own, and the war seems to be raging in an altogether different world . . .

Dinner is frugal by peacetime standards, but rich in comparison with our normal meals. We lay the pink, Basque cloth on the old kitchen table. The stone and wicker wine jars stand in their accustomed place, against the bulging wall. Margo and I have a glass of whisky each. Then comes the main course, a succulently tender leg of lamb, served with balls of mincemeat, leeks fried in batter, and mashed potato.

Christian suggests that we should drink toasts. Margo gives him a little whisky in a glass of soda-water; he stands and says gravely, 'To Helen Anne Bonington, because . . . because . . . she is so nice.'

I get up and propose, 'To Christian John Bonington, who has contributed so much to the happiness of our home.'

More toasts follow, each of us jumping up with a proposal: 'To Margo, who runs the house so well and cooks so beautifully.'

Last of all, Christian gets to his feet and with suitable solemnity says, 'To Stalin.'

1944 saw the raids on London reach a new intensity. Helen became increasingly frightened. Trying hard to hide her terror: 'We talked as cheerfully as we could, though my legs were trembling and my mouth felt dry. Once when the racket was very bad, Christian disappeared under his eiderdown. "Just like a rabbit," he said when he emerged.' She read an article in the *News Chronicle* in which a doctor recommended distractions to cope with the claustrophobia of the shelters. She took his advice and from then on poetry reading, knitting and, for Christian, drawing, became diversions, though they weren't always successful. There were a few bright interludes. It was a cold winter with frequent snow flurries and the ponds on

the Heath were frozen. One Sunday she took Christian for a walk:
'Mothers pushed prams past the coils of barbed wire that sur-
rounded the anti-aircraft guns and everywhere a peaceful life went
on.' She shared a make believe game: 'I am a German spy making
for an ammunition dump, he a Home Guard bent on shooting me.
He slunk behind trees and along ditches and I pretended not to see
his bright red face and blue eyes framed by his new balaclava.'

Though he was progressing well at school he was dogged
throughout his schooldays by a complete aversion to organised
sports, particularly ball games. In the first volume of Bonington's
autobiography, *I Chose to Climb*, he confesses, 'Games at first were
sheer purgatory. I detested cricket and was frightened of the hard
ball.'

Football wasn't much better and one Sunday he was invited to
a friend's birthday party:

When the day arrives, Martin calls in the morning and takes him
to play football on the Heath. Chris comes home to lunch, muddy
and tremulous. He limps and says he will not be able to go to
the party, as his ankle pains him. I gather that he hasn't enjoyed
the football and was frightened of another boy, who will also
be at the party. He telephoned Martin and comes downstairs,
red-faced but relieved. 'Let's not be depressed any more,' he says.

In the afternoon I take him to see the Russian film, *The Magic
Seed*, and Christian limps carefully all the way there and back.
I refuse to accept the limp, and aver there's no occasion to go
to parties if you don't want to, but there's equally no need to
deceive yourself about your reasons. Christian retorts, 'Sometimes you treat me as if I'm an old man of thirty.'

I guiltily realise that I do expect considerable self-knowledge
from him and apologise humbly.

Unfortunately, such trivial incidents awaken my memory of
Charles who so often evaded obligations by various subterfuges
and finally put a shot through his shoulder to extricate himself
from the necessity of working.

It is a curious fact that an unusually high proportion of top rank
British climbers seem to lack ability at other forms of physical
activity requiring co-ordination or ball sense. Joe Brown, Martin

Boysen and Alan Rouse are just three that spring to mind but there are many others whose obsession with an individualistic activity like climbing seems to have its roots in making up for a lack of achievement in team games. As puzzling is the number of very good all-round sportsmen who, on their first introduction to climbing, have instantly and conclusively demonstrated no aptitude whatsoever.

After a year at Heysham School Chris's behaviour seemed to have improved, though Helen noticed that his spelling was still very poor (it still is). She decided to enter him at University College Junior School in Hampstead. In wartime there was no written exam, just an interview:

When the day for this arrived, Christian and I repaired to the Junior School and were admitted to the headmaster's study. After initial greetings, I sat down in a corner of the room and Christian stood in front of the headmaster's desk. Even to my adult eye, Dr Lake was a terrifying man – tall, white-haired, and stern, with blazing dark eyes.

He asked the child a number of questions, practically none of which he could answer. Then a more personal one:

'Christian is an unusual name in this country. How did you come by it?'

'It is my grandfather's name, sir. He is called Maximilian Christian.'

'Is he British?'

'No, sir, I think he was Danish, but he became British.'

'Danish, eh! Well, Christian, my young Dane, what is the capital of Denmark?'

There was a short silence. Then, 'Belgrade, sir.'

'No.'

'Warsaw.'

'No.'

'Stockholm.'

'You're getting nearer, but you still don't know. The capital of Denmark, Master Bonington, is Copenhagen.'

Not once during this interrogation did Christian glance towards me. He stood firmly on his feet, looking the alarming Dr Lake straight in the eyes. Perhaps because of this independent

attitude the school to my surprise accepted him for the coming
autumn term.

Though it remains a public (i.e. private and fee-paying) day school
University College has little of the traditional pomp and ritual of
the great English boarding schools like Eton, Winchester or Rugby.
It was marked from its earliest days by a rejection of corporal
punishment, flexibility in teaching method and a welcoming of science subjects that were spurned by more traditional schools. The
young Bonington settled in quickly and was to stay there until 1952.

By February 1945, with the end of the war in sight, London was
subjected to the V2 rocket bombardment. For Helen, nerves frayed,
it was almost the last straw:

I wake early in the morning to the concussion of another rocket.
It must be the most awful sound that human beings have ever
heard. Something hard seems to be struck and the impact rocks
the house. A long knife of blast pierces the room as if to disem-
bowel it. Because the rocket travels faster than sound the roar
of its descent follows the crash of its explosion . . . nobody was
injured and I felt somewhat reassured. Christian was more
alarmed, as he had persuaded himself that no rocket would fall
on Hampstead. Last night he went to bed with his Indian shield
on his chest and his flintlock pistol and spear on either side.

By now aged ten, he had already experienced his first great and
enduring passion: an almost obsessive interest in military history.
He would plan and fight imaginary battles in his mind, as well as
playing war games with a large collection of toy soldiers. It was an
interest fuelled not just by the war. From the earliest stages it seemed
to have been more than merely a childish phase. Strategy and planning were involved, before the sheer fun of knocking over lead
soldiers in mock battles. It has remained an interest to the present
day. No Bonington expedition sets off without a few weighty tomes
of military history or biography and, if the lead soldiers have gone,
it is only because they have been replaced by sophisticated computer
games that are played at virtually every spare moment at Base
Camp.

Toward the end of the war the Americans liberated the POW

camp in which Charles Bonington had been incarcerated and he returned to England. At first he entertained hopes that he could resume his marriage to Helen. She felt however, that the years of separation and imprisonment had made little fundamental change in him. He wrote a long typewritten letter to his son making a number of wild suggestions that they meet in Ireland, the Hebrides or Manchester, to all of which destinations the boy would travel alone. The letter upset him and Helen wrote back saying Charles could visit him as often as he wanted in London, but the offer was not taken up, Helen noting 'a series of outings, treats and frequent disappointments for Christian when Charles fails to appear'.

Chris confirms that his father's performance left a lot to be desired: 'He took me out once or twice. I desperately wanted a father and idolised him. I remember he bought a toy submarine and an SS dagger looted from the Germans – my mother insisted on having the end blunted so that I couldn't stab anyone, or myself. But he would say he'd be taking me out and not turn up and I remember vividly being very hurt.'

At last the war ended. On VE Day Helen took Christian by bus into town to watch the celebrations in Trafalgar Square. In the evening he was awakened for more festivities: a giant bonfire, fireworks and a display of searchlights. But somehow it all failed to move him: 'He stands shivering, hands in pockets, and withdraws completely into himself . . . giving nothing, receiving nothing.'

3

Mountain Dreamer

IF THE END of the war was an anticlimax for Chris, it was much more traumatic for Helen for whom the ending of so much stress and tension, combined with intense job pressure, provoked a severe nervous breakdown. In the summer of 1946 she was admitted first to New End Hospital, then to Bethlehem Royal Mental Hospital and then to a private nursing home, Parkdene, near Uxbridge. Here she had a leucotomy, an operation severing the nerves of the frontal lobes of the brain, an operation that has since fallen out of favour.

By now Christian was twelve and had been sent on holiday to a farm in Devon that catered for children. On his return to London he was met by Nan, whom he hadn't seen for three years, and told of his mother's illness. Uprooted again, he went to live with his grandmother in a flat in Rosslyn Hill, Hampstead, where he spent the next year. By the time he moved back to Helen, he had been admitted to University College Senior School. Chris remembers that at that time money was a real problem and that in desperation Nan wrote to his father asking for a contribution towards his school fees. Charles had never before been asked for, or indeed given, a penny towards Chris's upkeep and he said he couldn't afford it, which made Chris very bitter.

Helen got a new job at a small agency in Soho, and Christian settled into the senior school: 'He seemed resigned to school life, rather than actively enjoying it. Although the school is not officially

streamed I am fairly sure that it is unobtrusively divided into two
streams and that Christian is clearly allocated to the "B" one.'
Nevertheless, by the time he was thirteen he was, by any standards,
extremely well read, for which he is eternally grateful:

> The great thing Mum did for me was introducing and encourag-
> ing me to read. I remember, when Mum got out of hospital in
> 1946, and all she could afford was a big bed-sitting room, reading
> most of the English classics – Thackeray, Dickens, a lot of the
> Brontës, Jane Austen – I never got into George Eliot – then Balzac
> and Tolstoy – I've read *War and Peace* twice; the first time I was
> about thirteen. After that practically all my reading was military
> history – it still is.

Looking back, Bonington is not sure whether the war itself had
much influence on his reading matter:

> I was more interested in the Napoleonic Wars and the American
> Civil War. The irony of all this was that when I eventually got
> into the sixth form and started getting interested in politics I
> inherited Mum's interest in Communism. Mum was typical of
> those bourgeois idealistic intellectuals who blinded themselves to
> what Stalin was doing and it was the same for me. The trouble
> was that walking round the Heath dreaming of leading armies
> into battle didn't square very well with joining the Young Com-
> munist League. They were so bloody dreary and their meetings
> were so boring. So in parallel with going round collecting Peace
> Petition signatures, I was still fighting these battles in my mind,
> imagining I was a general.

Until he went to the UCS Upper School he had never been able to
share this obsession with anyone else. One evening he confided in
his mother.
   'I'm considering making a new friend at school.'
   'Who is he?'
   'A boy called David Hellings, but I haven't decided about him
yet.'
   'What makes you hesitate?'
   'I want to make sure first by watching him and getting to know

what he's like. He's clever, but we've got a lot in common.'

In the event a favourable decision was made and their friendship has continued to the present day. David Hellings still lives in Hampstead, in the house his parents used to own, and in which he and Chris used to play. He recalls their first meeting, using the same phrase Helen had noted, half a century earlier: 'One day he came up to me, rather out of the blue, and said that he thought we had a lot in common and would I like to come to tea?' The 'lot in common' was of course, military history and a passion for toy soldiers. For David Hellings it had started during the war with what he described as 'a dreadfully gung-ho naval history of England which I devoured from cover to cover. After that I never looked back. Chris shared my interest but I don't think he was as passionate as I was. We both had, by modern standards, rather feeble collections of toy soldiers and fought our battles up and down our respective play rooms.'

Like Bonington, and many other wartime children, David Hellings had had a disturbed education, came from a progressive school, and found himself a year behind at UCS. He was also useless at games, claiming to be even worse than Chris, who at least ended his school career in the murky depths of the rugby third fifteen. Their friendship, like so many that last from childhood, has continued unchanged and Hellings doesn't consider that Chris has altered much since he first met him.

The years at UCS up to 'O' levels passed uneventfully. Bonington normally came in the bottom third of class positions and worked just hard enough to avoid any sort of trouble. Helen found his progress, or lack of it, frustrating and was particularly irritated that even just before his 'O' levels he still couldn't spell the simplest words. She described a UCS speech day that she attended with Nan, with disturbing honesty.

I come to dread the annual school Prize Day in both junior and senior school. Christian always insists that I shall wear a 'nice hat' and on each occasion I go to Scotts of Bond Street and buy myself an expensive, but possibly over-austere one.

At the end of his second year at the senior school Nan and I join the flock of parents drifting through the main gates. Christian, who went to school earlier, appears for a few minutes to greet us. He is still very short for his age – the smallest boy in his class, in this taking after the Boningtons, who are all well below average height.

He is wearing the customary prize day outfit of maroon, striped blazer, white trousers and white shirt. Despite his fairly long residence in London, he has preserved his childish fairness and his hair is only a little darker than it was in babyhood. With his round, high coloured cheeks, small, bright blue eyes and slight build, he looks considerably younger than his age and is on the whole a decidedly plain child.

When the parents and their guests are assembled in the hall, the hundreds of boys begin filing in. As they are all dressed alike, I fail to pick out Christian but suddenly Nan presses my arm and whispers, 'Christian is definitely the best looking boy in the school.'

Having experienced one Senior School Prize Day, I have been forewarned and bring a book this time, which I lay on my lap and unobtrusively read.

When all the speeches have been made and the many prizes awarded, the more social business of the day begins. We take a stand-up tea and individual parents seek brief talks with their son's class-master. I find Christian's teacher and suspect, from his replies to my questions, that he cannot clearly identify Christian among the boys who cluster near the bottom of the class.

By the time Christian was due to take his 'O' levels Helen had little confidence in his passing. He – or maybe Helen – became so worked up before his mock 'O' levels that she got the doctor to prescribe him tranquillisers before the real thing, which must have done the trick as Helen records her son's confidence at each examination:

> . . . especially the English paper. I read through the questions of this, including one on an untitled poem, which I recognise as 'Going Downhill on a Bicycle'.
>
> 'What did you make of the poem, Chris?' I ask.
>
> 'Oh, that was easy. It describes a girl ice-skating.'
>
> My heart sinks but, despite this glaring error of interpretation, he passes in English and five other subjects, and is qualified to continue at school to take three A-levels in two years' time.

Just after taking his 'O' levels he was invited to spend part of his summer holidays in Ireland, visiting his grandfather Maximilian and his wife, now living in Blackrock, a suburb of Dublin near the Wicklow Hills. Helen had maintained contact with her in-laws and they had occasionally visited them in London, so the Irish holiday did not come entirely out of the blue. As far as Christian was concerned a certain element of hero-worship of Maximilian was involved from a boy who had little experience of adult male company. The journey however proved to be a turning point as the teenager from London suddenly became aware of mountains. The train to Holyhead skirts the North Welsh coastline and, though the mountains inland are not dramatic, the northern slopes of the Carneddau fall quite steeply almost into the Irish Sea. Bonington remembers gazing enthralled out of the carriage window. 'There was something strangely exciting about the way the deep-cut, utterly desolate valleys wound their way into the mountains. There were no crags, just big rounded hills that gave a feeling of emptiness, of the unknown.'

He found the Wicklow Hills more friendly ... but was very cautious about exploring them. It was on his way home, however, when a second revelation hit him. He broke his journey to stay with his Aunt Poll in Wallasey, and they went to visit friends. Bored by adult conversation, Bonington picked up a book and was suddenly riveted.

> My imagination was jolted in a way I had never previously experienced. The book was full of photographs of mountains: the Cairngorms, huge and rounded; the Cuillins of Skye, all jagged rock and sinuous ridges, but what impressed me most of all was a picture taken from the summit of Bidean nam Bian in Glencoe, with serried folds of the hills and valleys, merging into a blur on the horizon. To me it was a wild virgin country, and yet it was almost within my reach: I could imagine exploring these hills for myself ... I spent the rest of the holiday examining every picture; I no longer planned battles but worked out expeditions through the mountains instead.

In those very earliest days it was Chris Bonington's *exploratory* instincts that were roused, rather than a desire to rock climb. It was the adventurous spirit of his grandfather and, to a lesser extent, of his father showing itself. As for that book, whatever it was, would in itself have been quite a find. In the late 1940s and early 'fifties there simply weren't very many mountaineering books around of any sort. The picture book of Scotland could well have been by Walter Poucher, *Scotland Through the Lens* perhaps, or *Highland Holiday*. Or it could possibly have been a book on mountain photography by C. Douglas Milner. Even ten years later I remember having to scour Ealing Public Library before minutely examining every climbing book on its shelves. In a way their very scarcity, combined with what by today's standards were very average sets of black and white photographs, gave them an almost grail-like rarity value. For Bonington they sparked off new dreams and like the generals of his bedtime reading he set about devising a plan of campaign.

During the following term he planned a trip to North Wales and persuaded a classmate called Anton to go with him. After Christmas 1950 they hitchhiked up the A5, taking two days to reach the youth hostel at Capel Curig, just a few miles from Snowdon. To those not brought up in the days before Outward Bound courses, adventure holidays and the proliferation of climbing clubs, the journey to the mountains was very much part of the romance. In London car-owning climbers were scarce and for a boy like Chris Bonington, discovering the hills for the first time, hitching was the norm rather than the exception. Once in the mountains finding things out for yourself was also commonplace. Those who shudder at the thought of their offspring going to the mountains in this way (with little or no equipment either) might take heart from the fact that accidents then, as now, were uncommon, and ambitions were much lower. It could even be argued that the practical difficulties to be overcome meant that only the dedicated few persevered and most of their adventurous urges were comparatively easy to fulfil.

Even so, the young Bonington and his friend nearly came to grief when on a grey snowy day they managed to get themselves avalanched off the slopes of Crib Goch in an attempt to follow the Miners' Track up Snowdon. Luckily, neither suffered any injuries. For Bonington it was 'the most exciting and enjoyable day I had ever had'. For Anton it may well have been the most exciting, but that was all, and the next day he hitched back to London, never to return. Bonington, clad in his school Burberry and army surplus boots, tramped round the roads from hostel to hostel, dreaming of future adventures but uncertain how to set about achieving them.

Returning to school, he read whatever he could find. Inevitably they were books like *Let's Go Climbing* by Colin Kirkus (probably the best beginners' book ever written), and John Barford's *Climbing in Britain*, a popular Pelican paperback. Perhaps best of all was W. H. Murray's *Mountaineering In Scotland*, a classic that has inspired thousands of young climbers since it was first published just after the war. But the real problem was to find a partner who was also keen, and to get at least some elementary instruction. Finally he tracked down Cliff Bayliss, an assistant to Charles Gilbert, a photographer who had married Helen's sister. Bayliss agreed to take Bonington to Harrisons Rocks near Tunbridge Wells.

Harrisons was already an established outcrop, and is the only worthwhile climbing to be had near London, along with the neighbouring crags of High Rocks, Bowles, Eridge and, slightly further afield, Stone Farm near East Grinstead. The rock is a soft friable sandstone, never much more than thirty feet high, and the tradition is that the climbs are normally top-roped; that is, a rope runs round a karabiner and sling attached to a tree at the top of the crag. The climber is belayed from below and as he ascends the rope is taken in. This means that he is in no danger of falling and will simply dangle on the rope if he comes off. It is therefore possible to climb to your absolute limits in near perfect safety. The only alternative at Harrisons is to solo, which of course is far more dangerous. This has ensured that climbing standards on southern sandstone have always been extremely high. The downside has been that many climbers trained on the steep fingery walls and overhangs have found the transitions to the bigger crags of Wales, the Lakes, and Scotland hard to make, particularly as they are unlikely to have had much experience of leading. This is probably less apparent nowadays with motorway networks making the West Country, Wales and the Peak District easily accessible, but when Chris Bonington was first taken down to the Rocks, set deep in the hop fields of the Kent/Sussex border, it was uncommon for habitués to travel further afield.

For the young Bonington the day surpassed his wildest expectations: 'I felt a sympathy with the rock; I found that my body somehow slipped into balance naturally . . . I found it stimulating. I knew that I had found a pursuit that I loved, that my body and my temperament seemed designed for it, and that I was happy.' Once he had been to Harrisons and become instantly hooked, Bonington was a frequent visitor in 1951–52, and climbed there regularly until he left London several years later. He developed into a more than adequate performer and eventually was good (and confident) enough to solo an impressive set of favourite climbs, including Birchden Wall, Birchden Corner, Crowborough Corner and the Niblick. All these were graded 5b or 5c, at that time the highest grade at Harrisons, which was the first British outcrop to adopt numerical grades. (Curiously, 5c in 1951 is remarkably consistent with 5c in the late 1990s on virtually every British crag.) On one occasion David Hellings accompanied Bonington to Harrisons: 'He dragged me off a couple of times, once to North Wales and once to Harrisons. At Harrisons I disgraced myself – I remember it with shame to this day. Chris was soloing quite a difficult climb and making his way up it rather slowly. I started a barrage of facetious comments as he struggled from hold to hold, and he remained silent until he got to the top then rounded on me furiously because he was actually at the limits of his skill and I hadn't realised this.'

After his first visit to Harrisons, Bonington was keen to return to North Wales and do some proper climbing. Reading *I Chose to Climb*, his first book, it is easy to visualise a young somewhat over-intense youth desperately trying to persuade Cliff Bayliss to go with him. But he couldn't make it and introduced Bonington to Tom Blackburn, a schoolteacher who promised to spend a few days in Wales with him during the Easter holidays of 1951.

Equipped with a new pair of nailed boots two sizes too large, an old hemp rope that would undoubtedly be thrown away today, and a cut down school mackintosh, Bonington hitched up to Wales again, this time to the newly opened Climbers' Club hut of Ynys Ettws. Bonington was sublimely unaware that the CC at that time was an exclusive club for the élite of British climbing. There was only one occupant whom he quickly recognised as being a bona-fide climber. In fact it was Tony Moulam, one of the leading activists of the post-war period, who, with Peter Harding had raised climbing standards in Wales and was responsible for many of the CC guidebooks in the 1950s. Instead of Tom Blackburn there was just a telegram saying he would by delayed by his children having mumps. The weather was typically Welsh and Bonington wandered around on his own until Blackburn arrived. Then, 'he did his duty manfully, taking me out every day. My first climb was Flake Crack on Dinas Bach, an undistinguished climb on a scruffy little crag, but to me it was the ultimate in excitement and difficulty.'

When Tom Blackburn had to return home, Chris was left on his own again with Tony Moulam, who kept a detailed record of his climbs and recalls that the weather had been pretty bad and he had taken part in two all-night rescues, so was not best pleased when Chris asked him to take him out. They did the Crevice, which today is graded Very Severe and described as 'a pleasant route for the slim but a fiendish problem for the corpulent and those of above average girth'. Tony Moulam remembers 'Chris did very well, when he abandoned his bendy boots and resorted to stocking feet, although he did grunt and sweat a lot.'

The novice remembers reaching the final ledge rather differently: 'completely exhausted, sobbing for breath. It was the only time I have been pulled up a climb and it was agonisingly uncomfortable, but it was also useful for I had become over-confident even in my first few days of climbing, and this showed me all too clearly how much I had to learn.'

I asked Moulam if he had taken Chris up the Crevice to bring him down a peg or two, which he dismissed: 'I seem to recall I chose it because it was near the hut and because it was a climb I wanted to do – I thought it might stretch him a bit though – and it certainly did.' The next day the weather reverted to rain. Moulam thinks that he and Chris did Crackstone Rib, a classic Severe, as a holiday finale, though Bonington remembers doing it before the Crevice. Either way he found it steeper and more exposed than anything he'd climbed before.

That evening Bonington innocently asked Tony Moulam if he could join the Climbers' Club. Moulam, embarrassed, explained that the Club couldn't really accept beginners, however enthusiastic they were, and that he'd have to have climbed for at least five years before he could realistically apply. Bonington took the reply badly: 'I sat and listened in a state of dumb misery. It sounded like a sentence of eternal banishment'. Some time later Tony Moulam heard that his young protégé had fallen off Scars Climb, a stiff Very

Severe on Tryfan, which caused him to comment that he would either be very good, or very dead! In the event, Bonington was accepted into the Climbers' Club in 1955 – a year ahead of Moulam's schedule. During the next year Bonington went back to Wales at every opportunity, made his first trip to Scotland and generally went through the normal development of any keen young climber, steadily increasing his experience and slowly working his way through the climbing grades.

All too soon he had to face another unwelcome challenge, that of passing his three 'A' levels in English, History and Latin. With his head full of climbing dreams and another attack of exam nerves, Helen again feared he would fail, particularly in Latin, which he found very heavy going. He had been offered a place at University College, London, conditional on getting good grades. After another visit to the doctor for more tranquillisers, Bonington sat his 'A' levels then, liberated, he hitchhiked up to Scotland to spend the whole summer holiday climbing.

During his early climbing days Chris Bonington's natural shyness and reticence were frequently overcome by his overwhelming drive to go climbing. He seemed to have no inhibitions about approaching strangers and asking them to climb with him. Maybe it was an extraordinary belief in his own ability that enabled him to do this, or perhaps it was just that he knew if he didn't push he wouldn't get any climbing done at all, but it was very characteristic of the young Bonington that many of his earliest climbing adventures were with people he hardly knew at all and never met again.

It was while he was at Glen Brittle youth hostel on Skye that he received his 'A' level results sent on by his mother. He had passed Latin (to his surprise) and History, both with low grades, but failed English. Apart from his spelling, something had gone drastically wrong. David Hellings remembers: 'He didn't just fail it, he got a 9, the lowest possible grade.' Whether or not he had mixed up his papers and handed in his rough copies (and Bonington admits that they were very rough indeed) or whether the outside examiner had developed an extreme prejudice against him is impossible to know. But neither his school nor his mother did anything about it. In the early 1950s the questioning of authority, like an exam board, was something that did not occur.

Disillusioned and frustrated, Bonington went back to school in the autumn, but was forced to study all the three subjects again. If it had just been English he would have stuck it out for the whole year but to retake History and Latin, which he had hated, was too much, and after only one term he left, electing to do his National Service. In making this decision his chances of going to university vanished. It is hard to know what effect this has had on him since but he has occasionally ruefully remarked that the various honorary degrees that have been awarded to him over the years have almost made up for not getting a proper one at the time. Nevertheless, Bonington has had the last laugh on the 'A' level exam board: not many of their failed English candidates have since written thirteen bestselling books, been translated into several languages, including Japanese and Russian, and been read in virtually every country in the world. At the time, though, a meagre brace of 'A' levels put a questionmark over a professional career.

Cenotaph Corner - Llanberis Pass

4

Down to Earth –
The Road-Menders' Hut

THERE ARE SOME mountain views in Britain that never fail to impress. The first sight of the Snowdon Horseshoe from the long straight A5 at Carreg y Drudion, the sudden revelation of the East Face of Tryfan from the same road as it emerges from behind the lumpy form of Gallt yr Ogof, and, perhaps best of all, the imposing monolith of Buachaille Etive Mor guarding the entrance to Glencoe and dominating the bleak wastes of Rannoch Moor. All three have a classic simplicity of line and all give the impression of huge scale. In winter the illusion is even greater and the Buachaille in particular can look positively Eigerish. For the eighteen-year-old Chris Bonington, free of school at last and waiting for his call-up papers, the view was inspirational. He had hitched up from London to spend the Christmas holidays climbing around Glencoe with John Hammond, an older and more experienced climber Bonington had got to know at Harrisons. They stayed at Lagangarbh, a Junior Scottish Mountaineering Club hut, and it was there that Bonington met the first of his really significant climbing partners.

Returning to the hut one day they found three Scotsmen helping themselves to their tea. They were members of the legendary, or notorious, Creagh Dhu, a club that had been formed on Clydeside during the Depression. Its members were famous for hard living, hard climbing and an uncompromising contempt for anything that smacked of Sassenach softness. The young, well-spoken Bonington

must have instantly raised their hackles. One of the three was
Hamish MacInnes, three years older than Bonington but already a
figure to be reckoned with in Scottish climbing. Somehow Bonington and Hammond inveigled themselves into joining MacInnes in
an attempt to make the first winter ascent of Agag's Groove on
Rannoch Wall, possibly the most popular easy rock climb on the
Buachaille. It had, in fact, been climbed in December 1937 by
Murray, Dunn, Mackenzie and MacAlpine but, despite low tem-
peratures and frosty conditions, they had found the route completely devoid of snow and ice and effectively just a very cold
rock climb. In December 1952, however, it was in genuine winter
condition and, despite being relatively short, it is high on the mountain and feels remarkably exposed for its grade.

They climbed in two ropes, MacInnes leading the first and cunningly landing the other pair of Bonington and Hammond with
an aspirant member of the Creagh Dhu who proved to be quite
exceptionally slow. Bonington led his rope of three and, despite
finishing in the dark, he obviously acquitted himself well on his
first winter climb of any significance. Hamish MacInnes still has
clear memories of their first encounter. 'My first impression was
that he was incredibly young and boyish-looking. It was quite amus-
ing how the other members of the Creagh Dhu reacted to him –
they thought he must live in a dolls' house! But he was, even then,
a very competent rock climber and they had a lot of respect for
him, even if it was rather grudging.'

John Hammond returned home and Bonington stayed on with
MacInnes doing two more first winter ascents on Buachaille Etive
Mor. The first was the Direct on Crowberry Ridge, the second was
the much sought after prize of Raven's Gully, a route that had
already given MacInnes himself a cold bivouac only feet from the
top. The gully is a dark vertical gash between the aptly named Slime
Wall and the steep Cuneiform Buttress. It is only 500 feet long, but
very sustained (it is still given Scottish Grade 5) with strenuous
technical climbing over chockstones and onto the steep side-walls.
Even in summer Raven's Gully is graded Very Severe, which in
Scotland covers a multitude of sins. MacInnes led almost the whole
route, only handing over to Bonington for the last pitch, which was
mainly on rock.

With these three new winter climbs Bonington was undoubtedly catapulted out of the mass of aspiring young climbers and pitched into the small élite of leading British mountaineers. More importantly, he had found in Hamish MacInnes a partner who would, in the years to come, give him the confidence and the benefit of his own hard-won experience to attempt climbs in the Alps beyond his wildest dreams.

But first there was his National Service to consider. In 1953 conscription was still in force and the two years of National Service was obligatory for all young able-bodied males. It was possible to defer it until after university but most joined up at eighteen. Rather surprisingly, given his interest in military history, Bonington opted for the Air Force rather than the Army. This was simply because he wanted to join the RAF Mountain Rescue in order to keep climbing and possibly make a future based around mountains. At school he had been an unenthusiastic member of the Junior Training Corps, a precursor to the Combined Cadet Corps (CCF) that most public schools run to this day. He was, on his own admission, a pretty hopeless cadet and found it impossible to keep his boots shiny and his belt blancoed. Nevertheless, a career in the forces appealed to him. To his surprise he found that he enjoyed service life. Perhaps after leading a solitary, fatherless childhood, when he had always felt different, in some ways inferior to other boys at school, he was now an integral part of a large organisation, in effect a family, in which he could submerge himself.

Having opted for the RAF Bonington was quickly diverted from his Mountain Rescue plans. Because of his public school background he was automatically put up for a National Service commission, to become an officer. There he was asked if he wanted to try for a flying commission. Feeling it would be unwise to say 'no', and convinced he would in any case fail the aptitude tests, he said 'yes'. To his amazement he passed the tests, though to this day he suspects there was another mix-up in his papers, and some highly motivated, well qualified young man with lightning fast reactions and lynx-like eyesight is still bemoaning his lack of opportunity to be a fighter pilot.

While Bonington was doing his introductory square-bashing on Coronation Day on a dusty parade ground he has a vivid memory of the announcement that Everest had been climbed – conquered was the word favoured by the press, but not by John Hunt. But it was only the news that impressed him, for his horizons at that time were solely limited to rock climbing and Scottish snow and ice. Everest was another world and it was not one he could imagine ever being part of.

Bonington was posted to the Royal Air Force College, Cranwell in the autumn of 1953. Here, deep in the flat Lincolnshire countryside he underwent basic training. Looking back, he sees this as not much more than institutionalised bullying, which must have brought back unpleasant memories of his childhood. Once it was over he became a full flight cadet, and started pilot training. Almost immediately he realised his worst forebodings. Despite his aptitude tests, he was incapable of judging distances and heights. His mother had never owned a car and Bonington had never even had a driving lesson. Unsurprisingly, he found it hard to control the Chipmunk Trainer, even on the ground. All the insecurities he had experienced with ball games resurfaced as, one by one, his contemporaries qualified to fly solo. Eventually he was tested by the Chief Flying Instructor, who told him to fly to another unfamiliar airstrip. Here, in the words of Mike Thompson, a close friend he made at Sandhurst the following year, 'He made a perfect landing; unfortunately he was still about 500 feet above the runway!' His second attempt, according to Thompson, would have been just as good, though ending up well below ground level. The instructor's shredded nerves could stand no more. He had failed. Bonington was later told that with time and effort he could have qualified as a civilian pilot, but he would never reach the high standards set by the RAF. After some soul-searching, he decided to transfer to the Army and apply for Officer Training at Sandhurst. This would give him two months' freedom until the new term started in September 1954, though he was technically on duty at home and couldn't leave the country. Predictably, he spent the entire time in North Wales, living on his basic pay, which for a Sandhurst cadet in 1954 was seven shillings (35 new pence) per day. Not exactly a fortune, but with beer at 1/3d (6 new pence) a pint, and a large loaf costing 6½d (2½ new pence), it was adequate for the frugal lifestyle of a young fit rock climber, particularly if you didn't have to pay rent.

The Llanberis Pass runs between the Glyders to the north and the Snowdon massif to the south. The road twists and turns from Pen-y-Pass at the top and flattens out as it goes through Nant Peris at the bottom. Halfway down it crosses a stream at Pont-y-Gromlech and runs through a narrow gap between the stream on one side and some giant rocks on the other. These are the Gromlech Boulders, which in all probability fell from the steep right-angled walls of the Dinas-y-Gromlech high above. The most famous of these is Cenotaph Corner, first climbed by Joe Brown in 1952. The boulders have survived various proposals to blow them up for road widening and provided uncomfortable bivouac sites for the impecunious ever since rock climbing became popular in the Pass after the war. There are also a few grassy sites for tents. With no amenities, climbers go to great lengths to avoid paying the minimal camping fees to the local farmer. In 1954 Caernarvonshire County Council, as it then was, thoughtfully abandoned a small roadmenders' hut by the side of the road, which provided climbers with free accommodation, albeit of a primitive nature. It became Bonington's home for the summer and one he shared with another young climber who was also in a kind of limbo.

Anthony 'Ginger' Cain was born in Liverpool and, incongruously for those who know him now as an artist, he studied mining at Leeds University for two years before failing end-of-year exams. He transferred to Wigan Technical College to study geology. Finishing the course meant that National Service could not be deferred any longer, but Ginger was (and is) a man of strong socialist principles, so he was in the process of registering as a conscientious objector and was waiting for his interview with the appropriate tribunal.

He now lives in Llanberis, just down the road from the site of the old road-menders' hut, and is a successful practising artist. His prints of mountain views the world over are deservedly popular, owing a lot to his interest and understanding of geology, and he, like Bonington, has found a way of making a livelihood out of his love of the hills. He has fond memories of his sojourn in the hut, where they both lived on leftovers from weekend climbers, plus a staple diet of porridge, noodles and tomato purée. They used to walk over the Pass to the Pen-y-Gwryd, not so much to drink as to pursue the waitresses who worked at the hotel. Bonington, in fact, got banned eventually from the pub for leading his girlfriend up Kaisergebirge Wall, which was considered far too difficult and dangerous for a girl!

Ginger Cain remembers his first sight of Bonington climbing: 'At that time you knew everyone who climbed regularly, certainly at a hardish level, and one day I remember seeing someone up on Carreg Wastad doing Overlapping Wall. There were very, very few people doing Extremes that you didn't know. It turned out to be Chris and his friend Geoff Francis. Chris looked about seventeen.' It rained nearly every day that summer, but they worked their way through the climbing guide to the Llanberis Pass, to which they were limited by a combination of bad weather, lack of transport and laziness. Bonington thinks that Surplomb on Clogwyn-y-Grochan was their best effort – it was a Joe Brown route with a fierce reputation. But Ginger remembers a climb he and Bonington did with Geoff Francis. The climb was actually a new route called Sunset Boulevard, on Clogwyn-y-Grochan. It traverses the central section of the cliff and the crux and, as Ginger recalls, is a diagonal descending flake, which has to be laybacked backwards. The technique of laybacking is brutally simple: the climber holds the flake and presses his feet against the wall behind and walks up the wall. It is a bold technique and in ascent, as is normal, it is strenuous and committing. Reversing is not only unnatural, but must have been very frightening. Ginger remembers Bonington doing the moves without any hesitation at all, even though he faced a huge swinging fall if he had made a mistake. 'He was really pushy – just went and did it – his push was way beyond mine.'

The climb was one of the comparatively few new routes Bonington put up in North Wales, though at the standard he was climbing in the early to mid-fifties, he was capable of many more. He, like so many others, was living in the shadow of Joe Brown and Don Whillans, whose climbs and indeed, lives, were shrouded in myth and mystery unless you were part of the magic circle – the Rock and Ice Club – whose members were almost exclusively based around Manchester and the Peak District. With no glossy climbing magazines and few up-to-date guidebooks, their climbs received almost no publicity which, paradoxically, gave them immense charisma. Even early repeat ascents of Surplomb or Cemetery Gates, did little to dispel the aura the routes possessed. It is interesting to note that Bonington's single biggest crop of new routes a couple of years later, were in the Avon Gorge in Bristol, well away from the Brown/ Whillans limelight.

It is also worth remembering the equipment used by Bonington and indeed most rock climbers until the early 1960s. Footwear for hard climbs was a simple pair of tight plimsolls. Many still climbed to quite a high standard in nailed boots. Ropes were hawser-laid nylon; harnesses hadn't been thought of and the rope was either tied directly round the waist or, for the more sophisticated, into a waist belt that consisted of a long piece of hemp or nylon rope wrapped around the body. This hopefully would absorb some of the shock of a fall. Protection consisted mainly of long nylon slings of varying thickness and steel karabiners. The slings were simply draped over spikes and the climbing rope clipped into them. They were occasionally threaded round chockstones and the Rock and Ice climbers were particularly cunning in developing the skill of inserting their own small chockstones, by wedging them in cracks. The technique was developed later to include drilled out metal nuts of various sizes, which were the precursors of the modern purpose-built nut. Few climbers, including Bonington, were fully aware of how sophisticated the Rock and Ice Club had become in protecting their climbs. It was this technique which explains, in part, why Brown and Whillans could venture onto such steep and sustained areas of rock with such confidence. Only in part of course for, like the chicken and egg, it was just as true that the daring and vision of climbing on these vertical or even over-hanging walls caused the innovations to be made in the first place.

Finally, climbers operating at the highest standards would often carry a few pitons and a hammer, though then, as now, their use was kept to a minimum. There is no doubt at all that most, if not all rock climbing in Britain in the 1950s was an inherently more dangerous sport than it is today. Leader falls were to be avoided at all costs and the average climber operated at a far lower standard than today. The hardest climbs took a lot of raw courage to undertake, and to the modern scoffing rock athlete who thinks that they are comparatively easy, just putting on a pair of cheap tight-fitting black plimsolls and trying a few moves on small footholds might give a disturbing insight into the spirit of the age.

It was the very commitment required to get up the hardest routes of the day that worked in the young Bonington's favour, rather than exceptional technical ability. Every surviving partner from those early days speaks of his tremendous drive, his ability to push on into ever more committing positions. On Diagonal for instance, a Hard Very Severe on the Nose of Dinas Mot, Ginger remembers, 'He led the traverse pitch by going right up underneath the overhang – it was absolutely desperate doing it that way – I've never done it like that since. He was a poky lad, very capable but very poky – apart from the Rock and Ice, he was the hardest lad I'd come across.'

Their damp sojourn was broken briefly by interviews. Ginger went before his tribunal and was registered as a conscientious objector and was eventually sent to work in Forestry. Bonington travelled down for an interview with the Regular Commissions Board in a large country house. By now an old hand at this sort of thing, he undertook the sort of aptitude and intelligence tests that have since been the subject of popular TV documentaries – building suspension bridges from old pairs of trousers and paper clips, constructing rafts out of empty cornflake packets and elastic bands and demonstrating leadership potential by using the right knives and forks at dinner.

Despite their lives going in opposite directions, Ginger Cain doesn't think either of them resented the other's chosen life style. 'There may have been one or two pointed remarks but there were no arguments at all.' Bonington half-envied Ginger's independent and uncertain future, yet still clung to the concept of a steady well-mapped career, though perhaps his summer in the road-menders' hut saw the first faint manifestation of the dilemma that was to recur for most of his adult life – the alternative pulls of freedom and security, of eccentricity versus convention, of danger versus safety. Even today there is the conflict between his ever-expanding work commitments and endless escapist ambitions that time has done little to modify.

Celebrating their mutual success by getting drunk at the Pen-y-Gwryd, they then went their separate ways. Ginger and Chris have retained their friendship, though they rarely see each other and have only very occasionally climbed together since. Ginger, who has a reputation for not suffering fools gladly, retains both affection for the man and admiration for what he has become. 'We always hit it off OK. I've defended him – a lot of criticism he's had has been uninformed and unfair. We go back a long way, do Chris and I.'

· 5 ·

Sandhurst

THE ROYAL MILITARY College, Sandhurst, evolved from the first British Army training establishment for cavalry and infantry officer cadets formed in High Wycombe in 1802. Its purpose was then, as now, to give a broader education to the officer class rather than just a basic grounding in military discipline and theory. Originally, its intake came almost exclusively from the English public schools. Even before the outbreak of the Second World War, eighty-four per cent of Sandhurst cadets were from such public schools as Wellington, Marlborough, Eton and Harrow, but by 1946 this had dropped to only fifteen per cent. In 1954, when Chris Bonington enrolled, the Sandhurst intake represented a reasonably wide cross-section of social strata. Before he arrived Bonington completed three days basic training with his local regiment, the Royal Fusiliers, and spent it incarcerated with squaddies from the East End in the Tower of London. Then it was off to the rural setting of the Berkshire-Surrey border and the grandiose architecture of the Military Academy.

The curriculum for cadets was about two-thirds military and one third academic. It must have been a severe jolt to the Bonington system returning to maths, science, economics, languages and history at the age of twenty-one. On the military front he was taught to command a division. A contemporary, Dennis Gallway, noted, 'The standard joke about the Academy was that it was like a

Giant's Cave Buttress, Avon Gorge

provincial university where the OTC has run riot. One ended the course knowing very little about a lot of things.'

Bonington found the social scene difficult to handle: a passage from *I Chose to Climb* is revealing and it pinpoints an identity problem that perhaps he has never fully resolved to this day. He is writing about those 'pukka' cadets whose social credentials were impeccably upper-class:

They had the same backgrounds, went to the same parties, all knew each other or had mutual friends, and were going into the same kind of regiments – the Brigade of Guards, Cavalry and so on. They were full of self-confidence, at times were arrogant and had a firm though unspoken code of what was, or was not, good form. They undoubtedly had a strong influence on the rest of the Academy. For a start, one could not help being a little envious. I also should have liked to flit off to London to deb parties, to attend hunt balls, to have the same self-confidence. As a result, many of us with very ordinary, middle-class backgrounds aped some of their ways, conforming with the atmosphere that pervaded Sandhurst. I hid in the back of my wardrobe the unfashionable, double-breasted blue suit, which I had bought whilst at Cranwell, and acquired the Sandhurst leisure uniform: tight cavalry twill trousers, plain coloured waistcoat and tweed jacket. I even equipped myself with a bowler hat – bought second-hand, and an umbrella, for my forays in London, which rarely got farther than my home in Hampstead. My only girlfriend at the time, a straight-thinking, Northern lass, who was at a domestic science college in Leicester, was, I think, slightly appalled by my affectation. I became acutely conscious of my own social limitations and quite unconsciously began to add an exaggerated public school veneer to my ordinary south-country accent. I, and many others, were simply conforming to the Sandhurst mould, not consciously but because we were adaptable and wanted to be part of this society.

For the many climbers who even now think Bonington's image epitomises upper-class privilege, it is ironic that, while Chris has certainly never been accepted as 'one of the lads', it is also possible that he doesn't really believe he is 'one of the chaps' either. Clearly his lonely childhood had a lot to do with it, but there would soon be another rather odd historical anomaly at work. By the beginning of the 1960s, at the very point when Bonington's military career peaked, a sea change was sweeping through British youth. Epitomised by rock 'n' roll, skiffle, and above all, the rise of the Beatles, northern working-class culture became immensely fashionable. Their climbing equivalents, Joe Brown and Don Whillans, with their underplayed humour, flat hats, and matching accents, had immense charisma for most young rock climbers, even for the public at large when Joe Brown became a minor television celebrity. Almost overnight the clean-cut heroes of post-war Britain, in music, sport, film and particularly war, were replaced by increasingly anti-establishment attitudes and personalities. Almost everything that Bonington seemed to represent became, not just unfashionable, but derided. He himself appeared to be stranded on the wrong side of a new social divide.

However, the early days at Sandhurst were, hunt balls apart, enjoyable and fulfilling. Bonington's dream of becoming a Field Marshall moved a step nearer reality, though his old friend Mike Thompson remembers him even then 'being famous for being absent-minded and chaotic'. He relished the war games, the military ethos, and even the drill. He also found, with the Sandhurst emphasis on sport, quite a lot of time for climbing and for the first time in his career (apart from his brief winter escapade with Hamish MacInnes) he made a real impact with a succession of hard new routes in the Avon Gorge, the nearest worthwhile climbing area to Sandhurst.

In the UK in the mid 1950s limestone climbing was an esoteric and unpopular sidewater. True, the Rock and Ice members practised artificial climbing in the dales of Derbyshire but limestone was generally dismissed as unsound and impossible to protect without excessive use of pitons. Bristol's Avon Gorge, the ultimate city crag, was rather different. The cliffs are quarried and, though steep, are actually made up of complex overlapping slabs. The climbing is delicate and subtle, even quirky; on a good day everything seems possible, but once confidence ebbs, even the easiest routes feel alarming and insecure and poorly protected. The bold style of climbing was tailor-made for Chris Bonington, who has always excelled in complex balancing, bridging movements, rather than using pure finger strength.

By the mid 1950s most of the classic easier lines in the Gorge had been climbed by a group of talented Bristol University students, particularly Hugh Banner, Barrie Page and Mike Harvey. Harvey was tragically killed in Wales; Page will feature again later in this story, and Banner still climbs to an impressively high standard. All their routes skirted the daunting Main Wall, which is the biggest single sweep of rock in the Gorge. It was loose, steep and frightening. Bonington wrote, 'More impressive than any of the Three Cliffs [Llanberis], it was almost comparable with the East Buttress of Clogwyn Du'r Arddu.' This was doubtless an opinion based on the psychological difficulty of venturing onto unknown ground, but even so it was a rather extravagant claim as Clogwyn Du'r Arddu ('Cloggy') is one of the greatest and most challenging cliffs in Britain.

Apart from one short incursion on the far right-hand side of Main Wall, Pink Wall Traverse, nobody had dared commit themselves to a frontal assault. After several abortive attempts, Bonington, having bivouacked in a tiny cave at the foot of the wall, steeled himself (literally, with a small selection of pitons) and forced his way up a somewhat indistinct groove line that led to frighteningly loose but easier ground. He named the route Macavity after T. S. Eliot's famous gravity-defying cat and, presumably, because it started from a cave.

Bonington revitalised the Sandhurst Mountaineering Club; in his own words, 'It was frankly élitist – we actively discouraged beginners.' On Macavity and many other routes, he was accompanied by Geoff Francis, with whom he had made an early ascent of Cemetery Gates during his sojourn in the road-menders' hut. Francis had led the lower half and belayed in the middle of what is now one big pitch. According to Chris this was because the protection was very sparse, but Francis claims that he was so worried about Chris's reaction if he'd grabbed the whole climb that he let Chris lead the crux! Whatever the truth there is no doubt that Bonington and Francis climbed extremely well together over quite a long period, which was why Francis, though not a soldier but a medical student, was on several occasions co-opted onto Sandhurst meets to provide Chris with a partner of similar ability.

Perhaps Geoff Francis didn't get quite the credit he deserved in following Bonington on what was undoubtedly the best climb they did together in the Avon Gorge, the strangely named Malbogies which takes one of the very few natural lines straight up the middle of Main Wall. It has become *the* classic middle grade route of the Gorge but was not repeated again for five years. It is still given a respectable Hard Very Severe grading, though it has, like so many limestone gems, become so highly polished it is almost transparent, and the first moves feel considerably harder than the 5a grade given in the guidebook.

It was, on Bonington's admission, the line that cried out to be attempted but was actually the last of his major Gorge climbs. This was due to Chris's own perennial inability to spot the obvious – a fact brought home to me a few years ago when I lived in Bristol. Then, despite having already done the climb several times, I had quite a job to persuade Chris that we were indeed climbing this, his most famous Avon route which he had almost no memory of doing, and only the haziest notion of where it went.

Though Avon provided Chris Bonington with some of his best new climbs it certainly wasn't the only place the Sandhurst Mountaineering Club visited. Dennis Gallway remembers a week in Wales, stopping in Williams Barn below Little Tryfan when it never stopped raining and wet clothes were hung across the barn to be worn again still wet, the following morning. Though he couldn't recall the names of any of the routes they did, he clearly remembered that even then Bonington had the reputation for dropping things; pitons, hammers, karabiners, slings, guidebooks would regularly part company with their owner. So it must be comforting for Chris to know that at least he hasn't got any worse with the passage of time, only that many of his later losses were rather more expensive – cameras being a particular favourite. Probably the best-documented incident was when he was being filmed in the French Alps recreating the first ascent of the Grépon. He managed to drop the plimsolls that he was changing into for a particularly difficult pitch: the scene stayed in, together with the accompanying expletive.

Another contemporary at Sandhurst was Patrick Fagan who was virtually kidnapped and taken to Wales. He remembers:

There was a very good library at Sandhurst. Though I'd never done any climbing I was very interested – probably as a result of the 1953 Everest film. I was browsing through the climbing books and perusing, I think it was Bill Murray's *Mountaineering in Scotland*, when I felt a heavy hand on my shoulder. This cadet I'd never seen said, 'Are you a climber?' To which I couldn't really answer. But he said, 'Well, we're going to North Wales next weekend,' and before I knew it, I was bundled off with Chris and a group of cadets and found myself on the Saturday morning at the foot of the Milestone Buttress on Tryfan.

Though only a novice, and they have rarely climbed together since, Fagan has fond memories of Chris, both at Sandhurst and later on through meetings at the Alpine Club and Royal Geographical Society. Interestingly, Fagan thinks that Bonington would have made an outstanding soldier if he had had the motivation to pursue a military career. Despite the shortcomings of the Sandhurst system, it certainly equipped him with many of the organisational and leadership skills that he was to use so successfully later on as a professional mountaineer.

Without doubt the closest and longest-lasting friend Chris made at Sandhurst was Mike Thompson. Born in the Lake District and educated at St Bees School (where Chris's son Daniel would eventually be a pupil), Mike Thompson had been climbing since he was twelve years old. He started at Sandhurst six months after Bonington, and joined the Mountaineering Club. Though he would never claim to have the same ability or commitment to climbing as Bonington, Thompson was to prove over many years to have a shrewd eye for new routes, both in the Avon Gorge and, later, in the Lake District. Mike eventually became disillusioned with Army life at about the same time as Bonington and found an ingenious escape route. He went on to study anthropology and, though his direct involvement in climbing has declined over the years, his writing and concern about environmental issues has become highly respected. He is also one of the funniest climbing writers around.

The eighteen-month course at Sandhurst drew to a close and Bonington was faced with the choice of what regiment to join. Once again class and background played a part. The Guards or the Household Cavalry were not for the likes of Bonington who opted for the Royal Tank Regiment. The Tanks had been founded in World War Two and was seen as somewhat arriviste by the rest of the Army.

Mike Thompson, who *did* go into a cavalry regiment, wryly recalls Chris's choice: 'He was an ambitious soldier but he wasn't really appreciated, I don't think, by the Tank Regiment. You were supposed to be interested in tanks and things with engines. Rally-driving was approved of but climbing was a bit strange as far as they were concerned. My regiment, on the other hand, thought climbing was rather splendid.'

For the still fresh-faced Bonington, who was made an under officer in his final term and had graduated with a highly respectable nineteenth place in the Order of Merit out of his intake of over two hundred cadets, his commission in the Tank Regiment was a rude awakening. He was sent out to Germany where he realised learning to be an officer had taught him nothing about man management or tank maintenance. 'I often demanded the impossible and had to back down. I was too conscious of the pips on my shoulders and my own dignity – I hesitated to work in with the lads ... At Sandhurst we had been warned of the dangers of "familiarity breeds contempt" but in the close confines of this mobile steel box one had no choice.' It took Bonington a good year to repair the damage done in the first weeks, but his mechanical ineptitude never left him. On one occasion he was sent back to England on a tank maintenance course, his commanding officer commenting that he couldn't spare anyone to attend it, so Bonington would have to go! There is another anomaly here, for Bonington, who even today barely understands how to lift the bonnet of his car, is obsessed with all kinds of high-tech computer gadgetry, and is totally at home in the world of E-mail, the Internet, and laptop computers. But tanks and their mysterious innards remained a closed book for him, which couldn't have helped his Army prospects at all.

Socially, Army life wasn't much fun either: a rigid round of cock-tail parties, regimental gossip and, worst of all, an almost complete lack of available female company. There was virtually no fraternisation with the local community and, far from the family feeling that Sandhurst had engendered, Chris Bonington's first year in Germany was a lonely one. Perhaps the best bit were the exercises: 'tank training was a really magnificent game, the best I've ever played ... Juggernauts encased in steel, smashing through walls, scything through young trees, the wireless crackling in our headphones, giving us a picture of the course of the battle'. Not, perhaps the sentiments we might expect from the present President of the Council for National Parks, but they were written over forty years ago.

Time in Germany passed slowly, but in the summer of 1957 Bonington received a letter from Hamish MacInnes. While it is facile to suggest it changed his life, any more than any other random event can lead to all kinds of unexpected sequels, it did bring Bonington his first Alpine experience and with it his first encounter with the climb that would eventually bring him public acclaim, the North Face of the Eiger.

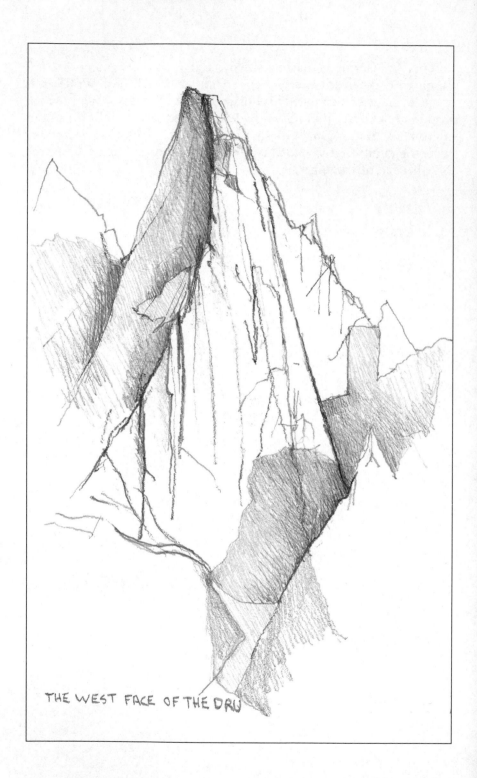

THE WEST FACE OF THE DRU

· 6 ·

Alpine Apprentice

It says a lot for Hamish MacInnes' faith in Chris Bonington that he should invite him, out of the blue, to attempt the most famous and notorious climb in the Alps, the North Face of the Eiger, as his first Alpine route. Luckily for them both, and for subsequent British climbing history, their attempts didn't get very far up the colossal wall before Chris, who was almost overwhelmed with trepidation, wisely decided that the weather wasn't looking good and persuaded Hamish to retreat. Was their attempt foolhardy? Even today MacInnes doesn't think so:

Chris, in his book [*I Chose to Climb*] plays himself down all the time. I mean I would never have gone on a climb like that, even then, unless I'd been with someone pretty competent – I'm not that stupid! True, he didn't have much snow and ice experience but he was always a better rock climber than I was; if there was anything really difficult I knew he could lead it. We hadn't much gear, but *nobody* had much gear in those days, just a lot of ex-Army stuff, all pretty useless really – but if we'd had a bit of luck with the weather we could have done it. We were pretty fit and technically we shouldn't have had much trouble. Chris actually made the right decision to retreat. I'd certainly have persuaded him to carry on if I thought the weather was OK.

While accepting that, given luck with the conditions they just might have done it, Bonington, on the other hand, thought that there was an imbalance in his and Hamish's experience which in a crisis could have proved critical: 'when struggling for one's life in a maelstrom of rushing snow and wind every member of the party needs to be equally capable, for one slip can bring disaster to all.'

With some relief Chris hitched from Switzerland to Chamonix, while Hamish drove across on his motorbike. Hamish's next plan was an ascent of the Walker Spur on the Grandes Jorasses which, like the Eiger, hadn't had a British ascent. Bad weather foiled this almost equally ambitious plan and in the end they settled for a minor new route: a rock climb on the comparatively insignificant Aiguille de Tacul. The route was neither great nor difficult but for Bonington the pleasure of his first new Alpine route and summit was immediately eclipsed by the horrors of the descent. Here Hamish's experience counted and Chris, like so many British climbers before and since, found down-climbing over complex and broken ground unroped both frightening and exhausting. The next day Bonington left to rejoin his regiment. It had been a baptism of fire; not many Alpine careers start with a new route. Once again Hamish MacInnes pushed Bonington into an arena, perhaps before he was quite ready for it, but with some success and without mishap.

A rather strange non-story has only just come to light regarding the furtherance of Chris Bonington's climbing career at this time. In the winter of 1957–58 Mike Banks, a Royal Marine, was planning to lead an attempt on Rakaposhi, then one of the highest unclimbed peaks in the Karakoram range in northern Pakistan. It was to be a Joint Services expedition. At an early stage of the planning Banks was told he could choose anyone he wanted from any of the three services – anyone, that is, with the exception of Lieutenant C. J. S. Bonington who couldn't be recommended. Neither Banks or Bonington himself have the slightest idea why he should have been blackballed, but Chris now maintains that whatever the reason, it was a blessing in disguise, for the summer of 1958 was to be a truly memorable one.

Hamish and Chris met up again in Chamonix. Hamish was as ambitious as he had been the previous year, and planned a new route on the South-East Spur on the Pointe de Lépiney. Not exactly a climb that cried out to be ascended but still a challenge, in fact it was one on which they nearly came to grief. After a cold bivouac halfway up the face, and a fall Chris took from an overhang when a wooden wedge pulled out, they had a desperate retreat down a water-worn gully, compounded with jammed ropes and a horrifying jump across a huge bergschrund at the bottom of the face. On their return Chris was adamant: 'You can keep your new route and stuff it. I couldn't care less if it's the last great unclimbed problem in the Alps. I just want to get to the top of one or two good standard climbs.' Hamish's answer, typically, was to suggest the spectacular South-West Pillar of the Dru, the Bonatti Pillar, as it is now universally known. In 1958 the Pillar was the hardest rock climb in the French Alps and a magnificent achievement by Walter Bonatti who had soloed the first ascent in 1955, taking five days of extreme effort and total commitment. In 1958 it had still only had four further ascents. It was scarcely Bonington's ideal choice of a 'good standard climb' but at least it was all supposedly on sound rock and would be playing to his strengths.

Hamish and Chris teamed up with Walter Phillip and Richard Blach, two excellent and experienced Austrian climbers. This boost to morale and confidence was redoubled by the appearance at the foot of the Dru of Paul Ross, a well-known Lakeland climber, and the legendary Don Whillans. Both have described the climb in great detail, Chris in *I Chose to Climb* and Don in *Portrait of a Mountaineer*. The story is well known. On their first bivouac on the Pillar, Hamish was struck by a rockfall and suffered a fractured skull. A huge rockfall down the approach couloir made retreat uninviting, so they decided the safest course of action was to press on to the top. It took two more harrowing bivouacs to get there and a concerted effort to get Hamish up and off the climb safely. Bonington felt he had been pushed to his limits but had gained a lot from the whole experience:

When we went on the South-West Pillar, I was afraid before starting it, and even more so on the climb itself, when things started to go wrong, for it was all so new to me. I could not know how serious our troubles were; whether I was capable of lasting out for several days on end, whether it was possible to get up the climb in bad weather. We got up alive because Don Whillans and Walter Phillip knew what they were doing. Their

self-confidence encouraged me at the time and I learnt a great
deal from them. My experience on the Pillar taught me that
however bad conditions become, whatever goes wrong, I could
extricate myself. I never again suffered the blind fear of unknown
dangers for, on all subsequent climbs, I was able to appreciate
the extent of any danger that threatened, and find a way of
avoiding it. I was still frightened at times, but it was a fear that
was quickly banished by action.

From those earliest days Bonington accepted that Don Whillans
was the better mountaineer, he was obviously far more experienced
and had already had several Alpine seasons behind him. In the last
resort he would invariably bow to Don's judgement. Whillans on
the other hand was impressed with Chris's push and drive, though
his first encounter with him in North Wales had been less than
impressive, as he described with characteristic bluntness:

> Mention of Christian Bonington among the Rock and Ice Club
> usually produced a few smiles. We had been sitting near the
> Cromlech Boulder sunning ourselves when a climber came run-
> ning down the scree from the crag.
>   'First aid. I must have some first aid,' the man called out as
> he neared us.
>   'Got a bloody plum in his mouth and he can't get it out,'
> remarked one of the lads, propping himself up on one elbow . . .
> It turned out that it was Chris Bonington and that in rapelling
> down Cenotaph Corner, he had burnt his shoulder rather badly
> . . . At the time we thought the posh accent and the appeal for
> first aid indicated a certain softness. Later Chris showed me the
> burn mark and it had been very severe.

On the South-West Pillar of the Dru, Bonington and Whillans
had been thrown together by accident and though big differences
existed between them of education, class, attitudes, it was the beginning of a formidable partnership that would survive, on and off,
for twelve years, culminating in the hugely successful Annapurna
South Face Expedition. A lot of water was to flow under many
bridges in the intervening years.

The following season, 1959's highlight was a first British ascent by Bonington of the Direttisima on the North Face of the Cima Grande in the Italian Dolomites with Gunn Clark, a talented climber who was killed years later in an avalanche in Glencoe. The Brandler Hasse, as it is now known, was another breakthrough, for the difficulties consisted mainly of artificial climbing on overhanging rock. Bonington had comparatively little experience of the complex techniques of piton placements and rope management, but still managed to lead the whole climb. It is still probably fair to say that in his long and varied career which has taken in virtually every major mountain range in the world, Chris has never been attracted to big wall climbing. This involves placing long lines of pitons or bolts, sleeping in hammocks and generally making very slow progress. He is too impatient, impulsive even, and one can't help feeling that if he were to attempt a long artificial climb in Yosemite for instance, he would probably fail because he would drop most if not all of his equipment on the first day.

Earlier in the year life in Germany had become almost intolerably boring and repetitive, so when he saw a notice advertising for instructors at the Army Outward Bound School in Towyn in mid-Wales, he applied for it. In retrospect it was the first significant shift towards the life of a professional climber, and one that in civilian life many climbers choose as a matter of course. But as a career move in the Army it was not a particularly good one and inevitably spelt the end of any long-term ambition to become General Bonington. Today it is hard to imagine Chris Bonington working in an Outdoor Centre, burdened with all the multiplicity of disciplines, leadership certification, endless knowledge of techniques and, like the Army, becoming ever increasingly immersed in bureaucracy. But in 1959 it was all much simpler. Young soldiers, from Junior Leaders Regiments and Army Apprentice Schools were given a three-week course in map-reading, mountain walking, camping, canoeing and basic rock climbing, culminating in a three-day expedition across forty miles of mountain terrain.

Initially Bonington revelled in both the freedom from Army discipline and the chance to get back into the Welsh rock climbing scene that he had missed for the last four years. Mention the summer of 1959 and many elderly climbers shake their heads and smile, for in that long hot summer, many of the myths that Joe Brown and Don Whillans had created over the last decade were demolished.

Suddenly their hardest routes were not just repeated, but actually became popular, and climbers like Hugh Banner even added two new hard routes on Clogwyn Du'r Arddu, over which Brown in particular had assumed almost proprietorial rights.

Bonington, on his own admission 'felt rather like Rip Van Winkle' on his return to Wales but quickly caught up with ascents of routes like Woubits and Bloody Slab on Cloggy and Joe Brown's most famous route, Cenotaph Corner on Dinas y Gromlech. Of this he wrote:

> I went climbing on every available weekend and even in the long summer evenings. On one such night I did Cenotaph Corner. Only a few years before, the Corner had seemed impossibly huge, as smooth as the corner of a giant concrete building but now, confident in the knowledge that many others had climbed it, and in my own experience on other climbs in the same idiom, it seemed to bristle with hand-jamming cracks and small holds. I was climbing no better than I had done earlier but now had the reassurance that many others had also found it easy: there was no longer any mystery.

Three years later Bonington was to team up with Joe Brown for the only time on a new route in North Wales. The climb was on Castell Cidwm, a ferocious crack line on a viciously overhanging little crag on the side of Mynydd Mawr, overlooking Llyn Cwellyn. Joe had attempted the climb the week before and wanted another go at it, but offered Chris the lead. Chris, one suspects, was slightly overawed and tense in Brown's presence, and couldn't make much progress. Inevitably Joe took over. One can't help feeling that Joe knew this would happen all along. He remembers it well:

> We were doing it in the traditional way, from the ground up. Today you'd just abseil down it and clean everything out. So the way we did it meant we had to use a lot of aid, in fact we only used about two or three points of direct aid: most of the moves we did free, but if you wanted to clean the crack or get a runner on it meant you had to hang off the one below. So for years it had a reputation for being done using a massive amount of aid, which it wasn't. I remember being absolutely knackered for about

three days afterwards. Chris told me he could never have led it himself.

Joe's wife Val was watching the pair on the climb and still recalls Chris saying, 'If I live to be a hundred I'll never be as good as Joe.' Brown named the route Tramgo after the celebrated Trango Tower in the Karakoram (now commonly spelt with an 'n' instead of 'm'). Today it is given a grade of E4, 6a and goes entirely free. But it is rarely climbed, simply because it is so strenuous. Joe and Chris later teamed up again with Tom Patey in the Alps and were together on the famous outside broadcast on the Old Man of Hoy. But even today when they meet it is not difficult to sense that Chris is still in awe of Joe and always seems slightly deferential. Joe, of course, has that effect on a lot of people but he has always felt that the rank and file of British climbers has unfairly treated Chris. I asked him to explain: 'Because he's known as a mountaineer people have assumed he's a not a good rock climber, which is not true; he's a very good rock climber indeed.' He paused and a great grin spread across his face. 'Not as good as me though, ha, ha, ha!'

Maybe the slightly arms-length nature of their friendship over the years meant that Joe was never an automatic choice on the Bonington expeditions to Annapurna or Everest. Joe himself suffers from the opposite problem to Chris, being seen just as a rock climber. This, for someone who made the first ascents of Kangchenjunga, Mustagh Tower and Trango Tower, is equally unfair. Chris eventually *did* invite Joe on two expeditions. The first was to Trango which Chris himself dropped out of to go to Everest in 1975. The second, which never happened, would indeed have been a huge Bonington enterprise, to Everest's North-East Ridge in 1989. After the news that Harry Taylor and Russell Brice had climbed the notorious Pinnacles the year before, it was felt that it was hardly worth going back to do a route that would actually cover no new ground at all. But one can't help feeling that Joe's presence on some of Bonington's earlier trips might have been less problematic than Don Whillans' were to become.

Back in 1959 the work at the Outward Bound School was far more fulfilling than the routine in his regiment, though Bonington found that teaching rock climbing was actually the least satisfying part of the course; endlessly repeating the same easy routes and cajoling beginners into an activity which many didn't enjoy or show any ability for. Nevertheless Bonington was happy as long as he didn't think too hard about the future. By now his regiment had been transferred to Libya which sounded even less promising than Germany had been. For the first time he contemplated a life outside the Army, but was unsure of what he could do, apart from becoming a climbing instructor which was the one job he *wasn't* interested in.

As the summer drew to a close all thoughts of leaving the Army were abruptly put aside. Whatever obstacles might have been put in his way to stop him going to Rakaposhi had by now disappeared or been forgotten. Out of the blue he was invited to go on another Joint Services expedition, this one to attempt the unclimbed Annapurna II in Nepal. For the twenty-six-year-old Lieutenant Bonington it offered the chance to go on the trip of a lifetime. In fact it was to be just the first in a seemingly endless line of expeditions, almost all of which have provided Bonington with a new set of superlatives – 'last great problems', 'ultimate challenges', 'hardest ways', 'elusive summits'. He was about to set out to find his own Holy Grail, a path which even forty years on he is still treading as enthusiastically as ever.

· 7 ·

Bonington Goes East

In the early 1960s the chances of climbing in the Himalaya were non-existent to all but an élite handful of British mountaineers. The cost alone was prohibitive and for the run-of-the-mill climber visiting Nepal was at best a fantasy. Even those who *did* go probably wouldn't have expected to make more than one or two trips in a lifetime. Only people like Eric Shipton and Bill Tilman mysteriously managed to return over and over again to explore new areas and climb new peaks. So when Lieutenant-Colonel Jimmy Roberts of the Indian Army assembled his nine-man team, only one member, Dick Grant had any real Himalayan experience. Roberts, who would later set up Mountain Travel, the first trekking company in Nepal, was an experienced mountain explorer and a natural leader. His planning, organisation and deep knowledge of the country he loved gave Bonington his first taste of expedition life and influenced his own leadership a decade later.

Annapurna II is only just under 8000 metres (7937 metres in fact), a big remote but, it has to be said, not very charismatic mountain, ten miles away from its higher and infinitely more famous namesake. Roberts planned a traditional siege-style ascent of the mountain with organised build-up of camps, heavy Sherpa support, fixed ropes on steep sections and oxygen for the summit bid. It was a very long but easy climb, apart from the final ridge leading to the top itself; it was in many ways an ideal Himalayan introduction

Swayambhu Nath Kathmandu

for Bonington who eventually made the summit with Dick Grant and the Sherpa Ang Nyima. He learnt that his own height ceiling without oxygen was probably just below 8000 metres (Nuptse at 7879 metres was to be the highest peak Bonington ever climbed without its use). He realised that youth and fitness were not in themselves the only qualities needed to succeed on a big mountain. Though he experienced immense satisfaction from getting to the top and had been highly competitive and single-minded in so doing, Bonington also realised that the whole expedition experience, the place, the people, the travel, the unknown, were just as important. His richest memory of the expedition was, in fact, when he left it for three days and walked out over a high pass with an old and experienced Sherpa. He felt in touch with the land and fulfilled by simply being there. As the years have gone by his love of Nepal remains as strong as ever. Despite the colossal changes and the double-edged sword of tourism with all the environmental problems it causes, Bonington is still entranced by the country. Even Kathmandu, with its overcrowding and horrendous pollution, still rather touchingly casts a spell over him, though he can remember the days when there was only one hotel and no roads outside the city.

On his return to Britain, Bonington resumed work at Towyn. After Annapurna II, the Alps were out for that year. Instead Bonington teamed up with Tom Patey and went on a magical mystery tour of north-west Scotland. Only new routes were contemplated and according to Bonington in *The Next Horizon* they completed fifteen, though this was reduced to only ten in his pictorial autobiography, *Mountaineer*. Tom Patey was without doubt the funniest climbing writer in the 1960s. He was a brilliant all round mountaineer, specialising in moving fast over mixed ground. Above all, he meticulously researched new routes, both in Scotland and the Alps. In the summer of 1960 he planned an ambitious itinerary. Two climbs stand out, both described by Patey in an article for the *Etchachan Club Journal* and since immortalised in *One Man's Mountains*, a compilation of Patey's writings and verse published after his death.

The first was unusual, a great classic easy route up the Nose of the Cioch of Sgùrr à Chaorachain near Applecross. It takes an improbable line in situations normally only to be savoured by doing much harder climbs. Patey's description of their first attempt is a masterly piece of understatement:

Bonington selected the driest and hence the most overhanging crack in the vicinity.

'Just keep an eye on the rope, I won't be a minute,' he remarked laconically, lacing up his favourite PAs.

True to his word he returned almost immediately, landing on the ledge in a heap.

'Mild XS,' he muttered. 'You have a go.'

An easier alternative provided a couple of undistinguished pitches and Patey belayed as Bonington led what looked like the crux:

I squeezed into a dry corner and lit a cigarette, resigning myself to a long wait. I was too pessimistic: 100 feet of rope snaked out in as many seconds and a triumphant yell resounded round the corrie.

'Come on, man – it's incredible!'

It was indeed. Great rough excrescence sprouted everywhere on the Nose like an exuberant eruption of 'acne vulgaris'. What had appeared from any angle to be an XS pitch up an incredibly exposed slab turned out to be a glorious Difficult!

Even the Lion of Llanberis, as Patey described Bonington, decided that the climb would 'fit comfortably into one of any number of favourite Welsh crags' and thought it was 'the Diff to end all Diffs!'

But the biggest and best route was on Skye, on the remote Coireachan Ruadh face of Mhic Coinnich on the Coruisk side of the Cuillin Ridge. Here an 800-foot sweep of vertical grey gabbro, a rock made for climbing, tempted them to try a series of corners.

Bonington disappeared round a corner on the right and I found him firmly established below a rather attractive *dièdre* looking as pleased as the goose that laid the golden eggs.

'This is the route for us,' he announced proudly, 'and here is an old tin can to prove it.'

As we were supposed to be climbing a new route I did not see the force of his logic.

Later Bonington led the crux:

For the rest of the way Bonington and the rough Skye gabbro were inseparable as a courting couple. I realised for the first time the value of PAs on a really thin pitch. Most of the current Welsh masters wear them; a few never take them off, even in bed.

PAs, the forerunner of the modern sticky-soled rock boot, were invented in the late 1940s by the great French climber Pierre Allain. The climb was called King Cobra and is still one of the great routes on Skye.

Their final route was a typically Pateyesque adventure on a crumbling unclimbed pinnacle just to the north of the Old Man of Storr.

It was a virgin summit modest by Alpine or even Cuillin proportions but nevertheless a potential Aiguille Bonington or Sgùrr Tom. We took the rope as an afterthought and lived to be grateful. After a scramble of 100 feet we came out on to the *arête* opposite the Old Man and had to readjust our scale of dimensions. There were still 75 feet to climb and it was not easy. We split it into three pitches in order to limit the momentum of any loose rock dislodged by the leader. A crash helmet would have been useful for the second.

At last, after a titanic struggle, Chris balanced delicately on the topmost block and performed the time honoured summit rites. It then occurred to him that the descent might present its own special problems. He would not consider climbing down by the same route and there was nowhere to fix a *rappel* rope. It was all very depressing. His only hope lay in adjusting the rope across the very tip of the pinnacle so that I could lower him down to safety, but the manoeuvre was fraught with danger for two very obvious reasons. In the first place the rope might slip from its moorings: again, and more important from my point of view, the whole top of the pinnacle might break off under the extra strain. In the event nothing untoward occurred . . .

It is tempting to consider how ironic it might have been for Bonington to achieve the pinnacle of his desire only to be marooned there for all time. One pictures a statuesque yet almost absurd figure sitting cross-legged on its lofty pedestal, contemplating the passing crowds with a jaundiced eye and being fed periodically from a long pole.

Patey's debunking style, funny without being malicious, has had its imitators, but he was the past master at it. Only Mike Thompson years later could compete with him. Though both men used their wit at the expense of other notables of the day, somehow their comments about Chris invariably are sharper and have survived. Perhaps Patey's most memorable effort was a song he later wrote to the tune, inevitably, of 'Onward, Christian Soldiers'. The closing lines of the first verse are what everyone remembers:

> Onward, Christian Bonington, of the ACG
>   Write another page of Alpine history
> He has climbed the Eigerwand; he has climbed the Dru –
>   For a mere ten thousand francs, he will climb with you:
> Onward, C . . . B . . . , of the ACG
>   If you name the mountain, he will name the fee.

This is ironic because they are simply not true. Certainly Chris has never guided for money and in fact has rarely if ever been paid actually to go climbing per se. As we shall see, Chris certainly knows what he is worth; as a lecturer, writer, TV performer, but as a climber pure and simple he has been, is, and always will be, in the best amateur traditions of the sport. Quite recently he described a visit to Innsbruck where he was giving a lecture and asked if there was anyone he could go climbing with. To his amazement he realised halfway through the day that he had hired a guide! The thought had never remotely crossed his mind, any more than, when climbing in the Lakes or Scotland he would even think of charging his partner for a day in the hills.

So Patey, while leaving thousands of climbers a wonderful legacy of humour, verse and song may not have actually done Bonington too many favours. His stories of climbs with Joe Brown and his classic article 'A Short Walk With Whillans' had quite the opposite effect: Whillans in particular emerging as the great anti-hero. But when it comes to Bonington, Patey reflects the disapproval of the traditional climbing community for the successful entrepreneur. Patey, after all, was a practising doctor and did not have to carve out a living for himself from his climbing.

The holiday in Scotland couldn't hide the fact that for Chris Bonington a future in the Army was becoming less and less attractive. His time at the Outward-Bound School was nearly up, and then he would have to return to his regiment. To complicate matters, he had fallen out with the commandant at Towyn who had no experience of mountaineering but was particularly enthusiastic about the merits of early morning sea swimming and canoeing. Bonington actually refused to carry out an order on a particularly stormy day, saying he couldn't be responsible for the safety of his cadets canoeing in those conditions (after he left there *was* a drowning in similar circumstances). Whether or not as a direct result of this, the commandant refused his promotion to captain, normally an almost automatic procedure. This would be a major blight on Bonington's career copybook.

His friend Mike Thompson had shared his career dilemma. Mike had returned from his regiment in Malaya and was embarked on a science course at the Royal Military College at Shrivenham. Like Bonington, Mike was disillusioned with Army life and looking for an academic career as an anthropologist, so he devised an ingenious scheme to get out of the Army by standing as a parliamentary candidate. Members of the armed forces are not allowed to be involved in politics, yet it is anyone's right to stand for Parliament. Faced with this Catch-22 situation, the Army reluctantly had to release him. Bonington decided to resign, too. Mike Thompson remembers: 'When he went in and diffidently suggested to his commanding officer he was thinking of leaving the Army, the officer had the forms ready in his drawer and said, "Sign here!" He was out just like that.'

He had already been invited on a civilian expedition, this time to Nuptse, the third peak of the Everest cirque. Having quit the Army, Bonington accepted the invitation to Nuptse for the spring of 1961 and planned a long alpine season afterwards. Naively, he persuaded himself that this was to be his swan song, after which he would settle down into a career in management. To this end he put in applications to the big companies like Shell, ICI and Unilever, eventually being offered a job as a management trainee with Van den Berghs, an associate of Unilever which sold margarine. With the knowledge that he wouldn't be starting work until September 1961 Bonington set sail for India, Nepal and Nuptse. He had the whole spring and summer to himself, before real life intruded once more.

Nuptse from Kala Pattar

8

Nuptse or Bust

THE 1961 BRITISH Nuptse expedition has gone down in climbing folklore as one of the most disruptive and bitchy expeditions ever to leave the country. At the time it received little publicity and no great acclaim when it eventually succeeded. Now, nearly forty years later, it can be seen as the forerunner of the great Himalayan face climbs of the 'seventies and 'eighties; a climb years ahead of its time and a distant relative of the ultimate Last Great Problem, the South Face of Lhotse, only a few kilometres away on the same great rampart that forms the south side of the Everest massif.

In concept, structure and execution the climb was significantly different from traditional Himalayan expeditions, like that to Annapurna II the previous year. A Manchester-based climber, Joe Walmsley, had led an expedition in 1957 which narrowly failed to climb Masherbrum in the Karakoram; he next planned an attempt on Dhaulagiri, at that time the highest unclimbed peak in the world, but a Swiss expedition, which included the Austrian, Kurt Diemburger, succeeded in 1960, and Walmsley, on the recommendation of Sir John Hunt, turned his attention to Nuptse, which from some views seemed to epitomise the unclimbable mountain, riddled with hanging séracs, knife-edged ridges and avalanche-prone gullies. Probably the most straightforward route on the mountain is actually the North Face, climbed alpine-style by Doug Scott, Al Rouse, Brian Hall and Georges Bettembourg in 1979. However this involved a logistically complicated approach via the dangerous Khumbu Ice-fall into the Western Cwm of Everest, before the climb itself was reached. The 1961 expedition chose the South Face, which avoided the Icefall but climbed a long difficult ridge leading to a steep face. It needed nearly 5000 feet of fixed rope just to equip the ridge and was almost a climb in its own right. Certainly the whole face was in a different league of difficulty and complexity to anything that had been tried before.

Joe Walmsley's team was a talented group of individuals: highly motivated and nearly all on their first Himalayan expedition. It is not hard to see how the stresses of coping with a long steep difficult and dangerous route contributed to a chain reaction of personality clashes that on one occasion actually led to a high-altitude punch-up. It had its problems even before the start. Don Whillans, one of the original members, had recommended Chris Bonington as his climbing partner, but Don managed to break his leg in a motorbike accident while returning from packing the expedition equipment in Manchester. He dropped out but it is interesting to speculate whether he and Chris climbing together at the height of their powers would have made an unhappy expedition better or perhaps even worse. Les Brown, a tall, gangly Lake District climber, was the youngest member of the team. Fair-minded and undemonstrative, he is even now unwilling to reopen old wounds. In the days before regular air travel access to the Himalaya was laborious and various. Les Brown had been part of the overland contingent with Dennis Davis, Simon Clark, Trevor Jones and Jim Lovelock:

I'd got my ear bent on the way out. The others had some misgiv-ings over Don's chosen partner, the gist of which was that 'He'll want to take over the whole bloody show, that bugger.' It was quite a strong feeling. I'd been indoctrinated by Trevor in particu-lar. I'd no idea what to expect. I got on with him very well throughout the expedition. Of course you can imagine what it was like, we'd just spent five weeks in snow, mud and deserts. Joe Walmsley and Jim Swallow had flown in and Chris had come out by boat and had some sort of romance on the way to Bombay and we'd been sleeping in −40° in Turkey . . . But he'd done his bit in getting all the gear up from Bombay through India.

On the walk-in, normally a time to relax and get focused, tensions were evident. Dennis Davis, with plenty of alpine snow and ice experience, felt that he was amongst a team of rock climbing prima donnas. This certainly had an element of truth in it. Trevor Jones was definitely a rock climber with not much snow and ice experience who, on hearing of Don Whillans' withdrawal from the team, was reputed to have said, 'Well, I'll just have to pull all the stops out now!' Dennis Davis had been turned back by bad weather very high on Annapurna II when he and Charles Evans had made a determined attempt to climb it without oxygen. Davis had another huge incentive to succeed on Nuptse, for he had given up his job to go on the expedition, the only one of the team to do so. Chris, of course, had given up the Army, but had something else to return to. The seeds of competition, even rivalry, were there from the beginning.

It would be tedious to describe the various comings and goings and ups and downs of the expedition. Incidents erupted for most of the usual reasons – failures in communication being the factor they all had in common. Thus, perceived selfishness in hogging the lead, apparent laziness in failing to carry loads in support, gluttony, sloth, and hypochondria all played their part. Perhaps a stronger leader might have curbed some of the backbiting, but the basic chemistry of an expedition is virtually impossible to change. By the time the team were in some sort of position to make a bid for the summit two members had gone home and the only serious contenders for the summit were Dennis Davis, Les Brown, Jim Swallow, two Sherpas, Ang Pemba and Tashi, and of course Bonington himself.

He and Davis had forced most of the route together but Chris had found Davis hard to relate to. He was organised, tidy and self-disciplined, none of which virtues have ever been high on the Bonington agenda. After the expedition Bonington, perhaps unwisely, tried to describe the kind of situation that an incompatible pair can find themselves in. It was a couple of sentences that were obviously an attempt to show his own weakness that caused the trouble. Predictably, they incensed Davis: 'He continued chopping steps in the hard ice. I cursed him with everything I could think of – imagined the satisfaction of smashing a fist in his face.' Later in the chapter he recognises he was at fault and apologises for his outburst but Davis, one feels, has never really forgiven him.

Later, Bonington and Les Brown were in support of Davis and Tashi and came to an agreement with them that, while he and Les Brown established the top camp, Davis and Tashi would prepare the route up the final gully that led to the summit ridge. But when they emerged at the top of the gully Davis saw his chance for the top and took it, to Bonington's chagrin: 'The bastard's gone for the top, I told Les.'

Yet, on learning of their success, Bonington tried to be magnanimous. The following day he and Ang Pemba, Jim Swallow and Les Brown repeated the climb, but for Bonington the principal feeling on getting to the top was relief rather than elation. Being second wasn't good enough.

The friction, which one might have supposed would have disappeared in the light of what should have been a totally successful expedition, was heightened on the descent when Dennis Davis discovered a tin of pears at Camp 3 and shared them out. Unfortunately, the tin had been hoarded by Trevor Jones who, on finding his treasure had been plundered, became apoplectic with rage.

Les Brown feels, in retrospect, that Jones, Davis and Bonington all exaggerated their differences to justify their own versions of events. 'It was all over my head – I was a youngster, twenty-four, madly keen to go to the Himalayas and a lot of the undercurrents, well, I didn't experience them at all, though I did have a big altercation with Jim Swallow.' In fact it was a punch-up that took place in two mountain tents tied together with a tunnel entrance and would have been hilarious to witness had anyone been looking on from outside. It is hard not to agree with Les Brown that incidents such as this obscured what should have been hailed as a brilliant success.

When Bonington looked across from the summit of Nuptse at Everest's huge South-West Face, he admits he had no idea that fourteen years later he would lead the expedition that would make the first ascent. Maybe he didn't even quite appreciate what the Nuptse team had just done, for it was to be nine years before the lessons learned on Nuptse were to be absorbed and developed on the South Face of Annapurna.

And that, one would have thought, was that. But now there was the little matter of getting home and Chris, having come out by

Winifride Storey – 'Nan'

Charles Bonington – Oxford 1928

Helen Anne Bonington

Charles and Helen

The infant Christian at eleven months
practising for the front cover of this biography

Aged four at Pets Corner of London Zoo   On holiday in Brighton, 1940

An early visit to Harrisons Rocks, on the Isolated Buttress. Note the hemp rope

Second lieutenant C. J. S. Bonington shortly after commissioning from Sandhurst

Great Central Route – Avon Gorge, 1955

(Above) Chris and Wendy
in 1961

(Left) Return from the Eiger

On the summit of the Central Tower of Paine

(Below) Leading the Right Unconquerable, Stanage

Unique meetings – with Walter Bonatti and Don Whillans . . . and the only Nuptse reunion ever held. Standing, *left to right:* Dennis Davis, Jim Lovelock, John Streetly, Jim Swallow, Les Brown, Simon Clark. Sitting, *left to right:* Trevor Jones, CB, Joe Walmsley

Chris with Conrad

The Old Man of Hoy

Chris and Mike Thompson revisit the
Avon Gorge

(Below) Wendy and Daniel and Rupert in
1972

Nick Estcourt

Doug Scott

Pete Boardman

Joe Tasker

boat, had to face the gruelling overland journey in the company of Les Brown, Trevor Jones and Dennis Davis. Unsurprisingly, the tensions that had beset the expedition didn't go away. Their frustrations culminated in an unseemly wrestling match between Chris and Trevor Jones which got out of hand when Chris, failing to appreciate that Jones was lying on a rock, nearly broke his back. He wrote in *I Chose to Climb*: 'at the end of it none of us was an enemy for life, as has happened after quite a few expeditions. Similarly, few friendships were cemented. We had remained throughout nine individuals – at best several small groups – but never a complete team.'

But despite their differences there is an interesting postscript to the Nuptse expedition. In 1962 Sir John Hunt was to lead a joint Anglo-Scottish expedition to the Russian Pamirs. Bonington was not included. In October 1961 he sent Hunt a very blunt letter criticising his choice of team:

> It is certainly not representative. Don Whillans, undoubtedly our best mountaineer (Brown has done nothing major in climbing for six years) has been ignored ... Quite a few of your party, though very pleasant people, are not particularly good climbers ... You might well think that this letter is a case of sour grapes. To be quite frank I was disappointed and hurt not to be invited – I was not aware that I was such an odd man out. However I could not have gone anyway since I have only just started a new career ... In conclusion I would strongly urge that if any vacancies *do* occur they should go to people like Don Whillans, Dennis Davis or even one of the younger generation like Ian Clough ...

So, despite all that had passed between them Bonington was still generously prepared to recommend Dennis Davis. It is also interesting to note that in 1961 Joe Brown was being written off as a serious mountaineer. (He went to the Pamirs in Hunt's team and climbed Mount Communism with Ian McNaught-Davis. Fourteen years later he climbed the Nameless Trango Tower in the Karakoram – at the age of forty-six!) It is fascinating to speculate why Bonington thought he was seen as 'an odd man out'. Today Chris can't remember what provoked this comment. Was it a feeling that the establishment wasn't quite sure about him? Tom Patey's song 'Red Pique' sums it all up. Here are the relevant verses:

> *Customs change and so alas*
> *We now include the working class,*
> *So we invited Good Old Joe*
> *To come along and join the show.*
> *He played his part, he fitted in,*
> *He justified our faith in him;*
> *We want the climbing world to know –*
> *That the chaps all got on well with Joe . . .*

> *The Noble Blood of an English Peer*
> *Adapts to a rarefied atmosphere*
> *And that is why the Old School Tie*
> *May be expected to Go High.*
> *Up they go! DAMN good show!*
> *Stamping steps in the Virgin Snow*
> *Hey nonny No! Fol dol dol!*
> *Jolly John Hunt and the Old South Col.*

> *Our climbing leaders are no fools;*
> *They went to the very best Public Schools.*
> *You'll never go wrong with Everest Men,*
> *So we select them again and again,*
> *Again and again and again and again.*
> *You won't go wrong with Everest Men;*
> *They went to the very best Public Schools,*
> *They play the game, they know the rules . . .*

> *One last question for Sir John –*
> *Where have all the hard men gone?*
> *Good Old Joe! Why not Don?*
> *Where was Christian Bonington?*
> *Sir John replied, 'The mountaineers*
> *Who showed the flag in the High Pamirs*
> *Were men of charm and tact and skill*
> *Overflowing with good will!'*

9

He Chose Not to Sell Margarine

By THE TIME the dust-encrusted Standard Vanguard reached Chamonix at the end of the 5000-mile journey from Kathmandu, Bonington was physically and mentally drained, not the superfit Himalayan athlete he had perhaps hoped he would be. He met Don Whillans, now recovered from his broken leg, and they did a short training climb on the Aiguille de l'M above Chamonix, which confirmed Chris's doubts. Whillans, pragmatic as always, suggested going straight to Switzerland to try the Eiger: 'You can do your training on the Face. By the time you get to the top you'll be fit – or dead!'

It was the first time the pair had spent any time together since the Bonatti Pillar. Superficially they seemed singularly ill-suited. Chris, lean, rather haughty, well spoken, absent-minded but the apparently self-confident ex-Army officer, and Whillans, short, powerful, abrasive, exuding common sense, but with the sort of Andy Capp stroppy I-know-my-rights mentality that one would have thought would have driven Chris to distraction. Don Whillans had made his name and reputation with Joe Brown but they had split up for a variety of reasons. Two big factors were that Brown inevitably got more publicity and his enigmatic personality was much more acceptable to the climbing establishment than Whillans' uncompromising, even aggressive, attitude. Don undoubtedly felt that Joe had reaped the rewards of their partnership while he to

Bonington and Whillans setting off
for the Eiger 1962

some extent had lost out. But another probably bigger factor was that Joe wasn't particularly interested in the climbs Don wanted to do, the North Face of the Eiger in particular. Don felt that Joe was over-cautious on big routes and realised that he and Bonington made a near-perfect partnership. Chris was the pusher, always prepared to carry on and Don became the wise counsel, ever calculating, weighing up the risks, using all his practical skill and judgement, in the knowledge that Chris could contribute inspirational flair and total commitment.

It is interesting that so many climbers have come to almost deify Whillans as the great Alpinist but still under-rate Bonington's abilities. It is self-evident that they wouldn't have climbed together unless they enjoyed it and both have written of the satisfaction they found in their partnership. First Bonington: 'Once we got on to a mountain we became a complete team, a single smooth-functioning machine. We never talked much, never seemed to waste any time, built up a rhythm of smooth steady movement that, to me, is the height of pleasure in climbing. I have certainly never enjoyed climbing with anyone as much as Don.' Whillans wrote: 'We were an ill-assorted pair but we balanced each other – his impetuosity: my stolidness; his vulnerability: my terseness. On a climb we made a sound partnership and I enjoyed climbing with him immensely. If Joe wasn't here, I could think of nobody better to share the climb with than Chris.'

Of course there *were* big differences. Don was always very aware of his deprived Salford background, though in later years he would frequently quip, 'People have always described me as working class – but I haven't worked for years.' He was at times both aggressive (punch-ups in bars being a frequent source of legend) and incredibly lazy; cooking for instance was out of the question under any circumstances and stories are legion of Whillans' refusal to even make a brew for exhausted climbers returning to camp.

Another bone of contention that would grow over the years of their partnership was money, or lack of it, and this, as it often does, probably undermined their friendship more than anything else. Bonington, from their earliest forays on the Eiger, could see the commercial possibilities in publicising their climbs. Though inexperienced, he apparently had no qualms in contacting daily papers and trying to sell a story. Many years later Don told me that 'Chris was fine until he got greedy.' This was a view he made no bones about, yet it is hard not to feel that, as with Joe's successes on TV outside broadcasts, Don was simply jealous that he hadn't been able to show the same sort of flair for self-publicity that he thought Chris had. Over the years Don, in fact, developed and marketed his own reputation very successfully but there was always the underlying feeling that somehow he had been outflanked by Chris.

In those early days Chris said, 'Don hated having anything to do with everyday money transactions and I had therefore been appointed treasurer and chief buyer – I did all the shopping.' It is easy to see that Don was happy to relinquish any responsibility for their finances but equally unhappy when Chris started to make money. Not that it was very much. After a couple of weeks' bad weather they had a tentative foray on the Eiger, finding it totally out of condition and plastered with ice and powder snow. Once again they returned to Chamonix where Chris managed to get a job advertising a camera, posing self-consciously above the Mer de Glace. (Whillans, typically, was turned down for the modelling role – too butch by far!)

Their objective was the then current Last Great Problem in the Alps, the Central Pillar of Frêney, high on the Italian side of Mont Blanc. This beautiful orange granite buttress is situated in as wild and remote a setting as anywhere in the Alps. It had been the scene that July of one of the worst disasters in Alpine history. The great Walter Bonatti and his two companions, Andrea Oggioni and Roberto Gallieni, had teamed up with four French climbers, Pierre Mazeaud, Antoine Vieille, Robert Guillaume and Pierre Kohlman. They climbed without too much trouble to the foot of the final pinnacle, la Chandelle, where a violent and prolonged storm broke. They tried to sit it out, in the hope that completing the climb and finishing over the summit of Mont Blanc would be less dangerous than a long avalanche-prone retreat, but after two desperate bivouacs Bonatti decided to descend. In the course of the next two days four of the seven men died. Only Bonatti, Mazeaud and Gal-lieni made it back to the safety of the Gamba Hut where a rescue was being organised.

Bonington and Whillans had only the sketchiest outline of what had happened when, in the middle of August, they teamed up with the Yorkshire climber, Ian Clough, and a Pole, Jan Djuglosz, whom they had met at the foot of the Eiger. By deciding to attempt the Pillar of Frêney they undoubtedly, if inadvertently, upset the French climbing élite, in particular Pierre Mazeaud, still shocked and grieving the loss of his friends. Today it is hard to see why. There have been many precedents for successive teams of different nationalities attempting the same new route. The Eiger and Walker Spur immediately come to mind. But for whatever reason Mazeaud took it personally and it was the source of friction with British climbers in general and Whillans in particular several years later when they were both members of the 1971 International Everest expedition. Perhaps in the end Bonington's and Whillans' real crime was to succeed in climbing the Pillar while just behind them a strong French team led by René Desmaison had to swallow their pride and ask for a rope to be taken up the crux pitch and fixed so that they could prussik up.

The ascent was by any standards a tour de force. The crux was actually led by Bonington after Whillans had fallen off trying to climb into an overhanging chimney crack. Bonington outwitted the hardest moves by using inserted chockstones in the Welsh fashion. La Chandelle had given several pitches of extremely hard climbing right at the end of a long route and was undoubtedly the best first ascent done by a British team since before the war when Graham Brown and Frank Smythe pioneered their classic routes on the Brenva Face of Mont Blanc.

Fresh from their success, Bonington and Whillans dashed back to Alpiglen and the North Face of the Eiger. Their travels had been eased by Bonington striking up a romantic involvement with an American girl called Anne who had a car. Bonington had made a deal with the *Daily Mail* for exclusive coverage of the first British ascent and inevitably the couple had to endure a photographer's attentions and the front page photo – 'A kiss before the Eiger.' This attempt was as inconclusive as their first but for the opposite reason: the constant fine weather now meant heavy stonefall and after one bivouac low on the face during which the temperature never fell below zero and running water seeped from the ice fields above, Whillans, safety-conscious as usual, counselled retreat. Their season was over.

Bonington, cutting it fine, bade farewell to Anne at Geneva airport, and started his new life only a few hours later at Van den

Berghs. After enduring a six-month training course he was given his first real job – selling margarine to grocers' shops in Hampstead. It is a moot point how well Chris Bonington persuaded himself that he was now destined to follow a business career, with climbing relegated to a weekend hobby. Mike Thompson remembers that for a time Chris was even prepared to sacrifice weekends. But his job, to open new accounts and close down the unprofitable ones, was really little more than that of a sales rep. Ian McNaught-Davis, an old friend already beginning to be a high-flyer in business, at first with Shell, then with his own computer company remembers, in his typically forthright manner, how the young would-be executive came to see him about his career. 'At that time they used to have things called management trainees – it was complete bullshit! They knew they couldn't tell an ex-Army officer his job was to flog marge. But if they imagined that if they called him a management trainee he would think Oh yes, that's it. I'm on the fast track to management. I'll end up being Chief Executive of Unilever. Chris saw that it was a nonsense very quickly. It was a con and he hated it, absolutely hated it.'

Bonington was certainly unhappy and, as the year wore on, his doubts about his latest career move increased. At the same time, however, he was to have what was probably the biggest stroke of luck in his life.

Wendy Marchant was the daughter of a former evangelical Baptist minister who, disillusioned with the church, had become a book illustrator in Hove, Sussex. She had inherited her father's artistic ability, attending the local Brighton Art College for three years before leaving at the end of what was then called the Intermediate Course to try and earn some money as a freelance illustrator. She remembers how a chance encounter by a friend in London led her to meet Chris:

> He was going to give a lecture and as usual he was in a hurry to catch a train. Sylvia was sitting in a compartment – the door opened as the train started moving and this man flung himself in and all these slides scattered all over the floor. She helped him pick them up and they got talking. She ascertained he lived only a few minutes away from the flat she shared with four other girls in Haverstock Hill and suggested he might like to come to a

party they were having at the weekend. So at some stage Rosa, my particular friend, rang up and said that Sylvia had met this fair-haired guy who had just come back from the Himalayas and invited him to a party. She actually said, 'I think we might have found your explorer'.

Wendy smiled at the memory and explained:

Very early in life, when I was twelve, and I can remember *exactly* where it was, I was standing outside our garden gate, talking to my best friend and I said, 'I'm going to marry an outdoor type – no nine to five person for me.' I had this idealised picture of someone blondish – I suppose I was thinking in terms of a Canadian lumberjack type. So I thought on my way up to London, right, I'm eyeing this one up. He wasn't there when I arrived but then someone said, 'Oh, look, he's just come in', and I looked over and saw this blue-eyed, rosy cheeked, incredibly young baby-faced chap. I'd imagined a sort of tanned rugged type with a hint of grey at the temples. It wasn't an immediate thing but I found some way of talking to him and it didn't take very long before we were dancing pretty closely – let's put it like that. I always remember the tweed of his jacket against my face and his warmth. I don't know, there was something about the way he talked, his enthusiasm. I've always liked enthusiastic people; that to me is the top drawer, people who sparkle with enthusiasm and that was so much him. Then he said why don't you come along and have a cup of coffee? Now I was very innocent – I thought he meant a cup of coffee . . . I really thought he meant a cup of coffee . . . so off we went.

For Chris, who had had several girlfriends over the years but nothing terribly serious, it was love at first sight. 'She was small and dark, wore a little black dress and rubbed herself up against me when we danced with the ecstatic pleasure of a kitten being stroked. Fortunately, she wasn't in the least bit conventional and was even more appalled by my future in the margarine business than I.'

By this time Bonington had succeeded in closing down over a dozen accounts in six months, but failed to open a single new one.

Cunningly, he now kept Fridays almost free to get away to Wales or the Lakes early. Slowly he realised that, like the Army, a career in business was not what he wanted. Marrying Wendy *was* what he wanted but after that? Bonington, insecure but ambitious, wrestled, as he was often to do, indeed still does, between the demands of security and freedom. Wendy remembers going for a long walk over Hampstead Heath with Chris agonising over what to do. Helen Bonington, despite her fairly unconventional career and lifestyle, thought her son should knuckle down to a career. Wendy, whose upbringing was emotionally far more secure, was all for Chris taking the plunge and trying to make a living out of climbing.

To complicate matters, Bonington had received an invitation to go on an expedition in the winter of 1962 to Patagonia to attempt the unclimbed Towers of Paine, a windswept collection of granite spires at the very foot of South America. Initially he had refused, but the temptation to go, and now the possibility of taking Wendy with him, was too strong. He wrote a letter to Van den Berghs asking for leave of absence. Not unnaturally they refused point blank and bluntly asked him to decide between mountaineering and management. Bonington at last took the plunge and, to quote Mike Thompson's play on the title of his first book, 'He Chose Not to Sell Margarine.'

· 10 ·

The Eiger Beckons

CHRIS AND WENDY married in May, only five months after they first met. His flatmate Billy Wilkinson was best man. Having made his make or break decision to leave Van den Berghs, with Wendy's full backing, Chris accepted the invitation to Patagonia and decided to take Wendy with him. But first was the little matter of the North Face of the Eiger, still without a first British ascent and consequently very marketable to the press, for whom the Eiger epitomised everything that was sensational, even mad in climbing.

Bonington, almost penniless, sold the story to the *Daily Express* who photographed him and Whillans leaving London on Don's motorbike: Chris, riding pillion with an enormous rucksack, is wearing a climbing helmet; Whillans, the Villain, as he was known, is wearing his usual flat hat and looks flinty-eyed into the lens. Once again the weather was against them: the face was running with melt-water and just below the infamous Hinterstoisser Traverse, which marks the start of the real difficulties, Bonington contrived to drop his ice axe. This time however, after a wet bivouac, and despite threatening weather, they decided to push on, reckoning that retreat was still a reasonable option. They reached the foot of the Second Icefield, a huge grey sweep of 45-degree ice leading to the steeper Upper Face. It is probably the most dangerous part of the North Face as it is totally exposed to stonefall from above. Just as they decided to retreat they heard a shout from below and were

Eiger North Face

told by two Swiss guides that a British party ahead of them had had an accident. Chris and Don agreed to help and immediately set off up the Icefield towards a tiny red figure they could just see where the ice met the rock above. The stonefall increased.

'It's as good as a bloody war film,' was Don's cryptic comment. Suddenly and horrifically they saw a figure shoot down the ice and hurtle, almost in slow motion, into space. Shocked and stunned, Chris swore and hugged the ice until he got a grip of himself. Slowly and methodically they carried on, towards the minute red dot which was still in the same position, praying that he wasn't injured. When at last they reached him, Chris recognised Brian Nally.

Nally had been climbing with Barry Brewster who, like Chris, had started climbing at Harrisons Rocks. He had gone on to study at Bangor University to be near the North Welsh crags. Brewster was a very talented and single-minded climber, utterly committed to hard rock climbs but comparatively inexperienced on snow and ice. Nally, a house painter from London, had more humble origins, but he had made the first British ascent of the North Face of the Matterhorn the year before. Nally had reckoned that Brewster was the brains of the team – 'I was the navvy.' It was a not dissimilar partnership that Chris himself had formed with Hamish MacInnes in 1957 and it is hard not to agree that, in the light of what happened to Brewster and Nally, Chris's earlier forebodings about an unequal team were justified.

Nally and Brewster had taken an age to cross the Second Icefield and on the first rock pitch above it Brewster had been knocked from his holds by stonefall, falling nearly 200 feet before Nally held him. Unconscious and with a broken back, Brewster had died in the night, despite Nally's desperate efforts to save him. His body had been swept from the ice by another burst of stonefall and Nally, now in deep shock, seemed unable to comprehend what was happening and asked Chris if he could tie on and go with them to the top. Chris, stressed out, exploded in anger and yelled that they'd come to rescue him, before realising how unfair his outburst had been. Taking control he began to untangle Nally's rope which hung like knitting around his neck. Don, 150 feet below and still in the line of fire from stonefall, could only stand and wait, silently imploring Chris to get a move on. At last they were ready, and moved down slowly and carefully. By now, rain, turning to hail, had started falling. Nally, bare-headed, was hit by a stone and staggered in his steps. Whillans later wrote: 'As they approached I could see that the worst was going to happen. Nally would be a complete liability on the descent. His eyes were blank and his expression wooden. Shock, exhaustion and exposure had reduced him to a robot state. How long could we keep him moving before the mental strain became too much?'

At the end of the Second Icefield the storm broke with full ferocity, thunder, lightning and torrential hail which threatened to sweep them all off the face. During a lull they managed to abseil to just above the Hinterstoisser Traverse where Whillans had a stroke of genius. In 1936 a team led by Andreas Hinterstoisser failed to find a way down in a similar storm, and couldn't reverse the crucial traverse that now bears his name. In attempting to descend all four were killed in harrowing circumstances. Don, instead of branching back right, went left to a point where a long abseil led to the far side of the traverse and effectively the end of the difficulties. As Tom Patey later wrote, 'If Hinterstoisser had realised that, he would probably not now have a Traverse named after him and the Eigerwand would not enjoy one half its present notoriety.'

From there the three climbed to one of the strangest features of the Eiger, the Stollenloch Window. A rack railway actually runs through the North Face and the window gives a vantage point for tourists to gawp down the face from a position of total safety. Once inside, Bonington wrote:

We were blinded by the flash bulbs of press cameras, and the whole ghastly nightmare reached its climax . . . a couple of Swiss journalists had laid on a special train to take us down, just to make sure of getting the story first . . . they got the full story from Nally, taking advantage of his shocked condition.

A couple of days later he was presented with the bill for his rescue – one for several hundred pounds, covering the employment of fourteen guides, the hire of a special train and the loss or damage to the guides' equipment. He didn't have the money; he could probably have sold his story for a large amount immediately after the accident but the Swiss journalists had already prised it from him, and anyway, the very last thing he had thought of was to sell the story of his friend's death to the highest bidder.

Both Chris and Don were disillusioned with the publicity surrounding the death of Brewster and Nally's rescue, and the following day they got on Don's bike and drove across to Austria, where Wendy and Don's wife Audrey, joined them. The pair enjoyed three weeks of magnificent rock climbing on dry sunny faces, culminating in a very fast ascent of the North Face of the Badile in Switzerland before returning to Chamonix, ostensibly en route for England.

Here, nearly at the end of August, they found perfect weather. Both acted in character, Chris, impetuous, opportunistic even, realised that a big route like the Walker Spur on the Grandes Jorasses was there for the taking. Don, however, had planned to be home by the end of the month and wouldn't be swayed. Not for the first time (and certainly not for the last), Whillans' seeming inflexibility of purpose worked against him. Chris teamed up with Ian Clough, who had been with them on the Frêney Pillar the year before, and the pair made a fast, uneventful ascent of the Walker Spur before Chris, once again seizing the opportunity, suggested that instead of merely descending the easy way down the Grandes Jorasses into Italy, they should make a long traverse of the Rochefort Ridge. Ian Clough agreed: 'All right by me, how about going the whole hog and doing a traverse of the whole bloody range – finish on the top of Mont Blanc?' Bonington was on cloud nine. 'It was wonderful climbing with someone who could respond so spontaneously to an impromptu change of plan – who had exactly the same enthusiasm as I had.'

In fact they didn't quite complete the project. After a very long day they arrived shattered at the Torino Hut. Despite his fatigue, Bonington had yet another idea and at first light woke up an unreceptive Clough.

'How about going for the Eiger?'

'Fuck off. Tell me about it later.'

Two hours later Bonington's persuasive powers had won him round and only two days later they were at the foot of the Eiger, sorting out their gear and leaving late in the afternoon to bivouac on a sheltered ledge below the Difficult Crack. Conditions were still perfect and the next morning they set off early: 'After a hurried breakfast, we packed our sacks and I started up the Difficult Crack – it was the first time I had led it, this had always been Don's pitch. I had a momentary pang of guilt as I looked up at it; wondered what would be Don's feelings if we succeeded, but then put the thought aside for I knew he would have done the same in similar circumstances.'

Their luck with the weather held and they climbed fast. So fast that by five in the evening they had reached the infamous White Spider, the hanging icefield near the top of the face with ice-seamed gullies spreading out above and below that gives the feature its wholly appropriate name. Here, as Bonington started onto the ice, a falling stone bounded past. Caution prevailed and the pair bivouacked in reasonable comfort as the night frost gripped the face and the stonefall ceased. Again they were away early and, despite a route-finding error they found the Exit Cracks above the Spider completely free of ice and little more than a scramble. In normal conditions the Exit Cracks have proved to be as hard as anything on the face. In a storm they are a formidable challenge to an exhausted party.

They reached the summit early enough to enjoy the view, eat dried fruit and sunbathe, and still get down the mountain in only a couple of hours where their joy was abruptly cut short with the news that behind them, a Scot, Tom Carruthers and an Austrian named Anton Moderegger had been killed on the Second Icefield. Like Brewster and Nally they had been climbing very slowly and had become exposed to rockfall late in the day. The Eiger had once more exacted its price.

The *Daily Express* got the story it wanted of the first British ascent, and Bonington and Clough received a congratulatory telegram from the Prime Minister, Harold Macmillan. In terms of Eiger history their ascent was not significant (it was the thirty-first) but for young British mountaineers it probably did more than any other climb to instil a sense of self-confidence and belief that they could compete with their European contemporaries. True, Brown and Whillans on the West Face of the Dru, and Bonington and Whillans on the Frêney Pillar had won similar accolades, but there was something about the Eiger that, despite the hysterical press coverage, struck a chord with aspiring Brits. Bonington's position at the top of British mountaineering was established almost overnight, and would be maintained for many years to come.

Another result of the publicity was that after a long gap Chris's father, Charles, made contact, which Chris felt slightly sceptical about. Suddenly Chris became aware of a new set of relatives – a young half-brother, Gerald, and three half-sisters, Alison, Rosemary and Liz. They lived outside Bristol with their mother. Charles, who was still a heavy drinker, was no better a husband the second time around and Chris feels he was actually less scarred by his father's absences than his half-brother and sisters. Gerald, in particular, was very proud of his new brother and, when Chris came to Bristol, everyone went off to see his Eiger lecture and Gerald became aware that he had a famous relative. Chris even took him as a five-year-old for a little climb in the Avon Gorge, which was the beginning of Gerald's interest in climbing, which continues to the present day.

As far as Chris and Wendy were concerned the Eiger could hardly have been better timed. What a way to start the uncertain career of a professional climber! The Eiger opened doors to lectures, articles and even a book. On a more immediate level it raised the cash for Chris and Wendy to travel together to Patagonia.

And what of Don Whillans? Some contemporaries were of the opinion that he and Chris would probably never have succeeded on the Eiger. Don was just too cautious. Indeed, Whillans never did, despite several further forays in which he probably chalked up more time on the North Face than anyone else before or since. There is no doubt that he was incensed with Chris's commercial exploitation of the climb and he wrote Chris a bitter letter accusing him of cheapening the whole experience. But the fact remains that if he had taken his chance with Chris and not gone home he might well have shared the glory. What was rather more awkward was that Chris, Ian Clough and Don were shortly to be thrown together again, for all three had been invited to go to Patagonia and the Towers of Paine. The potential for conflict must have given Chris and Don in particular some pause for thought. Could they ever swallow their pride and climb together again?

Not only would the answer be yes, but four years later the pair even set foot on the Eiger once more, albeit briefly. This was when Chris was involved in the Eiger Direct, an ambitious project that was to attract enormous publicity. Chris would be there ostensibly as a photo-journalist with Don (who hated the whole extravaganza) as his assistant. Though they didn't achieve much – Don suffered an attack of vertigo to which he was occasionally prone – it must have been a strange little episode for them both for Bonington was by now in full media flight while Don was, if anything, even more entrenched in his cynicism.

Perhaps symbolically the North Face of the Eiger came to stand for success for Chris, and to epitomise everything that appeared to be just out of Don's reach.

· 11 ·

Patagonia, Paine and Pain

WHEN CHRIS AND Wendy Bonington and the rest of the British Patagonian expedition set sail on the SS *Reina Del Mar* for Valparaiso they could be forgiven for thinking that they were quite literally embarking on a voyage that would lead to a new life, though quite what it was to be was another matter. The previous month had been a hectic round of lectures about the Eiger to raise enough money for both of them to go to Patagonia, as well as preparing for the expedition itself.

Derek Walker, at that time a school teacher in Cheshire, seems to have taken the brunt of the day to day organisation and still has a bulging file of letters from equipment firms and expedition members. Amongst them are many from Don Whillans (who was, rather surprisingly, a prolific letter writer). Some of his asides are revealing: 'would like to have done the Eiger but things went "beyond the pale". Too much bullshit and crazy loons about' and, tellingly, 'I've written to Chris . . . I told him to come back to earth and stop fucking about in the stratosphere!'

The letters from Bonington to Derek are remarkable only in the number of ways he manages to mis-spell Derek (Derrek, Derik, Dereck, Darek) and an early example of an incredible piece of Bonington optimism: 'I have talked to Unilever and told them I am going on the expedition. It is just possible they will keep me on and give me a higher salary.' Whillans clearly had a point.

Central Tower of Paine

Before they left Bonington had once again sold the story to the *Daily Express*. The paper ran a large feature on the team and its objective, as well as a column by journalist Nancy Banks-Smith praising the two women who were accompanying them. (Barrie Page the expedition leader was also taking his wife and small son with him.) The article is a telling example of how much times have changed. Banks-Smith praises Wendy and Elaine for 'following their men' to the mountain and writes approvingly of their abilities to cook, be hairdressers and generally remain subservient. The quoted opinion of Whillans ('the demon king with crampons on') was predictable: 'Women are out of place in a Base Camp. They fuss. They expect attention . . . It'll be "do this" and "have you done that?"' The 'more-trouble-than-they're-worth' women, the article concluded lamely, said nothing as they were too busy cooking curry, cutting cake and brewing tea for twenty!

However, as Wendy Bonington now remembers, being on a seven-man expedition did present problems for her. 'Elaine and I were supposed to be staying in the local estancia but it didn't work out and we ended up staying at Base Camp. The expedition was a very macho affair and we weren't supposed to put a foot into the Base Camp tent – all sorts of petty things which took me by surprise.' For Chris the presence of Wendy was both a pleasure and a problem, as he wanted to spend as much time with her, yet felt he was isolating himself from the rest of the expedition.

They had arrived below the Towers of Paine at the end of a long spell of fine weather, a rare event in Patagonia where high winds blowing off the Southern Ocean are the norm. The good weather lasted until the team set foot on the Central Tower, then broke as Bonington started the first pitch. He climbed only four metres before retreating with numb fingers, awed by the force of the wind hammering the walls of the Tower. From then on the expedition became a war of attrition with painfully slow progress on the very few good climbing days. Christmas came and went in a haze of alcohol and the weather stayed foul. Tents at the foot of the Tower weren't up to the battering and had to be collapsed every time the team retreated to the valley.

The arrival of an Italian expedition after Christmas with designs on the Central Tower focused everyone's mind on the problems of using every available piece of good weather actually climbing. Don came up with the idea of a wooden prefabricated shelter that could be assembled at the bottom of the Tower. Thus was born the concept of the Whillans Box, used to so much good effect a decade later on Annapurna and Everest. The Box proved to be the key to the climb. The Italians were pressing at the heels of the British, claiming with some justification that they had permission for the Central Tower while the British 'South Patagonian Survey expedition' didn't. There was real tension between the two groups, which probably wasn't helped by Whillans' potential for aggression. Bonington, on the other hand, rather enjoyed the cloak and dagger manoeuvring that had to be employed to keep ahead of their rivals. One day, while descending through the forests above Base Camp he and Barrie Page heard voices and took evasive action: 'we slunk through the trees like a pair of Partisans. I must confess I've always had a fondness for playing at soldiers and on the whole, found the Italian threat thoroughly stimulating.'

This competitive spirit has always been a driving force in Bonington's career, but Derek Walker remembers that he was so driven and single-minded on the Paine expedition that Don proved much easier to get on with. This, given Whillans' pent-up aggression and latent violence, seems very surprising. The two men had so far avoided climbing with each other throughout the expedition, with Eiger memories still rankling. But with the Italian threat they decided to team up again. In doing so they would be making the most powerful thrusting pair, and one that would be much stronger than any other combination, British or Italian. At last, in the middle of January, the weather cleared and very early one morning Chris and Don set off up the ropes that had already been fixed on previous attempts. It was on one of these that Whillans, climbing hand over hand, had a miraculous escape. On a steep slab, a rope, frayed by the constant wind blowing it over a sharp edge of rock, snapped. With lightning reflexes Don managed to get his weight onto his feet and somehow didn't fall backwards to almost certain death. Calmly he retied the rope and carried on. Chris remembers being more shaken than Don.

They reached the end of the fixed ropes and looked up at the new ground ahead just as, far below, the Italians, stung into action, prepared to follow them. So long as their route-finding was reliable Chris and Don would stay in front but if they made a mistake the

Italians might get past. So Barrie Page and John Streetly, climbing in support, began to remove the fixed ropes to slow the Italians down.

Now Chris, in the lead, began what he later described as the best piece of climbing he had ever done, a magnificent pitch on perfect granite. At first, trying to climb a small overhang, he fell off and dangled upside down five metres below the overhang. Angry rather than shocked, he put in an extra piton and on the second attempt he succeeded. Above the overhang the climbing was still hard and technical. According to Whillans progress was slow and pitons were used the whole way, but Bonington makes the point that he had a traditional British aversion to an excessive use of pitons and tried to use as few as possible. Above this Whillans led another long pitch, then it all gradually eased and they made quicker progress up complex ice-filled blocky terrain. The summit seemed a long way off and, racing the evening sky, they left their bivouac gear and climbed on unencumbered, hoping they would be able to get back to their rucksacks before it was totally dark.

The summit remained obstinately out of reach as each rocky projection revealed a higher one further on. At last Whillans climbed a final wall and gave the welcome news that he was on top. Together they shouted 'big Ned is dead!' – Big Ned being the nickname that the expedition had given to the Central Tower. Bonington remembered feeling a superstitious dread that they might be pushing their luck. Standing on the summit was one of those magic moments that in the end make climbing so compulsive. A great orange sun was dropping down behind the Patagonian Ice Cap, the wind had dropped, and all was silent. They photographed each other on Bonington's camera in black and white, both standing in exactly the same place and striking an identical pose. The shadows were lengthening and after only ten minutes they left and cautiously retraced their steps to the rucksacks, reaching them in the very last glimmer of daylight. It had been a fifteen-hour day, with no food or drink.

The cold bivouac was made more bearable because they had climbed the mountain. For Whillans it was also made easier by the discovery of his cigarettes and matches, which must have made it harder for the anti-smoking Bonington. As the first rays of the sun turned the Ice Cap cherry pink they resumed their slow descent, abseiling carefully and ensuring that the ropes didn't snag. They passed the Italian team on the way down to a mixed reception – two glowering silently but a third congratulating them and admitting that his party shouldn't have been on the British route at all. At last, with safety in sight, one long abseil would almost reach easy ground. Only five metres from the foot of the climb the rope jammed below them. So they trusted to an old rope, similar to the one that had broken on the way up. Don slid down safely but Chris stopped to free the tangled rope and, while tugging it, the old rope snapped and he somersaulted backward, somehow slithering to a halt just above a huge drop and suffering a hairline fracture of the ankle. The rest of the descent was a gruelling ordeal. On reaching their next campsite, Whillans, in what Bonington speculated might have been a masterly stroke of psychological insight but was almost certainly pure laziness, made Chris, still shocked and exhausted, do the cooking before he left him for Base Camp. It took Bonington two more days of agonising descent, helped by Vic Bray the cameraman, before an emotional reunion with Wendy at Base Camp.

With no chance of any more climbing the couple returned to Punta Arenas, the world's southernmost city on the Magellan Straits, where Bonington had his ankle put in plaster. He and Wendy had originally planned to spend an extended six-month holiday travelling in South America but Chris, in one of his many swings from adventurousness to caution, had decided against this even before they had left England. He was already worrying about the future which seemed financially so insecure, despite a contract to write his first volume of autobiography on his return. Wendy had been disappointed and then frustrated at being tied down to Base Camp. Now by way of recompence they had three weeks to travel around Chile and Argentina before joining the returning expedition to catch a boat in Buenos Aires.

Before they left Punta Arenas Bonington had a chance encounter with that doyen of mountain explorers, Eric Shipton. He had just finished a 200-mile circumnavigation of Mount Burney, ostensibly to find out whether it was an active volcano but, as with most Shipton ventures, it was probably more an excuse for the simple mountain travel that he loved and had excelled in since his 1930s ventures to Everest and the Karakoram. Bonington was impressed with Shipton, one of his early heroes, and contrasted his journey with his own expedition which had spent the same two months with their noses pressed against the Central Tower of Paine. One feels that perhaps neither man found a great deal in common with the other. Later Shipton wrote the foreword to *I Chose to Climb*, a strange, rather inhibited account of Alpine climbing advances since the Second World War, of which he had no experience. Almost as an afterthought, he mentions Bonington only once in the very last paragraph.

And yet, had they known it, they shared remarkably similar backgrounds. Both came from one-parent families and were brought up in London flats by rather strong but distant mothers. Both were shy lonely children, given to daydreaming and both discovered mountains mainly through books. While Bonington has always found spelling difficult Shipton, one of the most widely read mountain writers, was actually dyslexic. Their differences, of course, were profound; Shipton hated publicity while Bonington still embraces it. Shipton's philosophy of 'small is beautiful' in organising and executing his lightweight expeditions would be incomprehensible to Bonington whose personal kit for even quite modest ventures is more than most climbers will ever possess in a lifetime. But, again, their basic wanderlust *was* the same and as he has grown older Bonington is increasingly seeking out those wider horizons of mountain travel that were the mainstay of Eric Shipton's life.

In Patagonia Chris and Wendy, while not quite in the Shipton class, used the three weeks to travel by plane, bus and steamers from Puerto Montt around the Chilean Lake District to Bariloche. Now able to put climbing ambitions to rest and future doubts on hold, they enjoyed an idyllic period, wandering around the lakes, camping, swimming, even riding. Wendy was a keen horsewoman who could turn the tables on her husband who had once – but only once – taken her rock climbing in Derbyshire. Now on horseback he was as insecure as she had been on rock. All too soon their holiday was over. Now Bonington had to face the future. Having 'chosen to climb', how could he make it work? Or, to put it more bluntly, how could he make it pay?

Woodland Hall Lodge

Struggling to Get By

A LOT OF PEOPLE assume, quite wrongly, that Chris Bonington was the first British professional climber. This ignores the likes of Edward Whymper, Captain Noel and Frank Smythe, who, through their writing, lectures, and photography, managed to keep body and soul together. It also dismisses the ever-growing mass of instructors and guides who, increasingly after the war, used their climbing skills in the outdoor centres that sprang up all over the country. If there was anything unique in Chris Bonington's decision to follow in the footsteps of men like Whymper and Smythe it was that initially he was almost completely unqualified to do so. That he was an outstanding climber was plain for all to see, but writing, photography and lecturing were skills at which he was going to have to work.

In 1963 his and Wendy's worldly goods consisted of a new mini-van (paid for with a £500 book advance from the publishers Victor Gollancz), his and Wendy's clothes, her guitar and water colour paints and his own climbing gear, all of which fitted into the mini-van. Nothing else at all. Derek Walker remembers that at the time the newly wed Boningtons were always desperately short of money and certainly Chris wasn't seen as anything other than a struggling and rather uncertain figure. Until then Bonington had written four short articles for the *Climbers' Club Journal*, and taken a few photographs which, because they were of the Eiger of the Central Pillar of Frêney or the Towers of Paine, had been published. But he still knew very little about photography and even less about writing. Even public speaking, through which he has eventually become so well known, didn't come naturally to him. Mike Thompson remembers one of the very first lectures he organised for him in Keswick, not knowing if anyone would turn up and being absolutely amazed when they took about £70. It was all very speculative and for the security-conscious Bonington his plunge into such an uncertain, entrepreneurial world was a profoundly worrying time. By contrast Wendy, who had been brought up by a freelance illustrator and was one herself, had few of her husband's doubts and inhibitions and became (as she still is) a rock of reassurance and strength when Chris hit one of his frequent low points.

They decided to go and live in the Lake District. Neither could stand living in London and, though Chris had done most of his rock climbing in North Wales, it didn't appeal as much as the Lakes as a place to live. They imagined a sort of Beatrix Potter cottage which they could rent for about a pound a week and were horrified to find, or rather not find, anything remotely as cheap. They settled for a rented room near Ambleside. It was not much more than a hovel above a garage but it sufficed for a few months before they moved again, this time to Woodland Hall Lodge in the south-west corner of the Lakes, well away from the main tourist haunts like Windermere, Ambleside or Keswick. It was to be home for the next three years, during which Chris and Wendy were to experience their fair share of life's highs and lows and in which Chris was to hone his skills as a writer and photographer.

On the strength of the publicity surrounding the Eiger and the Central Tower of Paine he attempted in the summer of 1963 to get a documentary film of an ascent of the Eiger off the ground. Then, when this proved over-ambitious, he turned to the North Face of the Matterhorn. Neither came to any sort of fruition but Bonington had teamed up with Hamish MacInnes once more. During a miserable summer in Zermatt, it was Hamish who persuaded Chris, one suspects rather mischievously, to buy a second-hand Hasselblad 2¼-inch square format camera. As a climbing camera it could hardly have been a worse investment: bulky, complex and having the disconcerting feature of the image in the viewfinder being seen back-to-front. However it was an invaluable purchase for Bonington in that it forced him to think and learn about the basic tech-niques of exposure, film speed, apertures, composition and so on. A Hasselblad just can't be used for 'happy snaps', yet once the principles of photography are learnt they can be applied to any other camera.

Wendy, who through her family, training and natural talent has a discerning eye for a picture, remembers that Chris put in a huge amount of hard work in those early years and is still irritated by criticisms that imply Chris somehow doesn't deserve his success. 'It did seem very small-minded and hurtful when Chris first started making, literally, an honest living, by sharpening up his talents. He has always worked incredibly hard to give value for money, whether it's lectures, books or business presentations. You don't *force* people into the lectures or *make* them buy the books, so he must be doing something right.' In this, like so much of Bonington's professional life, he has had to put up with jealousy from his peers.

His photography is technically competent, incredibly comprehen-sive (on any expedition Bonington always tops the number of films taken) and, while never intended as high art, is easily good enough for a large coffee table volume of his work to have been published. Strangely, the interest in photography never really developed into an involvement with film and video. Bonington has, of course, taken part in countless TV programmes, but mainly as a performer or presenter. Maybe it was partly an early awareness that a camera operator inevitably plays second string to the star performers. But there is probably another more fundamental acceptance that while he is (again) conscientious and committed to 'doing his bit' he is, at least, not terribly interested in the moving image and all the time-consuming complexities of post production of a TV docu-mentary.

Back in Zermatt the weather was so bad that he and MacInnes only did one climb, soloing the *voie normale*, the Hörnli Ridge of the Matterhorn. As the summer ended there was a far more pressing event that put any possible film on the Matterhorn firmly in its place. Wendy was pregnant and due to give birth at the end of the year. Bonington spent the autumn struggling with his first book and lecturing about the Eiger. Neither was very fulfilling. The book was due at the publishers in November, yet by the following May he was barely halfway through it. (*I Chose to Climb* was eventually only just over 200 rather small pages long and set, it must be said, in rather large type.) The lectures were an ordeal. Lonely, missing Wendy, Bonington flogged the mini-van the length and breadth of the country, inevitably driving home late to Woodland. It was a far cry from today's three-projector or digital audio-visual productions in which Chris employs a roadie to set up the high-tech presentation and to help sell books and posters. Above all there was still the nagging uncertainty of what the future would bring.

The first thing it brought was Conrad, born on the last day of 1963, after a long and exhausting delivery. To many men (and now women) marriage and particularly the arrival of children spell the end of serious climbing. There could be no question of that with Bonington. He explained in *I Chose to Climb* that if he was going to climb at all it would have to be at the highest possible standard to make it worthwhile, and, rather simplistically, suggested that as most accidents happen on easy ground or in descent, it therefore wasn't really any more dangerous to climb hard. Now committed to earning his family's living through and around climbing there was even less choice, though Chris knew (and still knows) that ultimately it is impossible to completely justify his way of life with marriage and parenthood.

In 1964 at the age of thirty, Chris Bonington was probably at the height of his physical powers as an Alpinist. Yet the mid-sixties were strangely unfulfilling from a climbing point of view. His Alpine season was spent in the company of Tom Patey and Joe Brown and resulted in a couple of minor new routes in the Chamonix Aiguilles, but no great test piece to compare with the Eiger or the Frêney Pillar. At the end of a frustrating summer Bonington fled home to Wendy and Conrad, and also to another autumn of lecturing on the Eiger and tinkering with the book which was now a year late. During this period, Wendy Bonington remembers, he suffered from real bouts of depression and self-doubt. 'I'm not naturally depressive at all, and I tried to make him laugh at himself and not take himself so seriously. A lot of it was insecurity. He hadn't gone the way his mother would consider to be the safe way.'

In early 1965 came a break from out of the blue. Ned Kelly a young producer working for what was then called TWW, Television Wales and West, got in touch to ask him if he was interested in making a film of one of his classic climbs in the Avon Gorge.

Bonington was immediately interested but quickly realised that filming climbing in the Gorge wasn't really visually spectacular. What might work far better would be a route in the nearby Cheddar Gorge in the Mendip Hills which was both bigger and far more imposing. Unlike the complex quarrying at Avon, Cheddar has huge vertical sweeps of limestone, split by soaring crack lines. Above all it had High Rock, a vertical buttress 400 feet high and, what's more, still unclimbed, although a couple of routes skirted the imposing upper wall. It was one of the most obvious (and public) challenges and Bonington, when he realised that a plum was there for the taking, suffered agonies of apprehension that someone else would steal the first ascent before him. On his first venture with photographer John Cleare he reached a point about halfway up the wall before being stopped by the combination of encroaching darkness and a frightening shield of rock that looked as though it might peel away at any moment.

Unusually for the Mendips snow had fallen and, though High Rock was too steep for any to accumulate, it was bitterly cold. Perhaps for this reason competition in the form of Pete Crew and Chris Jones, two leading activists of the day, failed to materialise and a week later Bonington returned, this time with Tony Greenbank and Mike Thompson. Tony Greenbank also lived in the Lake District in similar hard circumstances to Bonington. They had first met at an Eiger lecture in Bradford. Tony had mentioned he was a freelance journalist, which instantly interested Chris who wanted to know anything and everything about how to get started. Neither, it must be said, were vastly successful but Tony had contributed several articles to the *Yorkshire Post*. Chris had climbed with him before and enjoyed his company. When Chris rang him late one evening and suggested he came down to Cheddar, Greenbank had no idea of what, where or why they were going. It was also snowing hard. His wife at the time was furious: 'Why has that man got such a hold over you? He only has to crook his finger and you come running!' Greenbank rufully describes Bonington as a 'climbaholic' who will climb with anyone at any time, which this biographer can wholeheartedly confirm.

Once again the Gorge was snowbound. They didn't bother to repeat the first pitches and abseiled down to the traverse to the Shield of rock where Mike Thompson, who was suffering from 'flu, dropped out. John Cleare was there as photographer, so Tony Greenback seconded Chris who set out across the Shield, praying it wouldn't part company from the main cliff, with him clinging to it like an airborne toboggan. It didn't, and remains there to this day. On the far side Bonington belayed to several pitons and hung uncomfortably while Greenbank joined him. It is an alarming place and changing over at the stance is complicated. At last Chris was ready to climb a vertical groove above him to a couple of small overhangs. To his amazement the whole pitch went free with several good placements for nut runners. Greenbank, who is even today one of the world's great enthusiasts, urged Chris on with extravagant praise. Chris, euphoric with the quality of the climbing, made short work of the upper crack and found a small ledge to belay on. It was perched right above the steep drop to the ground where the parked cars now looked like Dinky toys. One more slightly awkward slabby pitch and they were on top. A magnificent climb was in the bag.

Ned Kelly who had watched the whole climb felt that it would make a superb TV programme and in May the team returned, together with the film crew and sundry hangers on. Chris, Wendy and Conrad camped in a field near Cheddar village and Chris spent an enjoyable week practising the climb, establishing camera positions, learning to do live commentary and listening to instruction and questions coming in on headphones. Chris, who had been envious of the previous outside broadcasts that the BBC had staged in North Wales and on the Aiguille du Midi in Chamonix, now had his big chance to perform to the cameras and he revelled in the challenge.

Now all that was needed was a name for the climb. Tony Greenbank came up with Coronation Street after the soap opera, because it was being done for ITV. The name has since transcended its jokey origins and for climbers has become imbued with some of the grandeur of the climb itself. Bonington himself thinks it is the best new route he's done in Britain. It has become *the* classic climb of the Cheddar Gorge and every winter weekend (for climbing is banned in the summer months) sees a procession of climbers eager to add 'The Street' to their tick list. Many underestimate its length and difficulty and it has been the scene of a few unintentional bivouacs. Even Joe Brown has climbed it twice, a fitting accolade for a wonderful climb.

After two years living in furnished accommodation in Woodland Hall Lodge, the Boningtons wanted somewhere they could call their own, even though they couldn't afford to actually buy anything. Eventually they moved from the south-west Lake District to the Ennerdale valley in the north-west. They were extremely lucky to find and rent the unfurnished Bank End Cottage for £2 a week. Initially their only furniture was a desk, and they slept on the floor and cooked with a camping stove. Slowly their possessions accumulated, including a large tabby cat, the first of a long long line of cats and dogs that continues to this day.

Bonington's run of good luck continued when Tom Patey invited him to join him as British representatives at the Rassemblement International held every two years in Chamonix. National clubs all over the world were guests of the École Nationale de Ski et Alpinisme, wined, dined, given free access to ski lifts, téléphériques and huts. Though their time at the Rassemblement produced only two new routes of little importance, Patey and Bonington drove over to Leysin in Switzerland where Patey suggested meeting the American John Harlin, the 'Blond God' – a not wholly affectionate nickname for the man who ran the International School of Mountaineering there.

John Harlin had a larger than life reputation that was undoubtedly fuelled by his own desire for self-publicity and a capacity to exaggerate his many achievements almost beyond recognition. He was an ex-USAF pilot who had been based in Germany, which enabled him to climb frequently in the Alps. He had made the first American ascent of the North Face of the Eiger just before Bonington and Clough. He was, by all accounts, not a particularly gifted climber but he was strong, very well organised, and had the unusual ability to combine fantasy with practical solutions. He had also done the first ascent of the American Super Direct on the West Face of the Dru, a mainly artificial climb through colossal overhangs and overhanging walls.

Bonington had been toying with the idea of a Direct Route on the Eiger, for the original 1938 climb takes a wandering, devious line up the huge face, seeking out the line of least resistance. There was plenty of room for another climb but the Direct would inevitably be much harder. It would also be exposed to stonefall and could only be attempted in winter when everything would be frozen.

John Harlin also had designs on the Direct and, after some preliminary skirmishing and sounding each other out, they agreed to team up, with the Rhodesian Rusty Baillie as a third member. They hoped to do the climb in the autumn, gambling that it would be cold enough to stop the stonefall, but not as cold as in mid-winter. But the weather was against them and, though the three managed the first ascent of another big new route on the Italian side of Mont Blanc, the Right-Hand Pillar of Brouillard, September had turned to October, and they never got on to the face. It was time to go home.

That summer, when climbing with Harlin on the Dent du Midi, Bonington used jumar clamps for the first time. These are the sliding alloy ratchets that enable a climber to ascend a fixed rope far more easily than by the old-fashioned means of prussik knots, a tedious system that is normally used as a last resort in crevasse rescues. In America, on the big walls of Yosemite in particular, jumaring had been brought to a fine art and their efficient use would be critical in attempting a long and technically difficult route like the Eiger Direct. As Bonington was to quickly discover, their use on overhanging rock when the rope hangs free is unnerving. However efficient they may be, you are totally dependent on the security of the fixed rope. If anything goes wrong you are almost certainly dead. It was to be a lesson learnt the hard way the following winter.

At Bank End Cottage Bonington, now far away from the fantasies of the Blond God, began to have doubts about the whole idea of the climb. In particular he had difficulty in accepting Harlin's theory that every winter produced a ten-day period of fine clear weather in which the climb could be completed. Whether or not this was so wasn't really the point, the difficulty was knowing at the start of fine weather how long it would last. Retreating in the teeth of a winter storm after a week or so on the face would be life-threatening to put it mildly. A phone call from a journalist, Peter Gillman, asking to interview him about the Eiger Direct, forced a decision. Bonington wrote to Harlin telling him he was withdrawing from the team, a decision that instantly caused him a bout of depression. 'I had for the first time rejected a climbing challenge at a time when my ability as a climber was my only tangible asset.'

But again Bonington's luck changed with a letter from John Anstey, the editor of the *Daily Telegraph* Magazine, asking if he would photograph the climb with Gillman as their reporter. Anstey wanted Chris to take photos from the summit and from the West Ridge of the Eiger, which was beyond Gillman's occasional rock climbing abilities. It was the opportunity he had waited for since leaving Van den Berghs, and the chance to prove himself in a new role. It was also, of course, very exciting, for the Eiger Direct had all the ingredients of a media extravaganza. Bonington had had severe qualms about the gladiatorial aspects of performing in front of the media but harboured no such doubts about being a part of the media covering the event. He would be adopting, if not actually a risk-free role, then a much less committing position than the climbers themselves. Or so he thought.

Harlin had intended to climb the face in one continuous push but his plans were compromised by the arrival of a large strong German team who were prepared to fix ropes all the way up. Inevitably it turned into a race. ('If it's a race, it's the slowest race in the world,' observed Don Whillans.) Equally inevitably, Harlin was forced to use the same fixed rope tactics as the Germans and the climb turned inexorably into a prolonged siege. This actually worked in Chris's favour because he rationalised that by using the ropes and jumaring up the lower half of the face he could get much better photographs without committing himself fully to the climb. This he did, on one occasion with Don Whillans who found the whole circus 'a load of bullshit'. Inevitably though, Bonington got more involved than he had planned and ended up leading one of the hardest pitches on the route, a steep, delicate and poorly protected ice pitch which proved to be the key that unlocked the route to the White Spider and the upper part of the face.

During the first weeks on the face Bonington came to know a young climber who was to play a pivotal role in world climbing over the next ten years. He describes his first impressions of Dougal Haston from Edinburgh. 'On early acquaintance he seems silent and withdrawn, almost contemptuous of others. He dresses with an almost foppish elegance in a very mod style, but any risk of effeminacy is avoided in the cast of his features. His eyes are hooded, his face long and somehow primitive – a strange mixture of the sensual and the ascetic. Relaxed to the point of laziness, he has a single-mindedness which, when the need arises, enables him to direct his entire powers in the desired direction.' Haston, who had already proved himself with a series of hard routes in Scotland and the Alps, was totally committed to the route. When he and Bonington had been thrown together on the early part of the climb Bonington had been very impressed by the Scotsman's ability and self-contained strength. This was to be put to the test in the second half of the climb.

Returning to the face after a hiatus for bad weather, and with another storm forecast, John Harlin reckoned that there was just time to finish the climb which now had reached the foot of the White Spider. By this point the German and Anglo-American teams had been obliged to join forces and two Germans were out in front. Haston and Harlin jumared up the long line of fixed ropes to join them. Dougal got there first, but Harlin never arrived. Peter Gillman, observing the face through a large telescope from the terrace of a hotel in Kleine Scheidegg, was horrified to see an object falling through space. He was convinced it was a climber but prayed it was not so. Chris Bonington and the American Layton Kor skied to the foot of the face where, to their initial relief, they found the contents of a rucksack scattered in the snow. But then they saw something else. Bonington describes the moment:

> We plodded up the snow to where John Harlin's body lay, grotesque, distorted by the appalling impact of his 5,000 foot fall, but still horribly recognisable. There was a strange, terrible beauty in the juxtaposition of the bent limbs of this man, who had devoted everything to climbing and finally to this project and to the face towering above. It made a perfect photograph – a picture that said everything that could possibly be said about the North Wall of the Eiger. I was horrified with myself that I could even think this way: I knew I could never take such a picture.

Harlin, who had so confidently shown Chris how to jumar, had trusted his weight and heavy rucksack to a free-hanging 7mm rope that had been in place for several days and was running over a sharp edge. It had supported Dougal Haston who was considerably lighter, but snapped when Harlin had put his full weight on it. Ironically, it was the use of these thin 7mm ropes about which Don Whillans had had severe qualms when he first became involved in the climb. Now back in Leysin where he was instructing at Harlin's

International School, it fell to Don to break the news to John's wife, Marilyn.

After a lot of rapid discussion it was felt that it would be a tribute to the man whose idea it was if they finished the climb. Bonington and an English climber, Mick Burke were helicoptered to a point near the top of the Eiger to get the all-important summit photographs just before a violent storm broke. They managed to dig a snow cave below the summit and had an anxious two nights waiting while four Germans, plus Dougal Haston, fought their way through the teeth of the storm up the final chimneys and icefields to the summit. Bonington, despite the cameras freezing up, managed to get his photos of the ice-encrusted climbers, including two of Haston, one climbing the last few feet and a large close-up of his staring eyes and fixed grimace that was the nearest he could get to a smile. All of them spent a last grim night in the snow hole, along with several German would-be-rescuers. The Eiger Direct, the Harlin Route, existed. The climb did receive some inevitable criticism at the time from people who felt that the siege ascent was inappropriate in the Alps, and the route was eventually climbed in brilliant style by Alex MacIntyre and Tobin Sorenson in 1977. But, paradoxically, the 1966 ascent did influence the approach to Himalayan climbs like Annapurna South Face and the South-West Face of Everest.

The next day back at the hotel in Kleine Scheidegg Bonington removed his frozen boots and was horrified to find that he had three black frostbitten toes which necessitated several weeks in a London hospital where Bonington and Haston (who had frostbitten fingers) were guinea-pigs for a new form of treatment, spending hours in a cylinder filled with oxygen at twice the normal pressure. Whether or not it helped is now a moot point for it is a remedy that isn't used today, but both men made a full recovery. For Dougal Haston the Eiger catapulted him into a kind of cult pop-stardom, which was to remain with him for the rest of his life. For Bonington the successful completion of his photographic assignment, which had huge media exposure and public interest, meant a foot on the ladder, with another rung to follow, for halfway up the Eiger John Anstey had contacted him with the offer of another assignment, this one in Ecuador. Things were at last looking up.

Old Man of Hoy

· 13 ·

Photo-Journalist

BONINGTON'S SECOND ASSIGNMENT for the *Daily Telegraph* Magazine was to accompany the eccentric Old Etonian explorer Sebastian Snow, who wanted to climb Sangay, a remote but ferociously active volcano deep in the Amazon jungle. For the first time Bonington was to experience the difference between putting together a climbing project with friends and working for an employer who has chosen the objective and is paying you to get photos or find a story. Though Bonington got on extremely well with Sebastian Snow, it is not hard to detect in this adventure the seeds of doubt about the nature of the kind of work he was embarked on which later surfaced in the Blue Nile expedition when Bonington was nearly drowned.

Perhaps for a non-climber it is hard to understand why someone who is brave or foolhardy enough to choose to do something as obviously risky as climb the North Face of the Eiger should baulk at other forms of danger. The difference is precisely in that element of choice, to be free to weigh up the dangers for yourself and calculate the risk involved. Once you are employed by someone else to do this it is hard, if not impossible, to be objective; the external pressure to succeed will always have an influence and, if you are involved in risk that you have little or no control over, it becomes incomparably more stressful to undertake. For Bonington the days hacking through the jungle towards Sangay were claustrophobic and sinister. He was in an alien environment and, though Sebastian Snow appeared to be on home ground, Bonington was beset with doubts and fears about the future if he didn't bring back the kind of lurid photos of an erupting volcano that John Anstey obviously wanted.

With the threat of mutiny from their porters who were terrified and soaking wet, the realisation that they were rapidly running out of food, and the awful possibility of getting lost on the return, the bedraggled team got to a camp from which the summit might just be attainable. Bonington in a fever of impatience set off in the middle of the night only to have to descend when he realised that Snow was far behind. Snow's glasses had steamed up and he had never worn crampons or used an ice axe before. When the lava scree turned to ice he was virtually helpless. Feeling like a guide dog, Bonington led him up interminable slopes. 'We could have been in one of the circles of Hell, destined to eke out eternity plodding ever upwards . . . I was a good deal more frightened than I had ever been on the fixed ropes of the Eiger Direct but my fears were intangible, almost superstitious.'

With his conscience pricking him Bonington suggested that they retraced their steps to Quito, re-provisioned and then approached the other side of Sangay via a much shorter approach. He put it to Sebastian Snow who responded as only an Old Etonian could: 'My dear Christian, all I ask is a single bath in Quito and I'll go to the ends of the earth to help you get your pictures.' In fact they had a week in Quito, living in the luxury of the Intercontinental Hotel where Chris received letters from Wendy that made him homesick. After Sangay he had promised to join an expedition to Alpamayo in Peru, organised by the Yorkshire climber Dennis Gray, but now all he wanted was to get home. Dreading the thought of yet another adventure, Chris resolutely set off back to Sangay, determined to get his photos. This time the approach was much easier, the weather marginally better and there was a view of sorts from the rim, though still not the spectacular display of pyrotechnics that Bonington knew would be expected. Still dissatisfied, he planned yet another ascent of Sangay and was preparing to leave very early in the morning when his world fell apart. An Indian ran into the camp with a message addressed to him. It was the news every parent dreads. Conrad was dead, drowned in a freak accident.

Chris, beside himself with grief, set out on the long journey home, trying to keep himself together, and walked and rode on horseback through the night. Behind him Sangay erupted against a starry sky and a red snake of molten lava flowed down from the crater.

Chris and Wendy were reunited in their sorrow at Heathrow. Wendy had taken Conrad to her friend Mary Stewart who lived outside Glasgow. He had gone out to play with her children in what was normally a tiny stream at the bottom of the garden. A cloudburst had caused the waters to rise and somehow Conrad had wandered off and fallen in. Wendy herself had found him but it was too late. Conrad was just two and a half years old. Later Ned Kelly, who had found Chris a much gentler and more emotional person than he had expected, remembers showing Chris some black and white film he had shot during the week at Cheddar. There was a poignant shot of Chris walking up the street hand in hand with Conrad that had reduced Chris to helpless tears. Like any bereaved parents the scars never totally heal and for Chris and Wendy the loss of Conrad is something they both have to live with every day.

In the summer of 1966 Tom Patey, now working as a GP in the remote north-west Highlands, invited Chris and Wendy to visit the Orkney Islands to attempt a huge unclimbed sea stack, the Old Man of Hoy. Wendy decided to visit her parents in Sussex and Bonington joined Patey and Rusty Baillie for a rough crossing on the ferry the *St Ola* from Thurso to Stromness. On the way the ferry passed quite close to the Old Man whose summit disappeared into low cloud and white water churned around its base.

The Old Man of Hoy is fully 450 feet (150 metres) high and made of horizontally bedded sandstone. It used to be a headland but the pounding of the Atlantic eventually wore an archway which collapsed, leaving a slender free-standing pinnacle. In geological terms the Old Man could collapse at any time; it might last another thousand years or be reduced to rubble tomorrow. What was certain to the three climbers that evening as they peered nervously across from the clifftop behind it was that it was steep and very loose. Bonington even wondered whether the presence of climbers could cause it to collapse, provoking Patey to ask Chris where his spirit of adventure had gone.

In fact the first ascent of the Old Man relied mainly on the artificial climbing skills of Rusty Baillie who took the best part of two days to ascend the second pitch, a wide crack cutting through two overhangs. Today it is climbed free but in its original state, full of rotten rock that crumbled to sand, it was quite a tour de force involving precariously placed wooden wedges and the then new American bongs, wide-angle pitons that could be driven sideways into wide cracks. Bonington, perched halfway up the descent path took some excellent black and white stills of Baillie as he climbed. He also insisted that Tom Patey, who was spectacularly inept at artificial climbing, should second the pitch and remove the pitons, while Bonington jumared up a tied-off rope taking photographs. One in particular, looking down on Patey, cigarette in mouth and festooned with gear, has become a classic and has since appeared in many books and magazines.

By the time the three climbers arrived at the top of the long crack it was almost dark and Patey sensibly pooh-poohed the idea of a bivouac in favour of a bed and a bottle of whisky at the youth hostel in nearby Rackwick Bay. Patey wrote that the climb was taking longer than an ascent of the North Face of the Eiger! On the third day Patey took over the lead and quickly climbed easier but still loose ground to the foot of a final clean-cut corner where Bonington, who had been happy to follow, was determined to have a turn in the lead. In some ways it is the most enjoyable pitch on the whole route – the rock is weathered and sound and the hand jams give a great feeling of security. It is very well protected but Patey was impressed with Chris who . . . 'gleefully swung up the crack, the rope dropping cleanly from his waist to the coils at our feet'. They built a small cairn on the summit and lit a bonfire of sun-scorched heather that nearly got out of hand. Then they abseiled down.

Patey realised quickly that the Old Man of Hoy would make a brilliant outside broadcast and a year later it came to pass. The BBC gambled on a fantastically complex weekend extravaganza that involved a platoon of Scots Guards, an Army assault landing craft and tons of equipment ferried by tractor to the top of the cliff overlooking the Old Man. Three climbs were to be staged live: Bonington and Patey would repeat the original route, Joe Brown and Ian McNaught-Davis would do a new route up the South Face and Douglas Haston and Pete Crew would attempt to climb the overhanging South-East Arête. John Cleare and Hamish MacInnes masterminded the camera positions, which involved all Hamish's ingenuity in constructing gantries on the Old Man itself, and Chris Brasher, an old friend of Chris's who had actually done some rock climbing, supplied the commentary.

It was without doubt the best outside broadcast the BBC ever produced on rock climbing. It had everything – suspense, obvious difficulty, exposure and the strange convoluted sandstone architecture of the Old Man which somehow lent itself to black and white TV. The juxtapositions of the climbing personalities worked perfectly: Joe Brown's flat understated commentary, Mac, as always, over the top acting the clown, Chris totally serious and Tom Patey's whimsical lightheartedness. Only Haston and Crew, on the hardest climb, were monosyllabic and boring. A few fragments of the original videotape still exist and it is quite extraordinary how the excitement of the event still comes across, despite the stilted formality of the commentary to our ears today.

Millions watched 'The Old Man of Hoy'. Many people now in middle or old age can remember it clearly. It probably did more than any other single media event since 'The Ascent of Everest', the film of the 1953 expedition, to inform and entertain the general public. Inevitably it also raised the public profile of the stars, particularly Brown and Bonington. For Joe it was an event he took in his stride but for Chris it was an opportunity to further his own position. He recognised that the path he was going to follow would mean undertaking all kinds of work that in many ways would actually reduce his freedom to climb whenever and wherever he chose, but in the drive and excitement of furthering his photographic and writing career all the heartaches now began to seem worthwhile.

Chris Bonington's next assignment for the *Telegraph* Magazine was to go hunting with the Eskimos of Baffin Island in February of 1967. This time he was to be a one-man band, both taking the pictures and writing the story. In the extreme cold of mid-winter watching the Eskimos hunt caribou and seals was an ordeal but one from which Bonington got a great feeling of satisfaction. Despite the cold and the difficulty of taking photographs without the film snapping or the cameras icing up, it was an environment that he understood. He was also with people for whom he had immense respect as they eked out a precarious livelihood in a fast-disappearing nomadic way of life, living in igloos, dog sledding and relying largely on traditional methods of survival. This was in stark contrast to the new lifestyle of most Eskimos living in Pangnirtung, the trading post established by the Hudson Bay Company, who were fed, clothed and exposed to most of the 'advantages' of an industrial society, which in practice meant living on benefit and getting drunk whenever possible.

Bonington was also meant to write a story about a newly opened oil field in Central Canada, a project for which he had little sympathy or understanding, and the story never got written. Furthermore Wendy was pregnant and on his return she gave birth to Daniel on the 25th April 1967. Living in Bank End Cottage brought back so many memories of Conrad as a baby that the Boningtons decided to move and, now that Chris was making a reasonable living, they bought a house in Cockermouth in the far north-west corner of the Lakes. It was however a rather half-hearted move, for Bonington felt that if he was really to make it in the high-powered world of photo-journalism he ought to be living in London – a concept that filled Wendy with horror. A visit to London to look at houses was not dissimilar from their earlier hopes of a cheap cottage in the Lake District five years earlier. A house in Hampstead was completely out of Bonington's reach and a terraced house in grimy Muswell Hill in North London was not what he had in mind. They headed back up north and considered the possibility of a compromise – a house in south Manchester with easy access to North Wales, the Lakes and the Peak District, and with good communications to London.

But first, in the spring of 1968, there was what promised to be an interesting trip with *The Cruel Sea* author Nicholas Monsarrat to the kingdom of Hunza in north-west Pakistan. Legend has it that the populace is descended from Alexander the Great and that many live to incredible ages. Today Hunza has long since succumbed to tourism; trekking and climbing expeditions visit regularly, but Bonington was lucky enough to get to the kingdom before it opened up. Nicholas Monsarrat however didn't make it; forced to walk when the jeep road was swept away by flash floods, he soon beat a retreat to London. This enabled Chris to enjoy the peaceful isolation of the remote valley where at that time there was very little crime, no police force, no tax, no prison and no death penalty. He was however pessimistic for the future, fearing that the building of the Karakoram Highway, the road link from Pakistan to China, would inevitably bring industry, hotels and jobs but also crime, politics and all the corruption that goes with a sophisticated society. He was absolutely correct.

Returning from Pakistan, the Boningtons took the plunge and bought an old Edwardian semi in the south Manchester commuter belt at Bowdon. It was only a few minutes' drive from the M6 motorway, and several old climbing friends lived nearby. Before they could move in Bonington was off again, leaving Wendy to face all the stress of packing up their home in the Lakes.

This time he was to accompany the Great Abbai expedition, led by Captain John Blashford-Snell. Its object was to descend the Blue Nile from its source at Lake Tana, 500 miles through Ethiopia to the Sudanese border. The expedition was run as a military operation and featured shooting rapids, paddling through crocodile-infested gorges, and being attacked by tribesmen, the team actually coming under fire on a couple of occasions. Though Bonington got his photographs and story it is not hard to see that he had little rapport with Blashford-Snell, who behaved like a throwback to the days of the British Empire. Despite subsequent voyages with Robin Knox-Johnston to Greenland it would be fair to say that Bonington has never been at home on or in water and the Blue Nile was a truly gripping experience for even the most experienced team members. Twice Bonington's inflatable capsized, each time he was swept away, powerless to fight the power of the water, and each time, more by luck than good judgement, he managed to swim clear of the undertow. After the second capsize Bonington, suffering from delayed shock, doubted that he could carry on. In the end he did recover some confidence which was quickly undermined when Ian McLeod who had been in Bonington's boat was swept away and drowned while attempting what seemed to be a safe river crossing. Coming under fire put the lid on it as far as Bonington was concerned. He found it far more dangerous and frightening than any climbing expeditions he had ever undertaken. Like climbing Sangay, he felt out of control and powerless to influence the outcome.

The Blue Nile expedition marked the end of a three-year period where climbing had definitely been relegated to a hobby, which is more or less what it would have been had he stayed with Van den Berghs. When he returned to the UK, the Boningtons found themselves temporarily homeless, the house in Bowdon wasn't ready and they were forced to seek sanctuary with a climbing friend Nick Estcourt and his wife Carolyn, who had a two-bedroomed flat in Alderley Edge, a nearby commuter village in Cheshire. What was originally planned as a few days' stay turned into two months and, despite living on top of one another, with a small child as well, they all became close friends. It was during this period that Bonington first considered organising an expedition himself. Like the discovery of the book of Scottish photographs, the letter from Hamish MacInnes inviting him to the Alps and the dropping of the slides in the train, this was to be another life-changing event. This time it was to turn out to be exactly what he always wanted.

Annapurna South Face

WHEN HISTORIANS LOOK back at mountaineering in the twentieth century, one of the pivotal moments will be the ascent of the South Face of Annapurna on 27th May 1970 by Dougal Haston and Don Whillans. It was the culmination of a meticulously organised and brilliantly executed operation, but like many expeditions, the original concept was very much less ambitious.

Bonington, chafing in the confines of the flat in Alderley Edge, wanted to go on an expedition, as did Nick Estcourt and Martin Boysen, a brilliant rock climber Chris had first met at Harrisons and who lived nearby and taught in a Manchester school. Initially it was to be a four-man expedition to Alaska, Dougal Haston making up the fourth, though he didn't know it at the time. The choice of Alaska was made because all the great peaks of the Himalaya and Karakoram were out of bounds; closed for a variety of political reasons in both Nepal and Pakistan and quite out of the question from the northern approaches of Tibet and Chinese Sinkiang. Far-flung outliers of the Karakoram and Hindu Kush in Afghanistan *were* possible but Bonington felt they were overshadowed by the giants of the Himalaya and weren't worth it. Alaska, on the other hand, had hundreds of worthwhile objectives in the form of big new routes and unclimbed peaks.

Then in October 1968 the Nepalese government unexpectedly lifted the four-year ban they had imposed on climbers. Suddenly,

Annapurna South Face

everything was up for grabs. A lot of advances had happened in those four years, perhaps epitomised by the Eiger Direct. Could a similar climb be done at really high altitude? Martin Boysen remembers that somewhere he had seen a picture of the South Face of Annapurna, but accepts that Chris could also have the same sort of vague recollection at the same time. Bonington managed to track down a slide from David Cox at Oxford University. He had been a member of an expedition to Machapuchare, 'The Fish's Tail', a wonderful mountain in the Annapurna Sanctuary, which commanded a good view of the South Face. By now the Boningtons had moved into the Bowdon house and were putting up Nick and Carolyn in their attic, while they in turn waited for their new home to become habitable. Wendy became pregnant again and Rupert was born on 9th July 1969.

The slide arrived from David Cox and Bonington projected it onto the wall of his living room. He, Nick and Martin were awestruck – first excited, then frightened. Compared to the South Face of Nuptse, Annapurna was vast, the equivalent, as Bonington wrote, of four Alpine faces piled on top of each other. Yet there looked to be a possible line up the face, possibly even quite a safe one, standing proud of the avalanche runnels on each side. It couldn't be ignored. The 1970 Annapurna South Face Expedition was born, though it soon became obvious that a four-man team would not be sufficient for tackling such a huge project.

Bonington considered taking six, then eight climbers to Annapurna. Taking the Alaska contingent as a basis, he then fell back on tried and trusted companions: Ian Clough from the Walker, Eiger and Paine days and Mick Burke with whom he had spent a lot of time in the snow hole at the top of the Eiger Direct without driving each other mad. This left two vacancies. By now Chris had a literary agent, George Greenfield, who handled people as diverse as Sir Edmund Hillary, Sir Francis Chichester, the solo round the world yachtsman, and Sebastian Snow who had introduced him to Chris. He had been the agent for Fuchs' and Hillary's Trans-Antarctic expedition and was an old hand at raising media interest. Greenfield suggested it would make marketing books and films much easier if Chris chose an American. This Chris freely admits gave him some doubts, not because he was anti-American, but simply because he wondered about the wisdom of introducing a stranger into a group of reasonably close-knit friends. In the end he chose Tom Frost who had climbed in the Himalaya before, but was also a leading figure in American big wall techniques. The only snag was that Tom was a devout Mormon whose faith forbade alcohol, gambling, smoking, foul language, tea and coffee, all of which were indulged in to a greater or lesser extent by the rest of the team. Luckily he was not just a good Mormon but a tolerant one as well.

The eighth place went to the one person who could well test Frost's tolerance to breaking point, as well as the rest of the team's. Bonington needed someone with a lot more Himalayan experience than the team possessed. Remembering his days on Nuptse, he invited Les Brown who, just married and starting a new job, regretfully declined. Don Whillans would be the obvious choice but it was fraught with problems. Don was sliding into physical decline and drank far too much beer. He was also just as abrasive as he had always been. Chris decided to invite him for a winter weekend in Scotland and duly arrived at his house in Rawtenstall in Lancashire at 10.30 p.m. to pick him up. Don eventually returned home at 2.30 in the morning, having drunk eleven pints of beer. It is a telling sign of those pre-breathalyser days that in 1970 Bonington could write: 'We set off straight away – me in a slightly self-righteous bad temper. I kept the wheel most of the way, afraid that Don had had too much to drink.' They met up with Tom Patey and predictably did a first winter ascent, the Great Gully of Ardgour. Whillans brought up the rear all day until the last pitch which was an ice chimney. This he shot up without bothering to protect himself. Chris and Tom were hard pressed to follow him and, reassured that he could still turn it on, Chris invited him to Annapurna and also to be deputy leader.

Despite keeping the lead climbers down to eight Bonington felt he needed a Base Camp manager, a doctor and a support climber. Kelvin Kent, a captain in the Gurkhas filled the first position, Dr David Lambert from Newcastle the second and, perhaps inevitably, Mike Thompson the third. Mike was also responsible for the food; an inspired choice as he later supplied a hilarious appendix to the expedition book. On top of what by now had risen to eleven members, there was also a four-man TV crew from ITN/Thames Television, which included Alan Hankinson as the ITN representa-

tive. Hankinson ...
eventually beca...
go to Annapu...
seemed like a ...

So someh...
big team w...
from Sand...
he had t...
days ha...
comple...
Looki...
a far...
app...
ex...
m...
w...
he had ...
home, handling...
jobs and working th...
of this size involves.

Chris himself acknowledges a hu...
of the successful 1953 Everest expedition...
one of the expedition patrons and it is not ...
example and influences. In those days of plenty at th...
'sixties the Mount Everest Foundation agreed to underwri...
entire cost of the expedition, which was a huge relief, even though
it eventually paid for itself. Expedition meetings were often held at
the Bonington home in Bowdon. Years later Don Whillans told me
that at the end of one, to his utter bewilderment everyone else
present set off for a training run. 'Is there a bus strike?' he enquired.

The first major setback came when the boat carrying all the
expedition gear broke down in Cape Town. Don Whillans, who
had flown out to Bombay early to shepherd the equipment through
customs and accompany it overland to Kathmandu, cabled back
the news to Chris who offered to fly out early to 'pull strings'.

'The only useful strings 'e could pull would be a bloody great
big one attached to the ship,' was Don's dismissive comment.

In the event the ship *did* arrive, very late, and it fell to the conscientious Ian Clough to ensure the safe passage of the kit over the plains

of India. It was a demanding and
later felt Clough never fully reco...
long before he ever saw the m...
Chris had sent Don ahead...
down there was the awful...
dangerous line and the ex...
If anyone had a good ex...
differences, Chris had...
at least for mountai...
more than mount...
reasonably sure...
minimal. He t...
knife-edged ...
rock buttre...
But Whil...
yeti on...
have ...
Mik...
w...

responsible job and Bonington
ered from the efforts he had made
untain.

to get the first view of the face. Deep
thought that it might be a suicidally
pedition would never leave Base Camp.
e for a route it was Don and, despite their
a great deal of respect for his judgement –
neering decisions. But when they met Don had
ins on his mind. He had seen the face and was
t would 'go' and that the avalanche danger was
nought the climbing would be hard, particularly a
ce ridge less than halfway up the face. Above, a huge
ss, the Rock Band, could probably be turned on the left.
ans was just as excited about his possible sighting of a
moonlit night when he was alone in a tent. He claimed to
een an ape-like creature bounding along on all fours. Later
e Thompson was less than convinced, feeling that the bottle of
nisky he had with him at the time might have impaired Don's
judgement.

Once the whole team, and soon after them, the gear, arrived
at Base Camp, work started on what was undoubtedly the most
ambitious and difficult Himalayan climb so far attempted. The Ice
Ridge proved to be every bit as hard as Whillans had predicted and
it fell to Martin Boysen and Nick Estcourt to climb the crux section,
easily the hardest ice climbing done in the Himalaya at that time,
but it took five whole weeks to get to the top of the thin ridge. At
last Bonington himself led out a long rope-length to reach the crest
of the ridge and see that the way up the next section to the bottom
of the Rock Band was straightforward. Nevertheless, if the climbing
above was as hard as the Ice Ridge, chances of success were slim.

For those too young to remember the process of siege climbing,
establishing a long line of fixed ropes up a Himalayan face normally
involves the rotation of pairs of lead climbers out in front establishing the route, while those behind ferry supplies of rope, tents
and food until it is their turn for a stretch in front. The pair they
replace descend, sometimes all the way to Base Camp for a rest,
and then join the queue to get back to the front. It sounds simple
and in an ideal world, when each pair is as strong and fit as every

other pair, it should work. However, there are so many variables that the rotating scheme hardly ever runs smoothly. Illness, the nature of the ground to be covered and weather all conspire to make the leader's job of pre-planning a hit or miss activity at best. One is reminded of Harold Macmillan's reply when the Prime Minister was asked by a young journalist what was the hardest part of his job: 'Events, dear boy, events.'

So inexorably, as the climb progressed to the foot of the Rock Band and then, as Whillans predicted, took an ascending leftward line to avoid tackling it head on, the rotation of the lead started to break down. A major factor was that load-carrying in support was as hard, or harder than leading. Nick Estcourt and Martin Boysen, in particular, were approaching complete exhaustion. Mike Thompson, who had surpassed himself in support though he had never been expected to perform high on the face, actually ground himself to the point where he collapsed, hyper-ventilating halfway between camps. Both he and Mick Burke, who was with him, thought he was about to die and Mick felt powerless to help. 'I just stood there waiting for him to die and then, I suppose to relieve my own tension as much as anything else, asked him what he'd done with the nuts. This seemed to bring him round a bit.'

With dwindling manpower and the ferrying of supplies up the face becoming more and more erratic, success seemed still a long way off. Mick Burke and Tom Frost were in the lead, inching a devious way up the Rock Band. In theory, Martin Boysen and Nick Estcourt should have taken over from them, but in a long, convoluted and acrimonious radio call between camps in which Chris changed his mind several times, he eventually decided that Don Whillans and Dougal Haston should leapfrog to the front which everyone knew would place them in pole position for the first summer bid. It was a decision, as Chris himself wrote, based on expediency rather than fairness. Though it was probably the right one, it was to have many repercussions and though, ironically, Chris and Don were in full agreement that it was the right thing to do, it eventually led to their final break.

Don and Dougal were a curious pair. Don stocky, slow, fast becoming almost a living caricature of the stroppy, boozy Lancastrian, and Dougal, thin, rangy, and prone to self-analysis. Dougal later summed up the difference between them in one memorable sentence: 'Don had a job to do and was doing it. I had a life to live and was living it.' On their way through to the front they passed the exhausted pair of Boysen and Estcourt. Boysen remembers: 'Don always had a soft spot for me and I think he actually did feel a bit guilty about what was happening. Anyway he suggested I join them. I suppose I should have done but by that time I just thought – ah, I don't know – I suppose I'd sort of lost interest and suddenly it just seemed to be every man for himself. Perhaps I should have carried on.'

Over the next days Don and Dougal pushed the climb to the top of the Rock Band, with Don mainly living on a diet of water and cigar smoke. When they established the top camp it was obvious that the monsoon was about to break and moist cloud filled the valleys. It still seemed a long way to the top and the pair carried a tiny bivouac tent for their summit push. On the 27th of May they emerged onto the final slopes and realised that they might actually get to the top that day. They abandoned the tent and, climbing solo with Don now in the lead, picked their way to a final short rock wall that led to the summit ridge. Suddenly it was all over. The South Face of Annapurna was climbed.

Later in the afternoon they regained their top camp in time for a radio call. An anxious Bonington asked them if they had managed to get out that day.

'Aye, we've just climbed Annapurna.'

By now the monsoon was moving slowly in and the lower part of the face was becoming more dangerous day by day. Nevertheless Tom Frost and Mick Burke made an abortive attempt on the summit before Bonington ordered everyone off the mountain. Quite literally in the very last minutes of the expedition, a sérac on the glacier below the face collapsed, killing Ian Clough instantly. Mike Thompson had a miraculous escape and arrived at Base Camp as the TV crews were filming an interview with Chris. Ian's body was recovered and buried just above Base Camp at the foot of a slab where he had taught the few Sherpas they had used on the lower slopes how to jumar and abseil. The Sherpas collected wild flowers, Tom Frost said a prayer and Chris spoke a short moving tribute to the man with whom he had shared his best Alpine moments. The same day the expedition left Base Camp on the long journey home.

The success was accompanied by a huge media interest, fuelled by the ITN news reports, then the film and the book. In many ways both these last two were ground-breaking. The Annapurna film with its candid interviews of climbers just down from the face before they had time to compose their thoughts, gave the public a real insight into expedition life and Bonington's book *Annapurna South Face* was in my opinion his best expedition book. For the first time he used a montage technique of his own and others' diaries and extracts from radio calls (including a transcription of the whole of the crucial one). Above all, Bonington wrote with disarming frankness about his own weaknesses, admitting to being reduced to tears of exhaustion on the fixed ropes, acknowledging his outbursts of bad temper, and the torments of indecision he frequently succumbed to. Compared with, say, John Hunt's *The Ascent of Everest*, a rather formal account, *Annapurna South Face* was a breath of fresh air. A milestone book and film had complemented a milestone climb. It also made Bonington, and to a lesser extent Haston and Whillans, household names.

For Don, it was to be the high point of his career. Not only had he summitted on the hardest climb so far in the Himalaya, he had also designed the Whillans Box, the almost bombproof tents that were used on the face, and, more important, the Whillans Harness which for many years was to be virtually the only one in use in Britain. His financial future, whilst not assured, was made very much easier, particularly as Don never showed any great enthusiasm for regular work of any description. Don always cherished the memory of his return from Annapurna to his Rawtenstall home, where two letters awaited him, both from the same address in the Town Hall. One offered him congratulations and the freedom of the town; the other threatened him with a court appearance for non-payment of rates!

Hardly had Chris returned to Bowdon to write the book, when he was forced into making some awkward decisions about a project that was to consume his life for five long years and, on his own admission, put his marriage under great strain. One hundred and fifty miles east of Annapurna was the black, brooding South-West Face of Everest. It couldn't be ignored.

Rock Band on Everest SW Face

· 15 ·

'Big E' 1972

EVEN BEFORE LEAVING for Annapurna, Chris Bonington was aware of Himalayan climbing's next Last Great Problem – the South-West Face of Everest. Billed as the hardest route on the highest mountain, it never really had the same charisma for climbers as the South Face of Annapurna, the West Face of Makalu or even the nearby South Face of Lhotse. It was an ugly sweep of broken rock and long snowslopes that led to what would become a much more famous Rock Band than the one on Annapurna. This one only *started* at 8000 metres, almost at the height of the summit of Annapurna. To undertake difficult rock climbing would mean using oxygen at that height, which was both technically daunting and logistically challenging. Above the Rock Band there was still another 400–500 metres to the summit. Inevitably a camp would have to be placed above the Rock Band, very high indeed, and in order to do this, using fixed roped and oxygen, a logistical pyramid of colossal proportions seemed necessary. But, simply because it *was* on Everest – because it was there – it was to exert a spell over climbers for five years.

It was actually back in 1965, talking to John Harlin, that the possibility of climbing the South-West Face first occurred to Bonington but it was never more than a fantasy. With the death of Harlin, who might well have been a driving force in organising an expedition, the idea lay dormant. In any case there was no possibility of permission until Nepal opened up in 1969. Others had been thinking along the same lines and while Bonington threw everything into planning the Annapurna expedition for the following year, a small Japanese expedition almost immediately set out in the spring of '69 on a recce of Everest's South-West Face, getting into the Western Cwm to assess the possibilities of the huge face above them. They returned in force in the autumn of 1969 and climbed, relatively easily to the foot of the Rock Band. However, as Bonington pointed out, just getting to the foot of the Rock Band with no intention of going any higher is not too difficult. It's getting established there to make a realistic attempt to climb it and make a summit bid that is the real problem, and it would take another five expeditions to solve it.

In spring 1970, under the leadership of the seventy-year-old Saburo Matsukata (who stayed in Base Camp for the entire expedition), a huge Japanese team set out to climb the South-West Face *and* the original South Col Route as well as make a ski descent from the South Col. With these split objectives, plus the death of seven Sherpas, six in the Icefall, and one Japanese from a heart attack, the South-West Face was put on the back burner. In the meantime the most famous Japanese climber of his generation, Naomi Uemura, reached the summit via the South Col and South-East Ridge. The South-West Face team only got as far as the Rock Band before the expedition was called off.

Meanwhile an International expedition had been preparing for an attempt in 1971. It was led jointly by the Swiss-American Norman Dyhrenfurth and Jimmy Roberts, who asked Chris for advice on equipment. Chris responded by asking if he could go on the expedition and was invited to be climbing leader, which he accepted. The expedition would include French, German, Swiss and Austrian climbers. During and after the Annapurna expedition Bonington began to have doubts, rather like his misgivings about the Eiger Direct. To the secret delight of his friends, he then proceeded to resign from the expedition, ask to rejoin it, and resign again; a classic Bonington mind-changing exercise and one that plunged him back into self-doubt and depression – had he turned down a massive opportunity to consolidate his position as number one in the British climbing world?

In the event it proved to have been a wise decision. The International expedition was riven with dissent. It tried, as had the Japanese, to climb two routes; suffered the tragic and probably avoidable death of Harsh Bahuguna, who collapsed on fixed ropes descending the West Ridge, and in the end the expedition failed on both routes. Dougal Haston and Don Whillans provided most of the driving force on the South-West Face and were heavily criticised by the Latinos on the expedition. The whole saga attracted enormous media coverage and no one really emerged with much credit.

In spring 1972 another expedition was mounted, this one led by the Munich doctor, Karl Herrligkoffer. It was, if anything, even more acrimonious than the International expedition. Bonington was invited once more and, once more worried about the structure and possible personality clashes, pulled out, as did Dougal Haston. Whillans, Hamish MacInnes and the Nottingham-based climber Doug Scott did go, but all left the expedition before it ended, totally disillusioned with Herrligkoffer's leadership. (Whillans, memorably, nicknamed him 'Stirlingscoffer' when he seemed more interested in getting British financial sponsorship than getting the team together.) The expedition once again got no further than the foot of the Rock Band.

Unexpectedly, in April of 1972 Bonington obtained permission for a post-monsoon Everest expedition at very short notice. Initially he planned a lightweight ascent of the South Col Route with Dougal Haston, Mick Burke and Nick Estcourt, using only six Sherpas. This, at the time, would have been a very stylish ascent had it succeeded. But by May, Bonington knew that Herrligkoffer's expedition had failed. Could he walk past the foot of the greatest Himalayan challenge of the day and just ignore it? Yet again he changed his mind and in the middle of June he decided to go for it and try the South-West Face, which gave him only two months to plan, raise the money and the equipment to give his team a sporting chance. Bonington-watchers might be interested to note that from the first invitation from Dyhrenfurth to his decision to try the South-West Face in 1972 Chris had changed his mind no less than eight times!

His first priority was to increase the team and on the basis of his strong performance with Haston earlier in the year he invited Doug Scott. Then he added Dave Bathgate, Hamish MacInnes and Graham Tiso, a climbing shop owner from Edinburgh who was to handle all the equipment and stores. Kelvin Kent from Annapurna was again invited as Base Camp manager, with Jimmy Roberts as deputy leader.

When the team was announced it was greeted with general astonishment. Why had Whillans not been invited?

There were many arguments for and against leaving Don out. Since the row on the radio at Annapurna, which had caused so much resentment, attitudes towards Don had hardened. Some felt he was too selfish ever to work in a team, and too lazy to do his share of load-carrying. Others thought his omission was because he and Bonington were vying for the number one spot in British mountaineering and that if Whillans got to the summit of Everest he would seriously challenge Bonington. There was also the feeling that he was past his prime, though he had been high on the South-West Face twice in two years. Bonington rationalised it by saying that it would be difficult to lead an expedition where another member knew as much or more about the problems of the climb than the leader himself. He felt that the majority of his team was against the inclusion of Whillans, and that was that. But the news of Don's exclusion was greeted, as *Mountain* magazine put it at the time, with the same sort of disbelief as when the then Manchester United manager Frank O'Farrel dropped George Best. (Younger readers can substitute the names Hoddle and Gascoigne here to the same effect.)

Bonington's team selection over the years has frequently been criticised for 'cronyism', and pressure was put on him to make his teams more representative of British climbing. He has also made some unpopular exclusions, of which Don was only the first. But, unlike the England football manager, Chris isn't actually handling a national team. Though his expeditions are generally called the British Such-and-Such expedition, so are many others. In fact they are *his* and, though they always have the backing of bodies like the Mount Everest Foundation and the British Mountaineering Council, this again is no different from many other expeditions. If there *is* a difference it is that most Bonington expeditions end up paying back their grants and even making a contribution to the funds. So Bonington is free to select whoever he likes and, inevitably, they will be people he knows and trusts. Again, this is exactly the same way that most expedition leaders operate.

Looking back to the early 'seventies, it is also striking that comparatively few of Bonington's contemporaries ever seemed to get it
together to organise their own trips. Whillans in particular, had he
been bothered, could surely have got an Everest expedition off the
ground. If he had, would he have invited Bonington? There is no
doubt that climbing on board the Bonington bandwagon makes
expedition life very much easier, for Chris puts in a prodigious
amount of unseen work to ensure that they run smoothly. Few
climbers would be prepared to sacrifice all that time and energy,
yet are only too happy to avail themselves of what Peter Boardman
once described as 'one of the last great imperial experiences life can
offer'.

There is no doubt that the 'Bonington Boys', as Martin Boysen
called them, felt themselves to be part of an élite, and to the outsider
they often behaved as if they were. Inevitably over the years Bonington's teams have had to change and it must be said that Chris
doesn't always handle dropping people well. Even Prime Ministers
like Harold Wilson and Margaret Thatcher hated that part of the
job and Bonington is not good at sacking friends. He either becomes
defensive and self-justifying, which to the recipient of the bad news
tends to make it worse, or the person concerned simply finds that
his name is not on the team sheet with no explanation or apology.
Of course, there is no pleasant way to be told you have been cast
into outer darkness. Today company executives are sent on seminars
to learn how to make people redundant. Chris, without benefit of
this invaluable training, has never quite known how to soften the
blow. Perhaps it goes back to childhood and his lack of social
contacts, as he takes refuge behind the stiff upper lip of Sandhurst
and his Army days. Yet, paradoxically, Chris is someone who is
not ashamed to show emotion and he cries easily in public.

Before he had left England he contacted Ian McNaught-Davis
who was now managing director of Comshare, a computer firm in
London. Chris supplied Mac with all his logistical calculations and
asked him to work out a program for climbing the South-West Face
of Everest on his main frame computer. The results provided more
of a frame to work within than a blueprint to follow, for there are
far too many variables for that to be viable on an expedition. The
programming, which took weeks in 1972, could be done easily on
any laptop today, but it was Chris's introduction to the addictive

power of the computer. Already a compulsive player of board games, he became an early convert to the world of the word processor and computer war games. Later this would blossom into a dependence on his Internet and E-mail services that borders on the obsessive. Certainly, by 1998 he seemed to be spending more hours at Base Camp glued to the little screen than he did climbing the mountain.

So on 21st August 1972 with his slightly revamped team Bonington set off for the South-West Face of Everest. It was due to a major effort on Chris's part that they left, as he says, fairly solvent and, through the efforts of Graham Tiso, as well equipped as possible. The walk-in to Everest was a time to relax and then plan ahead, though walking through monsoon-drenched Nepal, replete with leeches that swayed from every twig or blade of grass seeking human blood, wasn't quite the pleasure that a pre-monsoon expedition experiences. The vanguard of Dougal Haston and Hamish Mac-Innes reached Base Camp on the 14th September as the last monsoon snowfall cleared and the weather appeared to settle into the calm and cold of autumn. Would the team have the time to climb the face before the winter winds (in fact the jet stream) settled over Everest's summit and made climbing, indeed life itself, impossible?

Aided by its computer program and also by a very experienced team of Sherpas, the expedition made excellent progress to begin with. From very early, in order to avoid the rows on Annapurna of who should lead what, Bonington had given specific roles to each pair of climbers. Thus Nick Estcourt and Dave Bathgate had the task of making the route from Camp 5 to Camp 6 at the foot of the Rock Band, Doug Scott and Mick Burke were to actually climb it, and Hamish MacInnes and Dougal Haston to make the summit bid. Bonington himself would adopt a similar role to John Hunt's on the 1953 expedition, leading from just behind the front pair, from where he could get a good idea of what was going on above and below. At first progress was steady and by mid-October Camp 4 had been established halfway up the face. Then out of a clear sky the first of the winter winds hit the mountain, scouring the face and battering the box tents with the sound of an express train. Life on the mountain was almost intolerable but Bonington, marooned in Camp 4, managed to stick it out for a week.

Below, an interesting addition to the team had arrived. Ken Wil-

son, the ever outspoken editor of *Mountain* magazine had travelled
under his own steam to see and report on what was happening.
Ken had written extremely knowledgeable, balanced and factual
reports on the complexities of the International and Herrligkoffer
expeditions, and Chris, in a characteristic burst of enthusiasm, had
invited him to see for himself what it was all about. (Needless to
say he had forgotten the conversation when Ken rang him to say
that he was coming!)

As if to punish him for his verbosity and assertiveness Ken found
himself in the first storm looking after Camp 1 for a whole week
on his own, before being allowed up to Camp 2 in the Western Cwm
at the foot of the face, where he spent a few nights stormbound in
the company of Chris and the others, cooking, chatting and inevitably arguing over climbing politics. In a lull in the storm, Ken,
who had to get home to work on the magazine set off down to
Base Camp, leaving with the jokey farewell of, 'You're mad – you're
all mad!' Later when the book was written Ken was mildly
aggrieved to see this written up semi-seriously with the comment
that he was a gregarious rock climber with no aspirations to be an
expedition man. But he did report the expedition in his usual forthright style, and would later make some fairly trenchant comments
about the 1975 expedition.

On the face the war of attrition continued. It got colder and the
winds got stronger. Then on the 1st November Chris made, in his
own words, 'A right bloody mess – a real cock-up.' He started
tinkering with the batting order – the way in which his pairs of
climbers would operate, and managed to infuriate both Doug Scott
and Nick Estcourt in particular by trying to swap pairs out of turn.
But worse was to come when on the 5th November, with the team
stretched almost to breaking point, Chris changed his tactics again
and proposed pushing Dougal Haston and Hamish MacInnes up
to the front to tackle the Rock Band instead of Mick Burke and
Doug Scott.

'Up to your old tricks is it, Chris?'

Mick, on the radio call, was referring to the Annapurna row
when it was Haston and Whillans being pushed through for very
similar reasons. Whereas on Annapurna the aggrieved pair of Estcourt and Boysen could just about accept the decision with good
grace, Doug Scott was not so easily pacified: 'In some ways you're

no better than Herrligkoffer, the way you're manipulating people.'

Chris tried to justify his decision until he lost his temper and suggested to Doug that if he couldn't accept it he should leave. Then both men pulled back, aware that they could destroy the whole expedition. Mick Burke meanwhile, who always had the reputation of being rather argumentative (though not in the Whillans league), decided he couldn't face another row and somehow the crisis passed.

In the event the whole argument was academic. When Haston finally reached the foot of the Rock Band on the 14 November and looked at the gully that he and Whillans had seen on the International expedition, it was now almost free of snow and the wind had become intolerable. Technical rock climbing in those conditions was out of the question. There was no alternative. The expedition had failed.

While the exhausted team were retreating off the mountain, a young Australian named Tony Tighe, who had been helping out at Base Camp, asked if he could just make one trip through the Icefall and into the Western Cwm. With an uncanny similarity to Ian Clough's death on the Annapurna expedition, Tony Tighe was killed by a falling sérac near the top of the Icefall. No trace of him was found and once more a Bonington expedition left Base Camp shocked by the tragedy that had waited until the very last moment to strike. There had been literally hundreds of trips up and down the Icefall, yet this had happened to Tony Tighe on his very first venture above Base Camp.

Again Bonington quickly produced an expedition book with the help of his secretary Betty Prentice, who typed the whole manuscript. Like *Annapurna South Face*, it was at times disturbingly honest, particularly in assessing his own failings. In his analysis of why they failed he obviously blamed the extreme weather but also interestingly, the choice of route through the Rock Band, which traversed rightwards below it until a weakness – the gully that Haston and Don had spotted – near its right-hand end. Even in 1972 Bonington was wondering whether that choice of route was a mistake. He also compared the South-West Face expedition with the six pre-war British Everest expeditions. Though all these were unsuccessful, they all learnt from previous experience and certainly, by the time of the fourth in 1933, the problems were understood and, once they were understood, they could be solved. It was to be another three years before Chris could learn from previous mistakes, come to grips with the problems and find the solutions for himself.

Changabang West Face

16

After Everest '72

Life in Bowdon was a series of mixed blessings. For Chris at least, the company was stimulating. The Estcourts, the Boysens and other keen climbers all lived nearby and were nicknamed, not entirely affectionately, the 'Altrincham All Stars'. His life was full, climbing in the summer evenings and weekends, writing, lecturing and increasingly travelling not just in the UK, but to Europe and the States. Wendy hated the suburban lifestyle and pined for the Lake District. She admits that at the time, 'I felt as though I was in a little cockleshell boat being tossed around in the wake of the great liner that was Chris, ploughing remorselessly through life.'

In 1971 they had bought a shepherd's cottage in the north-east corner of the Lakes. Badger Hill became a weekend refuge, though it needed a vast amount of work to make it habitable. In 1973 Chris was working in the garden when he made a characteristically impulsive proposal. 'There's no reason why we shouldn't live up here, is there?'

This time, Chris and Wendy put down roots and Badger Hill has become the focus of their existence. All the conversion work has been done tastefully but modestly. The Boningtons even now live a remarkably frugal lifestyle with the occasional indulgence. But when they first moved up to the cottage in 1974, Wendy had to live in a caravan with the children while the builders finished the conversion. Chris took himself off to India.

In 1973 and '74 Bonington went on two comparatively low-key expeditions. The first in 1973 with Nick Estcourt, Chris remembers fondly as one of the most enjoyable he has ever been on, more of an extended Alpine holiday than a Himalayan expedition. It was to Brammah I, a 6516 metre peak in the Kishtwar Himalaya, an area of beautiful and quite difficult mountains that used to be easily accessible but have now become out of bounds due to the fragile political situation in Kashmir. Chris and Nick climbed Brammah alpine-style and it cemented a deep friendship between the two. Nick had always been a loyal support climber and undertaken horrible jobs like being expedition treasurer. Now he could enjoy the simple pleasure of climbing a virgin peak by a difficult and fairly committing route, for there is a world of difference between nearly all climbing in the Alps, where rescue is a definite possibility, and an alpine-style ascent in the Himalaya when you are out on a limb if things go wrong. It has always been a puzzle to me that Chris, who enjoys this sort of climbing more than anything else, should have done comparatively little of it in the Himalaya until the 1980s and '90s when, by rights, he was getting a bit long in the tooth. But perversely some of his very best routes were done like this, long after the big expeditions to Annapurna, Everest and K2.

The following year came another joint Indian expedition. This time a venture with the Indian Army. The objective was without doubt one of the most charismatic mountains in the world with a name to match. Changabang, at 6864 metres, is a shark's fin of white granite in the Garhwal Himalaya. Tom Longstaff, the great pioneer and explorer, described it in 1907 as 'the most superbly beautiful mountain I have ever seen', and in 1936 Eric Shipton wrote, 'I sat for an hour, fascinated by the gigantic white cliffs of Changabang.' But it was W. H. Murray, whose book *Mountaineering in Scotland* had so inspired the young Chris Bonington, who found the words to sum it up: 'Changabang in the moonlight shone tenderly as though veiled in bridal lace; at ten miles distance seemingly as fragile as an icicle; a product of earth and sky rare and fantastic, and of loveliness unparalleled so that, unaware, one's pulse leapt and the heart gave thanks – that this mountain should be as it is.'

Bonington and his co-leader, Lieutenant-Colonel Balwant Sandhu each chose three climbers to make up a team of eight. Chris chose

Martin Boysen, Dougal Haston and Doug Scott; Sandhu chose Kiran Kumar, Ujagar Singh and D. J. Singh. Like many Indian mountaineers, the Army had made them very fit and determined but, by comparison with their British counterparts, they were not technical climbers, and Changabang would surely prove to be a technical peak.

An addition to the British team was Alan Hankinson, of the ITN team on Annapurna South Face. Rather like Ken Wilson on Everest, Hank, as everyone knows him, was the subject of an impetuous Bonington invitation to come on the trip and write a book, Chris having written two under great pressure and not fancying another one so soon. In the end Hank produced, edited and contributed to an amalgam of everyone's diaries and did a very competent job in describing the ups and downs of a fascinating and essentially happy adventure.

The first problem was to find the right approach to the mountain. Hankinson wrote that it seemed as though it might prove harder to find than climb. Eventually Base Camp was established near the foot of the Rhamani Glacier and commanding a superb view of the south side of Changabang. The skyline West Ridge was the route originally intended but it looked far too hard. In fact only two years later two extremely talented young British climbers, Peter Boardman and Joe Tasker, were to make a wonderfully impressive route on the West Face. At the time it was probably the hardest climb done in the Himalaya and certainly confirmed the original assessment, for it took forty days to achieve. In 1974 the Indian-British team didn't take long to decide it was out of the question, and that there must be an easier route on the other side of the mountain. The main snag was that they had come up the wrong valley and to get round to the north side of the mountain meant climbing a steep wall of mixed ground to Shipton's Col, the point where Eric Shipton had sat looking at the West Face. But Shipton had approached from the other side, the Changabang Glacier, which was no more than a walk. Martin Boysen and Doug Scott tried to force a direct route to the Col but were stopped by a steep headwall. Their second attempt was successful: a long ice face that led to the ridge above the col. It was quite dangerous and the pair descended to the Col with relief, then abseiled down to their previous high point. With fixed ropes in place it would be possible to jumar up the direct route. But it was a strange way to start the climb, and already some of the Indians were out of their depth on such steep ground. In the end only Balwant Sandhu and a Sherpa, Tashi, accompanied the four British climbers.

Chris was worried that without a reasonable Indian presence the Brits might be seen to have hijacked the expedition. It was a situation that would arise again in the 1990s on two more Indian/ British expeditions, and required a lot of tact and understanding from both sides. Seen from the British perspective, they undoubtedly make access to the remote and desirable mountains not just easier but possible, for expeditions to virgin summits in India have to be either Indian or joint expeditions. For the Indians, having smoothed out the bureaucracy and often used Army facilities to get the team to the foot of the mountain, it must be frustrating to say the least, to be abandoned by a team of technical climbers who suddenly want to do their own thing. But from a Western perspective it is a perennial problem, not only with joint expeditions, but any that require a liaison officer. Techniques of high standard Himalayan climbing are not acquired overnight, and mountains as serious as Changabang are not the place to learn them.

Despite Chris's single-minded commitment to succeed on his expeditions and his occasional high-handed treatment of fellow expedition members, he has probably been more successful than anyone in finding solutions to the potential conflicts of interest that inevitably arise on these expeditions. His Army background is, of course, a great help: most British climbers find an Indian Army Mess a strange place, and are thrown by Indian Army officers, whose behaviour can seem like a caricature of the 'pukka' British Army officer of the last century. But Chris understands and enjoys their company. I have come to realise that he has a deep and abiding love, not just for the Himalayan mountains but for the varied cultures, people and religions as well. Certainly on Changabang Chris's friendship with Balwant was real and enduring. They shared a tent, played chess and made the expedition work.

Once the six climbers got over Shipton's Col and established a camp at the head of the Changabang Glacier the team was effectively cut off from the world. If anything went wrong they would have to climb back to and re-cross the Col and get down to the Baghiri Glacier before any help could possibly be given. It is tempt-

ing to think that the climb itself was something of an anticlimax
after all the effort needed to get to the bottom of it. As Hankinson
says, it took a lot longer to get to the bottom than to climb, and
the description in the book gives the ascent only twenty out of the
book's 108 pages. In fact, though it only took a couple of days, it
was no pushover and only a hugely talented team could have dis-
posed of the long knife-edged ice ridge to the summit with such
panache. Even so, all six only reached the top at five in the evening,
after a very long day with twenty roped pitches, and then Doug
Scott and Dougal Haston traversed to another summit that seemed
to be marginally higher. The descent to the top camp was completed
in the dark. It was a perfect starlit night with no wind. Chris thought
that if the weather had broken they would have had desperate
trouble to get back. As it was, the climb was completed on the only
cloudless day of the whole expedition.

The retreat over Shipton's Col was marred by an argument. The
Indians were prepared to carry colossal loads up the 500-metre
ascent to the Col, but the affluent Brits were prepared to abandon
what they no longer needed. (Things have changed a lot since 1974,
and Chris is now as conservation- and pollution-conscious as anyone.) In the end the Indian view prevailed, and in gathering gloom
and falling snow the six bore their loads back to Advance Base to
welcome food and hot drinks and the only letters from home on
the whole expedition.

Alan Hankinson's book finishes with some telling interviews with
the wives of the climbers, an interesting perspective. Wendy Bonington talked at some length about the pressures of living with
expeditioning, particularly the effects on Daniel and Rupert:

> They come out with some pretty straight questions sometimes,
> 'What if Daddy gets killed?' and once when he seemed a long
> time getting back home – 'Is Daddy dead?' Mostly though they
> come out with 'I want Daddy' just when I'm having to tell them
> off about something.

From Wendy's point of view expeditions gave her the time to get
on with her own work – at that time it was painting and pottery
– but she was all too aware of the reality of expedition life:

I am not a natural worrier, being basically optimistic, but hate being continually asked if I worry about Chris when he's away. It's a bit like walking a tightrope. You've got to be completely aware of the realities of a situation which is completely beyond your control and being asked to worry is like being asked to look down: it certainly doesn't help and makes keeping your balance that much more difficult.

Late in 1973 Bonington had learnt that a Canadian team which had been given permission for Everest in the post-monsoon season in 1975 had cancelled. He applied for the vacant slot. Once again he was attracted by the possibility of a lightweight attempt on the original South Col Route. He had also applied for permission to attempt the Trango (Nameless) Tower in the Karakoram in the summer of '75 and for a while he dallied with the thought of doing both. In Delhi, on his way to Changabang he received a telegram from Nepal. He had got permission for Everest. Almost immediately Doug Scott started to persuade Chris to change his mind and mount another expedition to the still unclimbed South-West Face. Throughout the Changabang expedition he, Doug, Dougal and Martin mulled over the problems and by the time Chris returned to London his mind was made up. The South-West Face it was.

17

'Big E' 1975

UNLIKE EVEREST '72, Chris Bonington had a whole year to prepare for his second attempt on the South-West Face. Three issues
occupied his mind. One, he needed a single sponsor prepared to
underwrite the whole expedition from a very early stage. Two, the
expedition should arrive at Base Camp much earlier than in '72
when they were caught by the winter winds. Three, after five
expeditions (for there had been another unsuccessful Japanese
attempt in 1973) it was clear that the route through the Rock
Band would have to be changed. All the expeditions except the first
Japanese reconnaissance had traversed a long way to attempt the
narrow gully at its right-hand end. This, as Haston had found out
in '72, could prove to be swept bare of snow and simply too hard.
Another gully on the left-hand side started lower down and cut
through the Rock Band to a large snowfield. A top camp would
still have to be made above the Rock Band but it would be lower
than a camp on the alternative right-hand route. Much more important, it would cut out the need for the extra camp that had always
been necessary at the far end of the foot of the Rock Band. Logistically it made much more sense. Suddenly Bonington could see a
way through the impasse that had stopped the other expeditions.
Perhaps the biggest unknown now was whether the left-hand gully
was climbable and whether it was safe. If it was a natural avalanche
shoot it could be suicidal, but after five expeditions, which had, of

MACINNESS BOXES ON EVEREST S.W. FACE

necessity, climbed underneath it without incident, it seemed a gamble worth taking.

But first and foremost was the little matter of money. The ever-optimistic George Greenfield flinched when Chris told him that he was looking for £100,000, but suggested he write to Alan Tritton, a director of Barclays Bank International. Tritton met Chris in London where he was 'sympathetic but non-committed', but said he would put Chris's proposal to the Board. With one of those delicious ironies that make expeditions both fun and fascinating, Chris returned home to live like a refugee in an extremely chaotic and tatty caravan in the garden of Badger Hill, while in a different world a decision was being made about a huge sum of money that might or might not be about to come his way.

After two weeks the news came that he could scarcely have dared hoped for. Barclays said 'yes' and accepted the possibility of footing the bill, even if Chris went seriously over budget. In October 1974 Barclays gave a press conference to announce their sponsorship, which was not received with unbounded joy by many of their customers, who felt their hard-earned savings were being channelled into someone else's summer holidays. Letters to this effect were sent to Barclays and the daily papers, and no amount of explaining by Barclays that this was not the case could convince everyone.

On a different level many climbers worried that this was just another publicity-driven extravaganza designed to promote the Bonington bandwagon, but with little chance of success. Ken Wilson, playing the devil's advocate, felt obliged to put the groundswell of popular opinion into words in a fairly hard-hitting *Mountain* editorial.

Is such a climb really worth the expenditure of £100,000 and should climbing remain so completely oblivious of this point when the country, and indeed the world, are in such dire economic straits? ... a successful conclusion (a remote possibility) would please everybody but a more likely outcome would be an embarrassing rehash of the 1972 affair with a few hundred feet of height gained and some ticklish explaining to do to an increasingly sceptical press.

A question was even asked in Parliament how Barclays could justify themselves, but Barclays stuck to their guns.

Throughout his expeditioning career Chris has worked closely with equipment manufacturers, developing climbing gear and clothing that have been tested in extreme conditions. There is no doubt that several companies benefited directly from the big Everest expeditions – Mountain Equipment, who made high quality down gear, Karrimor rucksacks, Javlin fibre pile, Viking ropes. By supplying the gear they often got huge television exposure, plus many high quality advertising shots for their own publicity purposes. Bonington has always been extremely careful to ensure good photos of everything from Base Camp frame tents to cigarette lighters. Inevitably, he has been associated with several of them, notably Belstaff, who were early users of Gore-Tex material, and Karrimor.

It is Berghaus from Newcastle with whom Chris has had a long and productive association. The firm was the brainchild of Peter Lockey and Gordon Davidson, and for many years they personally developed and tested their prototypes on the Cheviot Hills. Many leading climbers became involved in what seemed to retain the atmosphere of a family firm. Originally, they produced rucksacks, but expanded into a wide range of successful and innovative equipment of which the Yeti gaiter is probably the best known as the first effective over-boot system to ensure dry feet under any conditions. Chris was advisor to Berghaus for many years, essentially lending his name for their promotion. He now sits on the board as non-executive chairman. Like all his commitments it is one he takes extremely seriously. He has given Berghaus great loyalty and certainly earns his retainer.

On the question of sponsorship, and particularly sponsorship of major Bonington expeditions, which admittedly have been quite expensive, it must be remembered that compared with many other sports, the sums involved are still minute. The total cost of every expedition Chris has been on wouldn't buy a single Premier Division footballer. Also, some of the big expeditions, particularly Everest South-West Face, ended up actually making a profit for the sponsors. Instead of taking the author's percentage royalty for the expedition book Chris wrote it for a flat fee and the royalties for what became a bestseller went back to the sponsors. With only one or two exceptions, most major sponsors feel they have had a very good deal from Chris's expeditions. Network TV programmes give a very high profile to sponsors, in particular equipment and clothing firms, who effectively get fifty minutes advertising, which would cost a small fortune otherwise. In a commercial world Chris had made climbing a respectable outlet for sponsorship and this has undoubtedly had a spin off for smaller expeditions who can use Chris's trips as an example to attract sponsorship. This may seem a very unattractive, even downright mercenary, approach, but without expeditions like Everest South-West Face it could be argued that a lot of lesser expeditions simply wouldn't have got off the ground.

Meanwhile, Bonington threw himself into the detailed planning of the expedition. This time, with the experience of Annapurna and Everest '72 behind him he was determined that no detail was too small to be ignored. Once again Ian McNaught-Davis's computer was pressed into use and Mac himself was on the committee of management. This was chaired by Lord Hunt and also included Sir Jack Longland and Charles Wylie, all experienced Everesters. Chris freely admits that John Hunt's Army-based organisation of the '53 expedition was a role model he followed and all through the 1975 expedition army terminology seeped into his descriptions – 'command post', 'assault camps', and the like. Though John Hunt was Chris's mentor, he confessed that he couldn't remember giving Chris any specific advice. 'He had so much energy and enthusiasm there really wasn't anything I could tell him. But I was extremely flattered to think that Chris was influenced by my leadership on the 1953 expedition.'

In fact, once on the mountain Chris's own performance would prove to be uncannily like Hunt's, even to the point of load-carrying to the highest camp and putting himself down for a possible third summit bid. Hunt had done precisely those things in 1953.

Bonington's team was to be much bigger than either Annapurna or Everest '72, with eight lead climbers and eight in support (both increased by one later on), as well as a four-man BBC film crew (including producer Ned Kelly of Cheddar fame). In addition to the old hands of Nick Estcourt, Martin Boysen, Dougal Haston, Mick Burke, Doug Scott and Hamish MacInnes, who was to be deputy leader, he included Paul 'Tut' Braithwaite, who had a brilliant Alpine record, and a young mountaineer who was just beginning to make his mark, Peter Boardman. Both these last were the result of pressure to make his team broader based. By 1975 there were certainly several very talented younger climbers hoping to be invited. Already activists like Rab Carrington, Brian Hall and Al Rouse felt they deserved a chance and, strange as it may seem now, they felt in 1975 that several of Chris's team were getting too old. In fact the average age was only thirty-two, and this included Chris at forty-one and Hamish MacInnes who was forty-four.

Of the support climbers perhaps inevitably Mike Thompson was Chris's first choice. Once again he was in charge of food and once again his appendix in the expedition book was the funniest and most perceptive section. With such a large team Chris decided to take two doctors. One was to become very much part of the Bonington entourage and a close friend as well. Charlie Clarke, while never claiming to be a high standard climber, had led several small expeditions to the Kishtwar range. His first introduction to Chris was typical. Chris had asked him if he was free to go on the '72 expedition. Charlie did some quick manoeuvring to get the time off from his job as Registrar in Neurology at the Middlesex Hospital, and rang Chris to tell him he was available. But by that time Chris had invited Dr Barney Rosedale! Charlie proved to be the ideal expedition doctor, understanding that neurotic climbers suffer from hypochondria as much as anything else, but always alive to the possibility of serious illness. By standing back from the hard climbing, Charlie has been an invaluable source of advice to Chris and become a sounding board for his legendary changes of mind.

One of Chris's best decisions was taken at a very early stage. In '72 the outstanding high-altitude Sherpa had been a young man called Pertemba. On a trip to Europe afterwards he visited Dougal Haston, by now running the International School of Mountaineering in Leysin. Pertemba then travelled on to Badger Hill. For two weeks he went rock climbing with Chris, played endlessly with Daniel and Rupert, and helped Chris lay a lawn in front of the cottage. Pertemba, or PT as he is always called, is very much the modern Sherpa. He was educated at a school in Khumde, founded by Sir Edmund Hillary. Intelligent, ambitious and having a natural gift for leadership, he was the perfect choice for sirdar, the critical link between the local porters, the Sherpas, and the expedition. His real friendship with Chris has blossomed over the years and PT still considers Chris to be an 'older brother'. In 1975 Chris could delegate huge responsibilities onto his shoulders, which, despite his comparative youth (he was still in his mid-twenties) he could handle, keeping the respect of his own Sherpa group, most of whom were older, and working easily with the lead climbers who all recognised an exceptional human being as well as a first-rate mountaineer.

Remembering Annapurna, Bonington decided that all the expedition equipment should travel overland to avoid the possibility of cargo ships' unpredictable delays. Two grossly overloaded 16-ton lorries set out in early April for the 7000-mile journey to Kathmandu. Bonington commented that even if they were hijacked on the way out they would still have more time to replace their contents than they had to organise the whole expedition in '72. In the event, by driving day and night they completed the journey without incident in only twenty days, and by early June everything was safely stored in a barn in Khumde. This time there would be no last minute panics when the team flew out at the end of July. Despite this there were many who didn't give the expedition much chance of success. Even John Hunt, their patron, thought it was only 50/50, which was probably a realistic estimate.

From the start the expedition ran smoothly. Base Camp was established on 22nd August, three weeks earlier than in 1972. Bonington's logistical machine rolled smoothly and by 13th September Dougal Haston had reached the site of Camp 5 below the Rock Band at 8000 metres. Bonington himself established the camp, using Hamish MacInnes's new Superboxes. These, developed from the Whillans Box, were virtually indestructible and some are apparently still standing on the face today! For double security they even had bullet-proof cloth stretched over them, as in '72 falling stones had come right through the walls. Each box weighed 66 pounds and no less than five were established at Camp 4. As a final precaution heavy-duty tarpaulins were stretched over them in the hope that any avalanche would simply slide over the camp.

Bonington stayed in Camp 5 for eight days helping to make the route up to the foot of the left-hand gully through the Rock Band and ensuring that the Camp was properly established and stocked. The rotation of lead climbers and load-carrying Sherpas unwound like clockwork and the expedition reached its critical phase. As in 1972, Bonington had decided earlier on his pairs of climbers, and it fell to Nick Estcourt and Tut Braithwaite to tackle the Rock

Band. Perhaps inevitably Doug Scott and Dougal Haston, as the strongest pair, would make the first summit bid.

On 20th September they set out, and almost unbelievably climbed nearly all the 330-metre gully in a single day. The crucial two pitches gave first Tut, then Nick more excitement than they were looking for. First Tut:

> There seemed to be a gangway leading up to some snowy ledges
> . . . I edged my way over, stepped carefully up sloping ledges,
> nothing much for the hands . . . I was totally involved in the
> climbing. Suddenly my oxygen ran out. I don't think I shall ever
> forget the feeling of suffocation as I ripped the mask away from
> my face. I was on the brink of falling. Beginning to panic, felt a
> warm trickle run down my leg . . .

Although he too had run out of oxygen, Nick led through and soon found himself on steep ground, out of balance and hanging on by his left arm which was jammed precariously behind a bulge of snow:

> I was getting desperate, goggles misting up, panting helplessly
> . . . I was losing strength fast . . . but whatever happened I wasn't
> going to give up. If I had and let Tut do it, I'd have kicked myself
> for years.

He managed to tap a piton into rotten rock.

> It was obviously useless but if you pulled on it in just one direction
> it was safe. I managed to lean out on it a little bit, walked my feet
> up, jammed my other arm behind the bulge, dug into the snow and
> found something, I'm not sure what, and just kept going . . . Given
> the conditions it was the hardest pitch I've ever led.

It was also the hardest pitch on the South-West Face and with its completion the way was open to the summit. Later John Hunt wrote in appreciation:

> I think that all members of the party would concede (with the
> exception of the person I allude to) that the supreme example of

climbing technique, applied with exceptional determination, was Nick Estcourt's superb lead without the normal safeguard or oxygen at 8300 metres up the rickety outward-leaning ramp of snow-covered rubble ... This must be one of the greatest leads in climbing history.

The day after Nick and Tut's great effort, Bonington at Camp 5 forced himself to think of the implications. Doug and Dougal would be going for the top in the next three or four days. Then what? The weather seemed settled and all over the mountain were ambitious people who had each contributed to getting the route established. How could he be totally fair in giving just a few of his team the chance to crown their climbing career? Whatever he did would be criticised. After a lot of thought Bonington announced his decision on a radio call to all camps: Doug Scott and Dougal Haston for the first bid (obviously); Martin Boysen, Pete Boardman, Mick Burke and Pertemba for the second attempt, and Tut, Nick, Ang Phurba and Chris himself for the third.

Later that day Charlie Clarke made a private radio call to Chris, and told him that he was worried about Chris's condition. He pointed out the length of time he had spent at around or above 8000 metres, and said his voice was becoming slurred and his instructions muddled. He thought Chris should come down to Camp 2 at the foot of the face for a rest and direct the operations on the mountain from there. Chris didn't agree wholeheartedly, but realised that if he was in the third summit team he would have to stay at Camp 5 for nearly a fortnight, which was far too long in any circumstances, let alone before trying to reach the summit of Everest. He resolved however to help do a carry to the top camp before he came down.

Before Charlie signed off the call he put Hamish MacInnes on, who dropped a small bombshell by announcing to Chris that he was going home. Earlier Hamish had been caught in a powder snow avalanche and had inhaled powder snow into his lungs. He had made a reasonable recovery and had put in a huge amount of work on two expeditions in organising, rigging ladders through the Icefall, designing equipment, and undoubtedly felt that he had deserved a chance at the summit. He and Chris had been friends for too long and been through too much to fall out, but Chris could sense his disappointment. After the radio call he even considered a fourth summit bid with Hamish, but knew this was probably unrealistic.

On 22nd September Doug and Dougal completed the route through the Rock Band and dug out a platform for Camp 6. Chris, Mick Burke and Mike Thompson supported them, along with Ang Phurba, Pertemba and Tenzing. For Mike Thompson it was perhaps the highlight of his Himalayan career. As a support climber he wasn't expected to go high, and on Annapurna he had driven himself to collapse at 7000 metres, but now he carried a heavy load a thousand metres higher. With the loads at Camp 6 and a smaller Summit Box pitched, it was now up to Doug and Dougal. In the evening sunlight the others descended. For Chris and Mike it would be for the last time.

After a day fixing rope across the snowfield above the Rock Band to a gully that led to the South Summit, Doug and Dougal set off just after first light on 24th September. Through a telescope at Camp 2 Chris and the others followed their progress as the two tiny dots inched across the snowfield and disappeared into the gully. Bonington was racked with worry and when at 4 p.m. Nick spotted them at the top of the gully Chris prayed they were on their way down. They weren't.

Doug and Dougal had found the gully full of bottomless snow, and then Dougal's oxygen set had become blocked with ice. At last, hours later than they had hoped, they reached the South Summit. Technically the South-West Face was climbed, for they were now on the original South-East Ridge route. But both knew they would carry on to the top. Fortunately the snow conditions on the ridge were slightly better and at 6 p.m., with the sun setting through multiple layers of cloud, they reached the summit. Just time for some photographs, a quick look into the mysterious valleys of Tibet to the north, and it was time to descend in twilight to the South Summit where darkness overtook them. Doug and Dougal dug a makeshift snow hole and survived the highest bivouac ever without sleeping bags, oxygen, or gas for their stove. The night was interminable, and both men, hypoxic and drifting in and out of sleep, began hallucinating: for Doug, his feet became separate beings that needed help and he started talking to them. Meanwhile, Dougal had a long and involved imaginary conversation with Dave Clarke, the equipment manager. At last dawn broke and far below at Camp

2 in the Western Cwm, Chris and the others were hugely relieved to see two tiny figures moving, oh so slowly, back to Camp 6. At 9 a.m. they radioed Chris with the happy news and Chris, over-joyed, broke down in tears. His joy didn't last long.

As with Annapurna, he had to suffer a second summit bid. Before the successful ascent he and everyone else were thinking upwards. Now, with success assured, he could only sit it out in a state of increasing anxiety. He had to give his team members the chance of standing on top of the world, but in his heart he would have liked to be able to call everyone down and go home. On the 26th the second team set out from Camp 6 for the summit. Martin Boysen left first, followed by Pete Boardman and Pertemba, with Mick Burke some way behind. Before he reached the end of the fixed ropes Martin's oxygen set failed him and then he lost a crampon. Weeping with frustration and self-pity Martin retreated to Camp 6 while Pete and Pertemba forged ahead. Now following Doug and Dougal's tracks they made quick time and reached the summit just after 1 p.m. But the weather was deteriorating and there was no view. On the way back to the South Summit they were surprised to see Mick Burke soloing along the summit ridge.

Mick was filming for the BBC and desperately wanted to get summit footage on his little clockwork autoload 16mm camera. He tried to persuade Pete and Pertemba to return to the top, but Pete, worried about the weather, said he would wait for Mick at the South Summit. When they got there the weather broke down com-pletely and soon they were facing a full Everest storm. Pete waited, and waited and waited, but Mick failed to reappear. At 4.30 p.m. Pete decided he had to get down, and he and Pertemba just managed to regain Camp 6 by 7.30 p.m. The storm raged for another day and Martin Boysen spent thirty-six hours clearing snow off the tents, brewing up, and digging spare oxygen cylinders out of the snow. On the morning of 20th September the weather cleared and Chris ordered everyone down. There was no possibility that Mick Burke could have survived. He had almost certainly reached the summit, and probably fallen through a cornice on the summit ridge on the descent in a white out. As if to confirm Bonington's decision to call off the expedition a huge avalanche nearly destroyed Camp 2. Amazingly, nobody was hurt and when the face had been cleared everyone retreated safely to Base Camp.

And so the South-West Face of Everest was climbed. It was without doubt the height of Chris's Himalayan career as a leader. A brilliant campaign had been quickly and efficiently executed. Ned Kelly, the BBC producer, remembers Chris's leadership as being incredibly calm and controlled throughout, handling all the potential conflict with quiet diplomacy. Of course the death of Mick Burke marred the achievement; for the third time in succession Chris's expedition had ended with the death of a friend. Nothing can justify this and nobody would try to. It is simply a fact that climbing is dangerous and the bigger the mountain the more dangerous it gets. As Chris wrote later: 'I know that I, and I suspect most other members of the team, would have followed the same course as Mick in similar circumstances. In pressing on alone he took a climber's calculated risk, in principle similar to the ones one often takes equally on British hills, the Alps or other mountains of the Himalayas.'

Historically the climb probably marked the beginning of the end of the importance of huge fixed-rope expeditions. Not that those expeditions stopped, they continue to this day, but the success of Everest South-West Face did show that if you have enough manpower, money, leadership and, of course, good luck, then virtually anything is possible. As if to underline this, 6000 miles away a newspaper headline announcing the successful ascent was on display outside a shop in Salzburg. A young Tyrolean climber saw it and, in that instant, he knew with absolute certainty that the next step forward would be to climb Everest without oxygen. His name was Reinhold Messner.

For the rest of the team the ascent of the South-West Face meant different things. For Doug it opened the way to the life of a professional mountaineer, but the accompanying fame that came with it always weighed heavily on his shoulders. Mike Thompson on the other hand, felt it was all rather an anticlimax. The Annapurna expedition was the breakthrough and it was done with a small team. Mike felt that first expedition was part of the culture of the 1960s, and had its roots in Welsh and Lakeland weekends, pubs, mini-vans, close friends and, above all, a step into the unknown. By 1975 he felt it had all become a bit predictable; a huge machine that once set in motion would produce a result. He also began to wonder whether it was worth it in human terms. 'It was getting more like war.' He likened the loss of close friends to premature ageing, something you expect in later life but not in your thirties.

On a more positive note, Mike wrote an article for *Mountain* magazine called 'Out With the Boys Again', which has become a classic. It is a highly personal, wry look at the expedition, and pokes affectionate fun at the whole enterprise, and inevitably at Chris himself, who found it hard to see the jokes:

> 'Welcome aboard,' said Our Leader, using the terminology of the only one of the armed forces of which he hadn't been a member . . . [Our Leader] had now entered his Mad Madhi phase, running out drums of fixed rope in the wrong direction, ranting on at Ang Phurba about 'really good Sherpa food', working out logistics on his porridge-encrusted electronic calculator, and communicating his instructions to the outside world on a broken walkie-talkie that had been persuaded to work again by jamming a ballpoint pen into its circuitry . . . one needs a leader who changes his mind a lot and has difficulty in remembering from one day to the next what he has decided. We were very fortunate to have such a leader.

Unfair? Certainly. But in such a portrait there always lurks a grain or two of truth.

Martin Boysen agreed with Mike Thompson that Annapurna was a far better and much harder climb. As someone primarily interested in very technical climbs, he genuinely felt the South-West Face of Everest was overblown. 'Most of it you could do with your hands in your pockets.' For Nick Estcourt, Everest was in the end a disappointment. Carolyn Estcourt thinks that it was a turning point in Nick's career. 'He had put so much effort into both expeditions and really wanted to get to the summit.' Carolyn felt he never quite had the same bubbling enthusiasm afterwards, even though he had undoubtedly made a huge contribution to their success. Dougal Haston, enigmatic as usual, seemed to regard Everest quite simply as one more climb and not long afterwards, his appetite for hard climbing as insatiable as ever, he completed a new hard route on Mount McKinley (Denali) in Alaska with Doug Scott.

And what of Chris Bonington himself? It undoubtedly confirmed his position at the top of the British climbing tree. His book *Everest the Hard Way*, and the film of the same name, had tremendous exposure with the general public, and he was now a household name. In 1976 he was awarded the CBE in the New Year Honours list. An extensive lecture tour was a sell-out and a pattern was set for the next twenty years: books, posters, films, lectures, interviews, guest appearances, even TV quiz shows! There was no stopping him now. For one thing was absolutely certain: if anyone thought that, at the age of forty-one, Chris would hang up his boots and settle for an easy life, they couldn't be more wrong. Everest was a big landmark but that was all. Now other challenges loomed. His enthusiasm was, if anything, even greater; his ambitions were seemingly boundless.

· 18 ·

The Ogre Affair

Perhaps the most surprising thing about the 1977 Ogre expedition was that Chris Bonington didn't write a book about it and neither did anyone else. It was a quite intriguing expedition with a complex plot, near tragedy and eventually a happy ending. As it happened, I was able to hear first-hand accounts from most of the members as they struggled home. I was driving overland to India and before I left England the first arrivals were telling the basic facts. I then met Clive Rowland driving the expedition van back when our paths crossed in Peshawar, and I bumped into Nick Estcourt in the British Embassy Club in Islamabad only hours before he was due to fly out. By this point I had great difficulty in believing that they had all been on the same expedition, or even the same mountain. So for an outsider to tell the tale is presumptuous at best and I can only hope that I annoy everyone equally as I try to be even-handed in doing so. Inevitably though, it will centre on Chris's part in the epic events of July 1977.

The Karakoram range of northern Pakistan contains some of the world's highest and hardest peaks, K2 being the best known. After years of closure the range was completely opened up in 1975. Suddenly some of the most desirable plums of world climbing were up for grabs – Trango Tower, Paiju Peak, the Latok Peaks, and the Ogre itself were just a few of the better known names. Doug Scott had climbed (or rather not climbed much, for his expedition was

The Ogre

beset by porter strikes) in the Ogre region in 1975 and had permission for the Ogre itself in 1977. The Ogre, or Baintha Brak, is,
at 7285 metres, the highest peak above the Biafo Glacier, with its
sister peaks, the Latoks, not much lower. None of them had been
climbed, although a Sheffield expedition led by Don Morrison had
attempted the Ogre in 1975, but had also been foiled by porter
troubles.

Doug Scott's expeditions are very different from Chris's. They
are comparatively unstructured, though Doug in the end is still the
boss. For the Ogre he invited five other climbers so they would
make three pairs. All could attempt their own routes on the Ogre.
He and Tut Braithwaite would attempt a vast Yosemite-like prow
of granite that led directly to a huge snowfield below a complex
summit structure, while Mo Anthoine and Clive Rowland would
try a rather more traditional route up the West Ridge. Chris meanwhile, who had originally been paired with Dougal Haston, fancied
the South-West Ridge which shared the same lower section as the
West Ridge. In January 1977 tragedy struck when Dougal, who
had survived so many desperate Alpine and Himalayan epics, was
killed in an avalanche skiing near his home in Leysin. For Chris it
was a bitter personal blow. Since Annapurna they had become good
friends and, in addition to the big expeditions, they had spent a lot
of time in the Alps together. Inevitably Nick Estcourt filled his place
for the Ogre.

It must have been quite strange for Chris to be part of someone
else's expedition, but at least he was free of logistics, man management and the media. When the expedition left Skardu for the
walk-in he needed to do very little other than walk, for Doug and,
in particular, the irrepressible Mo Anthoine had all the experience
from previous expeditions to sort out the porters. Mo was a hugely
charismatic character, with a rapier wit (often at Chris's expense)
and a highly individual view of life. Chris always seemed slightly
wary of him, probably with good reason. Clive Rowland from
Sheffield was even more caustic, and had the archetypal York-
shireman's distrust of anyone not born and bred in that county.

The idea of three teams each doing their own thing received an
early setback when at the foot of their prospective buttress Tut was
hit a glancing blow on the thigh by a football-sized rock. (A direct
hit to his head would almost certainly have killed him.) Tut man-

aged to limp back to Base Camp but he was effectively out of the
expedition. Meanwhile Chris and Nick were champing at the bit,
for they felt that Mo and Clive were overtly cautious and deliberate
in preparing their route. Chris was increasingly tempted to cut loose
and go for the top alpine-style with Nick. When both teams had
shared the job of fixing ropes to the foot of the big Snowband and
their routes divided, he and Nick, with heavy sacks and about a
week's food, set out for the top, still over a thousand metres higher.
Chris was going strongly whilst Nick was racked with coughing
and suffering sleep loss because of the perennial problem of tent-
sharing with Chris. Nick's diary explains: 'The problem was probably accumulated lack of sleep aggravated by Chris's snoring and
thrashing about – how does Wendy stand it?' It has to be said that
the Bonington snoring is legendary. Chris always pitches his Base
Camp tent well away from the rest of his expedition, partly to be
slightly removed from the rank and file, but also, one likes to feel
out of compassion for the suffering of his friends, who have on
occasion been almost reduced to tears as the night air is riven with
his snores.

Now high on the Ogre, he and Nick wasted a day whilst Nick
recovered somewhat. The following day the weather showed signs
of breaking and Chris in his own words, 'lashed out at Nick,
bemoaning the fact that we hadn't gone to the summit the previous
day, though I immediately apologised for the injustice of the attack.'
In threatening weather the pair pressed on. In gathering gloom
Nick, who had become convinced that Chris was leading him to
his doom, led the hardest pitch of the climb himself, and in almost
total darkness they hacked a snow hole of sorts and spent a grim
night sitting in it. The next day Chris came to the realisation that
they hadn't enough food, gas or climbing gear to reach the summit,
which had suddenly appeared as a massive granite buttress that
would obviously give hard climbing. He suggested they should settle
for the West Summit, and once this decision had been made the
weather improved.

As they reached the ridge between the two summits Chris's spirits
soared and, typically, he suggested going for the main summit after
all. Nick erupted: 'For pity's sake Chris, can't you keep to a decision
for ten minutes? We decided to go for the West Summit for a
completely logical set of reasons that hasn't changed with a bit of

bloody sun. *You* said that we didn't have the gear or fuel, not me. At least try to be consistent for once.' Chris was forced to agree and they prepared another snow hole, this one big enough to lie down. Nick later wrote in his diary: 'If Chris had his way he'd have spent the rest of his days up there!'

By dosing himself with Mogadon Nick got some sleep, but still had an appalling sore throat and was coughing up blood. It was Chris who led up the final 150 metres to the West Summit and a fantastic view of the endless Karakoram peaks. Nick felt satisfied that they had climbed one of the Ogre's summits and was prepared to call it a day. On the way down they met Mo, Clive, Doug and Tut on their way up. Chris persuaded the four that they hadn't enough gear or gas to get beyond the West Summit and that they should all return to Base to restock. Though this was probably true, there was undoubtedly a degree of self-interest at work, for after a rest Chris would be able to have another attempt. Nick was disconsolate: 'It seems Chris has got his way ... so suddenly, just when I thought the trip was over, I was feeling satisfied and had survived, I have got another fortnight to contend with.'

In fact, neither Nick nor Tut, whose leg wasn't getting better, felt able to go back on the mountain, so Chris teamed up with Doug and, together with Clive and Mo, they set off up the hill after only two rest days. They took the alternative route up the West Ridge to the West Summit and regained the top snow cave, enlarging it to take all four climbers. The next day, 13th July, Doug and Chris were away at 5 a.m. on their summit bid, followed by Clive and Mo, who was filming for the BBC.

The summit buttress proved every bit as hard as Chris had feared. Doug had surged into the lead and wasn't to relinquish it, save for the odd easy pitch. It was hard, steep technical rock climbing at over 7000 metres, with a crux pitch that involved a pendulum, suspended from a wire nut. Chris lowered Doug about fifteen metres and he began swinging on the rope until he was running from side to side on the vertical rock until he could reach a thin crack. It gave precarious climbing and Chris, who had previously resented Doug hogging the lead, was now lost in admiration at his strength and determination. Below, Mo and Clive who had followed them realised that there was now no chance for them of reaching the top, and retreated to the snow cave.

In the last glimmers of dusk Doug pulled out onto the summit and brought Chris up. Just time for a few snaps and it was time to get down. Doug set off on the first long abseil and Chris savoured the still evening with views as far as K2 and Nanga Parbat on the horizon. Suddenly there was a scream from below. Had Doug abseiled off the end of the rope? No, it was still taut. In fact, he had abseiled diagonally down the wall to a piton but he wasn't wearing crampons and his foot had slipped on a film of ice. Suddenly he started a colossal unintentional pendulum and crashed against a rock wall, trying to brace himself with his feet. The impact had broken both his legs. He managed to bang in a piton and get his weight off the abseil rope so that Chris could start descending. As he swung into Doug he gave him the typically cheery Bonington greeting, 'What ho, mate!' It may have sounded confident, but deep down Chris had already had the awful thought, You may not get out of this one, Bonington. He managed to abseil another few metres to a snowy ledge on which they could both sit. Doug abseiled down to him, but when he put any weight on his legs he crumpled in agony. Crawling on his knees, however, seemed to work, and he moved over to sit next to Chris, as they settled down for a grim night spent massaging each other's feet to stop frostbite. Doug, with his Everest bivouac behind him, knew he could survive the night at least.

Across in the snow cave Mo and Clive had seen the accident and at first light they set off over a steep snowslope to give whatever help they could. To Mo's amazement Doug's first question to them was were he and Clive going to the top. But now it was all a matter of survival. They were about 3000 metres above Base Camp and the descent was complicated. If it had just been a vertical descent Doug would have had relatively little trouble abseiling, but much of it was diagonal or horizontal and the first bit over the West Summit was actually uphill. All four regained the snow hole, Doug finding that knee-climbing on snow, in which the others cut huge bucket steps, wasn't quite as bad as it seemed. They spent the afternoon re-hydrating. They had a few gas cylinders, but very little food. And the weather was breaking.

At Base Camp, Nick Estcourt had seen two climbers near the summit the previous day, 13th July, when the porters had arrived for the walk-out. Thinking that they would all be down in a couple of days, he decided that Tut should start walking out with as much gear as possible, while he waited with a few porters to clear Base Camp. On the evening of the 14th the weather broke. In the snow hole Bonington awoke to a darkened dawn and thought he'd mis-read his watch. Then he realised that a full storm was raging. He and Clive braved the teeth of the gale but after belaying Clive for an hour he had only managed to cover twenty metres through waist-deep snow. They retreated to the snow cave. Here, incongru-ously, they played cards and put whatever doubts they may have had to the back of their minds.

The following morning wasn't any better but they just had to move. Mo later said: 'It simply never occurred to me that we might die. Of course, I knew if we stayed up there we'd snuff it because no-one was going to come and help us ... We were four tough blokes and fortunately the toughest of us was the one that was injured ... He said he knew he was in good hands and that he was strong enough.' Doug, meanwhile, got into a 'one day at a time' mindset. If he got through each day then eventually he'd get to Base Camp, but he couldn't allow himself to think that far ahead.

Clive set off first again, and made desperately slow progress up to the West Summit, alternating the lead with Mo. Doug crawled, Chris followed. On the last steep slope Doug floundered in the deep powder snow and Mo in front and Chris behind pulled and shoved him to the top. By now it was midday and the storm still howled around them. At least it would be downhill now and the four managed to abseil 350 metres to another snow cave they had used on the way up. With only one tea bag between all of them and with sodden sleeping bags it was a miserable night. Dawn brought no relief.

Cold and tired they could do little to help Doug as he crawled stoically down towards the next rock step. Here Mo fixed an abseil rope and disappeared. Doug followed. Clive and Chris could hear shouts from below and the rope went slack, so Clive went down. After a long wait Chris followed, relieved to be on a rope. But suddenly he was falling headfirst – a moment of horror – had the anchor failed? – then a jarring smash and he flipped upright and stopped. What had happened?

The shouts they had heard were caused by Doug, who had abse-iled straight off the ends of the doubled rope. A death-fall seemed certain but a few metres below him was a fixed rope stretched horizontally. Somehow he managed to grab it and save himself. But in sliding off the ends of the ropes he had left one end longer than the other. Clive had abseiled down and tied the longer end round a spike of rock. When Chris came down he hadn't heard the shouted warning and the short end of rope whipped out of his abseil device. Chris fell about seven metres until the long end tied to the spike stopped him. His ribs ached but there was no time to inspect for damage and they resumed the descent, abseiling and traversing. At least now they were on fixed ropes and at last they could see the half-buried tents they had left on the way up. They dug them out and found a few tea bags and some Oxo cubes, and more importantly, some sugar.

All night the wind screamed round the tents. Chris by now realised that he had broken some ribs and probably his wrist, which was numb and swollen. Even worse, he was beginning to cough up bubbly froth – normally a symptom of pulmonary oedema, which is a killer if height isn't lost quickly. Mo, with whom Chris was sharing a tent, tried to encourage him with jokes about his condition, and was relieved that Chris seemed to be more his old self when he whispered, 'We're going to make a fortune out of this with the book!'

There was no hope of moving that day. They were camped on a plateau with no visibility. Another night dragged past and the wind roared constantly. As dawn broke there appeared no sign of a let-up, but suddenly sunlight hit the tents. The sky had cleared. By now they had been without food for five days. Chris was very weak and could only manage a few steps before sitting down and resting. Doug, crawling, later wrote: 'Despite following Mo's footsteps, I took many rests, flopping down flat out in the snow . . . but there were some compensations, for whenever I shut my eyes I went off into a hallucinatory world of lilac and purple colouring, incredible shapes and forms, caricature people and stylised views of distant times and places. It did not make a lot of sense, but it was one way to while away a few minutes and recover enough to take a further twenty or so crawling paces through the snow.'

For Chris every step had become agony, and he was coughing up a rich yellow fluid. He found, to his horror, that he couldn't even keep up with Doug. They had to camp again before the last

1000 metres of descent, but at least most of this was by abseil. At the end was a long snowslope, which Chris decided to glissade. He sat down and started sliding, but it rapidly got out of control and he hurtled down unable to use his ice axe to brake with his one good hand. Mercifully he landed in soft snow without doing any further damage, to find Mo waiting. 'We'd better rope up to cross the glacier,' he said. 'After all that I'd hate to end up in the bottom of a crevasse.'

When they arrived at Base Camp they found a note:

Dear All,
In the unlikely event of your ever reading this I've gone down to try to catch up with Tut so that we can come back to look for you . . . I can only assume something has gone badly wrong. I couldn't come up to see for myself as I've sent away all my hill gear. Tut and I will get back up as quickly as we can.

Nick

Mo found a few scraps of food and set off in pursuit, walking all night and catching up with Nick in the first village, Askole, next morning. Meanwhile Chris had staggered into Base Camp; Doug had taken hours to crawl down the moraines below the glacier and hadn't arrived until after dark. He had worn through four layers of clothing to his knees, which were rubbed raw and bleeding.

It took another four days before Nick returned with porters and a makeshift stretcher. Doug was carried down the long Biafo Glacier to Askole where a helicopter picked him up, promising to return for Chris. The others set off on the long walk to Skardu. Days passed and the helicopter did not arrive. In fact on landing at Skardu it had crashed, luckily without injuries. It took almost a week for a replacement to come. When it arrived the pilot offered the despairing Chris a lift all the way back to Islamabad where, to the amazement of a golfing party, they landed on the eighteenth green of the golf course near the British Embassy. Chris, scrawny, filthy and wearing only bright red long johns and vest, with his arm in a sling and his beard long and unkempt, looking like a cross between Robinson Crusoe and a demented Father Christmas.

This epic must go down as one of the most harrowing and protracted self-rescues in the history of mountaineering, rivalling the solo effort by Joe Simpson in the Andes ten years later. All four men showed extraordinary courage and endurance but, as they admitted afterwards, they didn't have any choice.

For Doug the accident meant several long periods in hospital and the insertion of various bits of metal into his ankles, but he made a virtually full recovery. Chris's damaged ribs were going to play him up for a year. But neither man was deterred from Chris's next project.

The Ogre debacle attracted a fair amount of media attention, particularly in the British press. With such a complex event it was perhaps inevitable that Mo and Clive were almost completely written out – Doug and Chris were both famous and injured, and that was all-important for a good story. Nick and Tut didn't even get a mention. Nick's perception of events was obviously very different from the others, and even Mo and Clive, who came down relatively unscathed, told their stories from a rather different perspective. It says a lot for the expedition that there were no major recriminations or blazing rows during or after the event, but it was not hard to detect some resentment from Mo and Clive who felt, probably correctly, that without their support Chris and Doug would not have survived. Mo wrote an account of the expedition for the *Alpine Club Journal* which was so understated that the whole nightmare descent only took up fourteen lines and ended with a deadpan comment: 'Strangely enough it was not a frightening experience and while not pleasurable, it certainly did not lack in excitement.'

In 1978 Chris, Doug, Nick and Tut were due to return to the Karakoram. This time they were going to try and climb the huge triangular peak they had seen in the distance from high on the Ogre – K2, the second highest point on earth.

Getting the
hump on the
Kongur
reconnaissance

The summit
of Kongur.
Left to right:
Al Rouse, Pete
Boardman,
CB, Joe
Tasker

Kongur

Pete Boardman and Al Rouse return from the summit of Kongur

Chris during the filming of the TV series, Lakeland Rock

(Above) Chris and Bodie with Melvyn Bragg above Wasdale, 1983

En route to Menlungtse with Jim Fotheringham

William Hill backing a winner

The Irish lecture tour receives a setback

CB on Fools' Paradise, Gowder Crag, Borrowdale

The author and Paul Nunn on
Rangrik Rang, 1994

Sign of the times: Jim
Fotheringham and CB sending
e-mails at Sepu Kangri base camp

(*Above*) Still as enthusiastic as ever – Chris eyes
the route on Sepu Kangri with Jim Lowther and
John Porter

High on Sepu Kangri

Back to where it all began –
CB at Harrisons

The author and his subject return from Tibet

The Boningtons outside Buckingham Palace. *Left to right:*
Ann (Rupert's wife-to-be), Rupert, Wendy, Chris, Jude, Daniel

· 19 ·

Tragedy on K2

W HEN HE APPLIED for permission for K2, Chris Bonington knew there was not much point in doing another big fixed-rope expedition, even though at the time the mountain had only been climbed twice, both by the same route, the Abruzzi Spur. The first ascent in 1954 was made by a large Italian expedition, the second by a truly gigantic Japanese one, which had fifty-two members and no less than 1500 porters. Echoing his original plan for Everest, Chris wanted to make a lightweight attempt on the long North-East Ridge, which had nearly been climbed by a Polish expedition in 1976.

Originally the team was to be Doug, Dougal, Nick, Tut and Peter Boardman. With Dougal's death Chris invited Joe Tasker who, with Pete, had made the remarkable ascent of the West Face of Changabang in 1976. But there was no place for Martin Boysen, one of Chris's oldest friends, who was deeply upset. At this time Martin was trying to establish himself as a professional mountaineer and his omission was a major setback for him. Now, twenty years later and looking at the terrible death toll of his contemporaries, Martin ruefully concedes that by dropping him, Chris may well have saved his life, for Martin became disillusioned with big expeditions and returned to his roots as a brilliant rock climber, which age has done little to diminish. If he had carried on he may have found the choice harder to make. But the sad part is that

The West Face of K2

the friendship between the Boysens and the Boningtons has never recovered.

Inevitably Chris' plans changed. Pete and Doug wanted to try the West Ridge, which had never been attempted. It looked to be harder than the South-West Face of Everest but Chris decided that it could be climbed with a reasonable chance of success with a small team. There could be no Sherpa support, for they would not be allowed into Pakistan, so the expedition would be almost completely self-supporting above Base Camp, though they did employ the odd high-altitude porter. Chris insisted that on a project this big they should take fixed ropes and oxygen for the summit attempt. At this period Chris's planning was in a transitional state. He could not at that stage commit himself to a pure alpine-style ascent – that would come three years later – but he knew that the big siege-style expeditions had had their day. He hoped that he would be getting the best of both worlds, though there was a distinct possibility that he might fall between two stools and end up with all the disadvantages of both. In this situation the logistics of fixed roping a long route by a small team, and then using a small amount of oxygen from the top camp might prove to be impossible. Indeed, his by now customary dry run on the computer predicted just that but, 'In the end I abandoned trying to climb the mountain by computer with the thought that we would have to rise above the logistic barriers – one usually did!'

It was about this time that the term 'capsule ascent' was bandied about, which seemed to mean using some fixed rope and getting everything you needed in position, say halfway up the ridge, then taking off alpine-style for the summit. It was the approach Board-man and Tasker had adopted on Changabang. This was a possible strategy for K2 which, sadly was never to be tried.

Whatever tactics were to be employed, a graphic illustration of how much smaller this expedition was compared with Everest, was that instead of two 16-ton trucks, just two British Leyland Sherpa vans made the overland journey to Islamabad. Tony Riley, the cameraman on the expedition, and Chris Lister and Allen Jewhurst of Chameleon Films in Leeds drove the vans, which got caught up in the opening salvos of the Russian invasion of Afghanistan. At one point they were buzzed by MIG fighters, and only just got through under escort to the Khyber Pass and into Pakistan before the border closed.

For Joe Tasker the contrast between a Bonington expedition and the extremely frugal low-budget trips he had made with climbers like Pete Boardman and Dick Renshaw was extreme. The Bonington machinery made him feel alienated and when Chris rang to ask him why he had not signed the expedition contract he 'felt the sting of his comments and the force of his authority'. Chris was irritated: 'I remember feeling defensive at the time, the more so because I could see his point, yet resented my authority being threatened. In the end he signed simply because everyone else had done, but it left me feeling that Joe was a bit of a barrack-room lawyer.'

Unlike Everest, Chris soon found out, as others have done before and since, that raising sponsorship for K2 is a real problem. Because it is the second highest it is hard for potential sponsors not to think of second best, even though climbers know that even the easiest route on K2 is far harder than Everest, and that K2 is undoubtedly the hardest of the world's fourteen 8000-metre peaks. Eventually Chris found the most unlikely sponsor in the London Rubber Company who manufactured Durex, and were trying to open a factory in Pakistan. Chris found himself doing a Prince Charles-style visit round the Durex factory in the East End of London, trying to ask intelligent questions about the manufacturing of thousands of condoms. Needless to say the climbing world greeted the news of his sponsorship coup gleefully, with suitably unprintable ribald comments around the theme of an expedition that wouldn't be taking any chances!

More seriously, Ken Wilson, questioned in *Mountain* whether such a small expedition stood any chance of climbing K2. As he had criticised the Everest South-West Face expedition for being too big, Joe Tasker in particular was irritated. Ken's defence, as always, would be that his job is to be the devil's advocate.

At home Chris's preparations for K2 were interrupted by a horrible bone infection in his ribs. Twice he had the infection scraped out under an anaesthetic, but this, combined with the general after effects of the Ogre, weren't the best preparation for the expedition. Chris had taken up running and he and his secretary Louise Wilson went for lunchtime runs up High Pike behind Badger Hill. Rumours that Chris deputised Louise to do his runs for him are, sadly, unfounded!

The approach to K2 is one of the longest and most rugged walk-ins in all the Himalaya. Joe Tasker thought it was as hard as anything he had come across that wasn't actually climbing. Today it has been shortened by a new road that (when it is open) goes as far as Askole, the last village. But the route by truck or on foot through the Braldu Gorge is always threatened by rockfall and the Braldu River itself has claimed several lives over the years. Once past the snout of the Biafo Glacier that leads to the Ogre, two more days of hard walking take one to the Baltoro Glacier, which is thirty-seven miles long, an endless switchback of moraine and dry ice that early in the season is snow-covered.

In 1978 the expedition faced a near riot, then strike by its porters at Paiju Camp just below the Baltoro, which was only averted by some quick negotiation on Chris's part. Once on the glacier, which became progressively more snowbound, Chris sent Joe and Doug and a few porters ahead to prospect the route to Base Camp. As Chris had feared, Joe did indeed question his decisions but Joe also found Doug to be opinionated and resistant to argument. Reading Joe and Chris's accounts one can't help feeling that this very compact team had thrown up different leadership problems to the monolithic Everest trips. On the South-West Face Chris thought that his role was similar to that of 'an admiral in his flagship, who had to be terribly careful not to interfere with the tactical day-to-day decisions of the ship's captain'. On K2, with such a small team of highly motivated members, he had to be even more conscious that he did not undermine their drive and self-confidence by questioning their decisions. It says a lot about his mental flexibility that he was prepared to adapt to change, and his approach was to continue to evolve in the 1980s and 'nineties to become almost excessively democratic and consultative, yet somehow he still retained his authority as a leader.

Base Camp was eventually established on the Savoia Glacier below the colossal West Face of K2. The approach to the West Ridge was uncertain – an outrider of the Ridge comes right down to the glacier but to climb it direct would be pointless if it could be bypassed. Nick Estcourt and Pete Boardman went to look at the northern side but found it far too hard, whereas a long straightforward snowslope led up to the crest of the ridge on the south side. Above, the ridge was a complex mass of rock walls, snow patches and icefields that looked as though they could be linked together to give a hard but hopefully safe route. Camp 1 was quickly established about two-thirds of the way up and then Chris and Joe pushed the route out, each finding the other's company easier now that they were actually at grips with the climbing.

Near the top of the snowslope an icy gully led to a point where there was a choice of routes: either an easy traverse across a snow basin below the crest of the ridge or the ridge itself. The snow basin cut out the ridge and seemed so easily angled that Chris and Joe plodded across without even bothering to rope up. At the far side they found a good site for Camp 2. Pete Boardman and Doug Scott followed them carrying loads of rope and hardware, then they all returned to Camp 1 where Nick Estcourt and a high-altitude porter, Quamajan, had brewed tea.

Chris knew imposing pairings Everest fashion wouldn't work on K2. But simply to let everyone do his own thing wouldn't work either. Nick suggested they draw matchsticks to see who climbed with whom. Pete and Joe picked the short matches. 'Changabang rules,' commented Nick as the pair teamed up again to lead the next stretch beyond Camp 2.

But when they reached and occupied the camp the weather broke and everyone was pinned in their tents for two days. On the third day Pete and Joe woke to wind and swirling snow, but it was a fine day and the new snow was just being blown about. Below, three specks toiled up from Camp 1, but in the deep snow they failed to make it all the way. Pete and Joe made about 200 metres progress before they dropped back to Camp 2. The new day dawned brilliantly fine. At Camp 1 Chris had developed a bad cold and once again gave Nick, with whom he was sharing a tent, an Ogre-like sleepless night. He decided to have a rest day, and the others set off to do a carry to Camp 2 where Pete and Joe were in danger of running out of food and rope.

High above, Pete and Joe were making good progress. Having regained the high point of the day before, it was Joe's turn to lead. Lower down, Doug, Nick and Quamajan were at the far side of the snow basin. Although Chris and Joe had walked across unroped, they decided to run out a thin line as a handrail to assist heavily laden climbers. Doug led off first and when he had gone about seventy metres Nick followed, clipping into the rope Doug was trailing. Quamajan stayed behind paying out the rope from a reel. When Doug had almost reached Camp 2 and Nick was in the middle of the basin, Doug felt a tremor in the snow. Then another. Pete, looking down from his belay high above, describes what happened:

> There was a great rumbling roar. 'Joe, Joe, look!' The whole bowl of snow started moving slowly. Because of the concave slope it accumulated around the lower part of the slope. The two figures were about a hundred feet above a sérac wall, one figure completely enveloped. I nearly took a photograph, checked by revulsion, horror, and couldn't believe it. A great cloud of snow right across to Angel Peak, a slab avalanche five hundred feet wide, three hundred feet high. Thousands of tons of snow. The figure in the middle struggled and was overwhelmed and disappeared from view. Three thousand feet to the glacier.

Doug, who was within a few metres of the Camp, was catapulted backwards into the path of the avalanche, but as he somersaulted his rucksack wedged into the snow and at the same time the rope snapped.

'I stood up and watched, horrified as the avalanche with Nick in the middle of it poured down the cliffs to the glacier below.'

At Camp 1, Chris and expedition doctor Jim Duff watched the huge billowing cloud sweep past. Chris grabbed his camera and started taking photographs but Jim shouted, 'For God's sake stop. The lads could be in that.'

Chris was doubtful, assuming it had started from the ice cliffs below the snow basin, but even so he stopped and switched on the radio in case anyone opened up. The minutes ticked by then Doug's voice came across.

'Nick's copped it. The whole bloody slope went and he was in the middle of it. Didn't have a hope.'

Chris switched off the set and sobbed. His closest friend who had supported him so loyally through all his major expeditions was dead. Nick, excitable, grinning Nick, with his thinning curly hair and teeth with such big gaps that Mo had once accused him of cleaning them with a bath towel, Nick of innumerable pubs, parties, of long boozy evenings in the Moon in Derbyshire, of the crazy night-club in Buxton, of days in North Wales and Scotland, was now lying dead under thousands of tons of snow.

The others descended and they had a tearful reunion at Camp 1. After a sleepless night everyone went down to Base Camp, Doug, setting off first and making a futile search of the avalanche debris on the way back. Shocked and grieving, the survivors met in the mess tent to decide what to do. Surprisingly, Chris was all for carrying on, justifying his decision by saying that Nick's death was a part of what they had undertaken and going home would achieve nothing. Doug, on the other hand, was adamant that, having escaped death by a hair's breadth and been so close to Nick when he had died, he couldn't carry on, particularly knowing that his wife, indeed all the wives and girlfriends, would be in agony until everyone returned home. Pete agreed with Chris, Tut, who had been ill with a chest infection since reaching Base Camp, clearly wanted to go home and Jim Duff felt the same. Tony Riley wanted to make his film but felt, as he also had been ill, that he couldn't vote either way. And Joe, normally so clear cut in his opinions, was ambivalent. But with Doug, Tut and Jim adamant that they wanted to abandon the expedition there wasn't really much choice and Chris reluctantly decided to call it off.

Early next morning he and Doug set off, desperate to reach Skardu and telephone the news to Carolyn Estcourt before the press got hold of any rumours. They double-staged all the way, Chris finding that, 'it didn't reduce my grief, but it was something I could control, store away while I coped with our daily functions. Each day's walk, the need to place feet carefully on the rocky moraines, the heavy fatigue all helped to alleviate the aching pain. But once we were back in Islamabad we would have to tell others what had happened.'

By coincidence I was in Altrincham, about to set off the next day on a small expedition to the Karakoram when Chris, exhausted, looking ill, old and grief-stricken, arrived from Pakistan to see Carolyn. We all met up in the Railway Inn and got tearfully drunk. Little did I know that eight years later I would have to make exactly the same journey home from K2 under the same circumstances. But one thing I didn't have to cope with, and still find difficult to understand, was the strangers who approached Chris in the pub asking for autographs. Chris, as ever the professional, gave them and even managed to say a few words to them. Not for the last time I was impressed.

He had only been home for two days when his ribs once again flared up. This time it required an operation in which a section of a rib was removed. If the problem had occurred at K2 Base Camp it could have been desperately serious. Although the loss of a part of a rib was not a problem in itself, and something that he could manage without, it did seem to be the beginning of a tendency to chest infections, one of which in 1981 was nearly to kill him.

K2 marked the end of Chris Bonington's big fixed-rope expeditions but it was also the beginning of a new partnership with Joe and Pete, who were to become central to his next expeditions. Doug was to start running his own very different trips. But Nick was irreplaceable, and even twenty years later the loss is no less keenly felt, not just by Chris but by all who knew and climbed with him.

As for the accident itself, it is self-evident that Chris' assessment of the safety of the snow basin was wrong, but it was a decision that everyone else agreed with and certainly, to be fair to Chris, all the photographs of it do show a very shallow-angled slope. Maybe Doug and Nick should have waited longer after the dump of new snow before crossing, but the bottom line is that climbing on big Himalayan peaks is inherently dangerous. If every decision were made with safety in mind, nobody would ever go above the snow-line. However, when Pete, Doug and Joe returned to K2 in 1980 for another attempt they chose to follow the ridge above the basin. One can only regret that this route was not taken in 1978, and imagine what might have been the outcome.

Pillar Rock

·20·

At Home

AFTER THE K2 expedition and the convalescence following his operation, Chris Bonington wondered what to do next and picked up an idea that George Greenfield his agent, had mooted. This was to write a book on the nature of adventure since the Second World War, and highlight outstanding examples of different activities ranging from polar exploration and round-the-world yachting to the moon landings and ballooning across the Atlantic. It was an ambitious project: for the first time he would be writing about events that he had not experienced first-hand, and even some that he initially had little understanding of. Could he use his writing skills to produce what would inevitably be seen as some sort of definitive statement?

It took two years of research and interviews to produce, and remains his biggest book, over 400 pages. Looking at it eighteen years later, one is struck at the immensity of the task he set himself. Re-reading it there do seem to be inconsistencies in the writing. The book is divided into sections: Oceans, Deserts, Rivers, Mountains, The Poles, Air, Space, Beneath the Earth. Each section is divided into chapters. Oceans, with six and Mountains with seven easily dominate. The Poles get three and the rest one each. Inevitably the mountaineering chapters stand out, as does the cave diving chapter which Bonington felt was the most impressive activity, and certainly the most dangerous, as the penalty for any mistake is invariably death.

Researching the book took Bonington to NASA to look at the space programme and to interview Neil Armstrong, the first man on the moon. Chris obviously felt he had little in common with him, though he tried to make the analogy between a test pilot methodically pushing the limits of his aircraft and a rock climber pushing his own limits on hard rock. It was not a terribly convincing comparison. A much more fulfilling interview was with round-the-world yachtsman Robin Knox-Johnston with whom Chris sailed from Oban on the west coast of Scotland to the Isle of Skye where Chris took Robin climbing. It was the beginning of a long and productive friendship that would lead to bigger adventures with him in 1991 and 1998, when they sailed together to Greenland to explore and climb.

Although the book could be criticised for being a little too biased in favour of mountains and oceans, it was still a wide and imaginatively eclectic choice. The lone traveller like Christina Dodwell or the cave diver Geoff Yeadon rubbed shoulders with household names: Thor Heyerdahl, Reinhold Messner and Sir Edmund Hillary, which certainly made for some interesting contrasts. But what, if anything, had all these adventurers got in common? Some of his conclusions were obvious – the ability to put up with discomfort, heightened perception and awareness of their surroundings, and a single-minded drive, even obsession to complete the project in hand. But to answer 'why?' Bonington got no further than many other would-be analysts did. He noticed that all his subjects had piercing eyes that looked into the distance, and had large capable hands, but as Chris himself wrote, these are characteristics that one could expect to develop from the individuals' chosen activity. It didn't answer the question, and the book concluded rather lamely that 'the answer lies concealed, mysterious, in the complexity of man.' Bonington is now in the process of updating the book in the light of the last twenty years which have seen some major advances in some of the areas covered (these words are being written only days after the first successful round-the-world balloon flight). But the answer to his last question might be a bit nearer, for there is now some evidence emerging that the genetic make-up of extreme risk-takers is slightly but measurably different from those people at the opposite end of the scale, who are virtually confined to their homes with extreme agoraphobia. This may go some way to explain why some of us like living dangerously but doesn't seem to account for people like Chris himself who has oscillated between very high-risk activities to a deep need for emotional and physical security. Perhaps if it *is* all explained then it will be hardly worth while doing it. Maybe the sensation of risk-taking will then be able to be precisely duplicated in some kind of virtual reality game. If it is, one can be absolutely certain that Chris himself will be playing it!

The book occupied Chris for most of 1979–80. Like most writers he found it very hard work and welcomed any distraction. At around this time Wendy became keen on orienteering. It was a sport they could both enjoy, for it doesn't depend on running ability alone, but requires a degree of cunning and certainly the ability to read a map. Chris became President of the British Orienteering Federation in 1986, which raised a few eyebrows amongst those of us who have got lost with him on a fairly regular basis over the years.

In 1973 Bonington had been interviewed by Peter Gillman for the *Sunday Times*. Gillman speculated that Chris would eventually follow in John Hunt's footsteps doing charity work and serving on various committees, becoming the elder statesman of the climbing world. Chris firmly rejected such a view: 'I'm too much of an individual . . . I've got a sense of responsibility to the climbing world, but I'm not a committee man. I want to go on doing the things I like doing. I've no great desire to educate and I don't think I'm particularly a do-gooder.' Recently I read these words to Chris who laughed a rather hollow laugh, which was hardly surprising for over the years his commitment to serve on committees has grown immensely, as well as his working for charities giving free lectures, acting as a consultant to equipment firms and taking on various presidencies.

Over the past two decades by far the most challenging voluntary work he has undertaken was with the British Mountaineering Council. When Chris was first involved as a Vice-President in 1986 it had become a slightly moribund institution. In the past, presidents, who served a three-year period, tended to see their role simply as figureheads. The real power was in the Secretary, who naturally knew the nuts and bolts of committees, sub-committees, Sports Council machinations etc. Chris made it his business to find out how the BMC worked and how it needed to change. When he became President in 1988 he had two powerful Vice-Presidents in

Ian MacNaught-Davis and Paul Nunn, and together they worked hard to modernise the BMC by making it more accountable and appointing Derek Walker as General Secretary. Chris himself was incredibly conscientious, attending and chairing every meeting he could. 'I still don't like sitting on committees but I do enjoy chairing them – I think I do quite a good job in balancing a variety of views and helping things to a conclusion.'

In fact his skill as a chairman has increased markedly over the years, and it is very noticeable how he will listen to minority voices and try and integrate them into the whole. Sometimes they even come to be the prevailing view. One suspects that his mentor, John Hunt, who was quite brilliant at making people think his ideas were their own, had a big influence on how Chris conducts meetings. It is hard to imagine that the rather brash young Sandhurst cadet who first crossed swords with John Hunt over his exclusion from the Pamirs expedition would eventually become as diplomatic and reasonable as Hunt himself.

Bonington's other mountaineering presidency was of the Alpine Club from 1995–98. This was an honour dear to his heart, but Chris likened it to being master of a supertanker, in that persuading the venerable institution to change course took so long that many presidents in the past had finished their term of office before any measurable change was effected. Chris again used a very hands-on approach, and for three years travelled down to London to chair virtually every committee meeting. The Alpine Club's Assistant Secretary Sheila Harrison maintains that in the bunkhouse accommodation at the Alpine Club's premises in Charlotte Road, Chris was single-handedly responsible for the installation of a shower – 'The Chris Bonington Memorial Shower'. She tried to get a photograph of the President having an inaugural sluice under it for inclusion in the *Journal*. Sadly she failed! More seriously, the Alpine Club secretary Glynn Hughes thought Chris not only showed extraordinary commitment to the Club, but also made a point of getting to know all the officers. He was very keen that the Club's Himalayan Index should go out on the Internet, which is now about to happen. To mark his farewell as President, Chris organised a symposium, 'Climbing into the Millennium', which was held at Sheffield Hallam University in 1999. His influence ensured a gathering of some of the biggest names in world climbing. Reinhold Messner provided the keynote speech and the 400-strong audience enjoyed a thought-provoking series of lectures and debates chaired as professionally as usual by Chris himself.

The voluntary work that has given Chris the most enjoyment has been the Presidency of the Council for National Parks, which he took up in 1992. Vicki Elcoate, a director of the Council, describes Bonington as being a great support, a leader and a spokesperson for the organisation, as well as, inevitably, someone who chaired meetings, spoke at dinners and led delegations to lobby government ministers. Chris has also urged the Quarry Products Association to adopt a Four Point Plan for National Parks which Vicki Elcoate sees as being his lasting legacy, helping to protect National Park landscapes from quarrying in the long-term.

In 1998, in an attempt to reduce road traffic in the Peak Park in Derbyshire, a climbers' bus service was set up to run from Sheffield to Stanage Edge. Chris was on the inaugural run, typically in pouring rain, and took a park official and a BBC reporter up a streaming wet climb. In the middle of the reporter's ordeal (for he had never climbed before and certainly never will again) there was a flash of lightning and an almost simultaneous clap of thunder. It would have been an ignominious end if Chris, standing on top of the crag, had been struck but, apart from leaving his change of clothes on the bus and somehow needing a small fleet of cars to get him back to his own, it all passed off without further ado and certainly got a lot of publicity. Typically Chris's hands-on policy includes an obligatory walk in whatever park he is visiting. Wendy has often accompanied him, finding it one charity she can enjoy as much as Chris. The walks are not just for fun; Chris wants to experience the parks in the same way millions of visitors do, and to appreciate the reasons why they were designated in the first place.

Chris Bonington's longest charity commitment has been to LEPRA, a medical charity raising money in the UK to support work overseas, particularly in India, which has 80 per cent of the world's leprosy patients. He has been President since 1985. As with his Presidency of the Alpine Club, he is conscientious in the extreme. Bernard Farmer, the Deputy Director of LEPRA, had only praise for the time and effort Chris has put into writing and broadcasting appeals, promoting fund-raising events, and regularly attending staff conferences where he both entertains and inspires. In 1994 he spent several days in the stifling pre-monsoon heat visiting patient centres around Hyderabad. He returned to Bombay (where I was staying with Indian mountaineer, Harish Kapadia), having suffered badly from dehydration and heat stroke, and with a renewed respect for the work of LEPRA in the field.

Perhaps the last words on Chris's charitable works should be from John Hunt, spoken only weeks before his death: 'Chris is a highly socially responsible person, and that, as much as his climbing, is what makes him a great man.' Whether or not the charitable works have made a difference, one overdue reward came in the New Year Honour's List in 1996 when Chris received his knighthood. Prince Charles performed the ceremony. Like most modern recipients, Chris is still happy being called 'Chris', and 'Sir Christian' is reserved for letterheads and formal occasions, (though I have to admit I enjoy calling Wendy 'Lady B'!).

Inevitably, all these good works, plus the day-to-day running of his office, have greatly increased the administrative workload at home and Chris's office has grown accordingly. Louise Wilson, Chris's secretary, has been with him since Everest South-West Face in 1975 and must be a candidate for the perfect Secretary of the Year award, if it exists. I have to confess that in the past I have likened her to Miss Moneypenny who copes with James Bond's wayward eccentricities with unflappable patience. Louise maintains that her greatest success, which shouldn't be underestimated, was to get Chris to Buckingham Palace half-an-hour early for a reception after the South-West Face expedition and that her worst moment was when Chris had to cancel a visit to India to do a presentation in Delhi because she had forgotten he needed a visa. But her formidable array of skills in dealing with the vicissitudes of the Bonington lifestyle is quite extraordinary. On one occasion I was making a film with Chris that involved an internal flight from Islamabad to Gilgit. Here, to our consternation, all the film equipment failed to arrive, despite us having supervised it being loaded onto the plane (it had been removed once we had boarded). Chris went into masterful leadership mode: 'This calls for some action!' he exclaimed, heading for the nearest phone, I assumed to give a tongue-lashing to some hapless employee in Islamabad. Not a bit of it.

'Is that Louise? Look, ring PIA in London and give them hell – we've lost all the film gear.'

Not only did it arrive on the next flight, but we also flew home First Class. I was impressed.

More recently, Louise and her husband Gerry (both being skiers and climbers) accompanied Chris and a motley team, including me, to the Caucasus to climb amongst other things Mount Elbrus. I couldn't help feeling uneasy. James Bond never took Miss Moneypenny out of the office – if anything went wrong what would Chris do? Once again I worried needlessly; Louise simply took charge. Chris enjoyed a holiday that ran like clockwork and Louise herself led us all up the final slopes to the summit of Europe.

Over the years the empire at Badger Hill has expanded and now consists of Louise, plus Alison Lancaster, Frances Daltrey and Margaret Trinder, all of whom exude the sort of calm competence that you get from flight attendants during bad turbulence. But you know that behind the scenes everyone is rushing round trying to get Chris to leave on time, take the right slides with him, finish his next chapter, and remember to do his TV interview. Chris himself may well have sneaked off climbing, if he isn't playing war games on his computer!

His reliance on the computer has been mentioned before but now he has a part-time assistant within the family, for Rupert Bonington is as enthusiastic as his father in using it to set up websites and to programme his audio-visual lectures. This is a story with a happy ending because both Rupert and Daniel had their problems in childhood and at one stage their rebelliousness threatened to get out of hand. Growing up in the limelight of a famous father produced a very real pressure, and there is no doubt that they found their adolescent years doubly difficult. Dan remembers at school being referred to by a teacher as the 'Bovril boy' (Chris having being sponsored by Bovril on the Ogre and seen clutching a brew in a bivvy on TV advertisements). It was an incredibly insensitive remark to make about a lad who was particularly uncertain of what life had to offer. Both boys were inclined to rebel but found it hard to do when they had a father whose lifestyle was itself fairly unconventional. Like the children of fathers who regularly go on expeditions, Daniel as a small boy found Chris's absences disturbing: 'you don't understand why your Dad's going off – why people you know better than your relatives don't come back – why there are women coming round to stay with Mum and there's crying and tears – when is my Dad getting back? You just don't understand all that.'

Daniel found a resolution of his problems on a family expedition to Kilimanjaro with his father, uncle and brother. Though neither of the boys have taken to climbing and really only did it occasionally to please Chris, Daniel found that on the summit of Kilimanjaro years of bitterness dissolved. 'I'd done some bloody stupid things at school and right through to my early twenties. I think it was to punish Dad, even though I was proud of him. I am very, very proud of Dad and up there I could suddenly understand what Dad felt on his expeditions. For the first time I felt really emotionally close to him.'

Rupert, who enjoys football and 'sports that have an instant buzz', found climbing too long and drawn out and claims not to have a head for heights. Despite being fit and athletic, the Kilimanjaro experience didn't move him as much as it had his elder brother. Rupert's earliest memory is of playing with Pertemba in the garden of Badger Hill, but he always knew his father was a bit different from other dads and what he did. Aged about eight, faced with a big abseil on an Outward-Bound course, he burst into tears at the prospect, and thought, this is the son of a famous climber and I can't even do an abseil. Rupert is now on a teacher training course with the idea of being a PE teacher. 'I'm a western boy; I like my home comforts. I'm not really an adventurer.'

Now both Dan and Rupert are happily married with a direction in life and the Bonington family is very close. Rupert knows just how much he owes his parents: 'To me my Dad is a hero and an inspiration. I know how hard it's been for him and it keeps me going when I find things tough. I know he and Mum will give me all their support and if I'm ever half the man he is I'll be happy.'

China at Last

DURING THE LATE seventies Chris Bonington often stayed or passed through Bristol on his lecture tours. At that time I was a lecturer in the Faculty of Art and Design in what is now called the University of the West of England. Chris's persuasive powers often led to my being kidnapped from college to do a climb in the Avon Gorge and I slowly got to know him. In 1978 I remember asking him if he was interested in climbing Everest from Tibet, which was on the verge of opening up to the West for the first time since before the war. There was a momentary pause and Chris looked away before shrugging off the question, but I knew straight away that something was afoot. In fact, it wasn't Tibet or Everest he had designs on, but an unclimbed mountain called Kongur in Chinese Sinkiang, to the north of the Karakoram. If anything, it was an even more mysterious area for Europeans. True, Eric Shipton had been British Consul in Kashgar during and just after the war, and he and Bill Tilman had very nearly climbed Mustagh Ata, a prominent isolated mountain to the south of the Kongur massif, but by comparison with the Everest region, very little more was known, save for the fact that Kongur, at 7719 metres was the highest mountain in the area.

The quest for permission to climb in China had largely been the brainchild of Michael Ward. He had been a doctor on the 1953 Everest expedition and was now an eminent figure in the rarified

Statue of Mao - Kashgar

(literally) world of mountain medicine, as well as a practising surgeon in a London hospital. In 1980 Ward, Bonington and Alan Rouse explored the Kongur massif and surrounding mountains. Al Rouse was very much a leading light of the time, a brilliant rock climber who, in the company of Rab Carrington, had done an extraordinary series of winter ascents in the Alps and some major new routes throughout the Andes. In 1978 he had undertaken a very bold lightweight expedition to Jannu, a spectacular steep mountain near Kangchenjunga in Eastern Nepal. In the company of Carrington, Brian Hall and Roger Baxter-Jones, Al had made an alpine-style ascent of the original French route on Jannu which, in its time, had been considered a long and difficult ascent. Bonington had met Al and Rab at the COLA outdoor equipment trade fair in Harrogate just after their return and was impressed. It was only a matter of time before Al Rouse was brought into the Bonington stable.

Al was obviously delighted to be asked on the reconnaissance but, to save face amongst his peers, he maintained that he had his doubts about going away with Chris who was the same age as his mother, and observed that the combined ages of Bonington and Ward added up to over a hundred!

Ward and Bonington had negotiated a sponsorship deal with Jardine Matheson, the famous Hong Kong trading company. It was the beginning of three years of close ties with Jardines, and a friendship with the then Chairman, David Newbigging, and his wife Carolyn which has lasted to this day. Through the combined efforts of the Mount Everest Foundation, Jardine Matheson and even some diplomatic support from such unlikely figures as Dennis Thatcher, Lord Carrington and Edward Heath, permissions were given and bureaucratic obstacles smoothed away. From the outset Michael Ward was to be the leader of the main expedition in 1981. It would have joint scientific and medical objectives. This could be potentially fraught with problems but it says a lot for the tolerance of both the climbers and the doctors that the expedition was a happy one. Chris was appointed climbing leader, which meant that from Base Camp upwards, he was in charge, though, as with Everest and K2, it was a democratic kind of leadership. Peter Boardman and Joe Tasker made up the four lead climbers who very much wanted to make an ascent of Kongur using pure alpine-style tactics. I was invited to come along as a one-man film crew and, in addition to the four doctors, David Wilson, at that time Political Advisor to Hong Kong, was also invited to climb and, as a fluent Chinese scholar, to interpret.

On the reconnaissance in 1980, Al Rouse in particular seemed to think Kongur would be a pushover and, when asked at a press conference if he foresaw any unexpected problems, he rather flippantly suggested that if there were any they might have to use a rope. In one sentence Kongur became something of a joke amongst the British climbing cognoscenti who could never take it seriously. (Don Whillans was heard to ask if it was some sort of dance and always referred to it as 'Aye-aye-aye-aye, Kongur'.) In fact, while the recce had painstakingly explored the approaches to Kongur from the north and south, Ward, Bonington and Rouse were all slightly coy about the mountain itself. I vividly remember when the main expedition first arrived below the mountain and gazed as the black summit came to view through scudding cloud, Peter Boardman's aggrieved comment to Al: 'I thought you said it was going to be a walk; it looks bloody big and serious to me.'

On this my first Bonington expedition I began to realise at firsthand just how much time and effort Chris puts into the organisation of his trips. He always seemed to be awake at least an hour earlier than everyone else and was constantly revising plans, writing reports and discussing tactics with Pete, Joe and Al. There really was no doubt that, though Mike Ward was technically the leader (and as far as all bureaucratic dealings with the Chinese were concerned he fulfilled the role perfectly), Chris took on virtually all the day-to-day organisation. Looking back to 1981 I can see that he was going through a transition period: on Annapurna and Everest he was clearly the sole decision-maker, however, much he consulted and discussed. In 1981 he was far more democratic, though still prone to suddenly making a snap decision on his own. By the late 1990s he has become so laid back that sometimes he seems almost content to let things just unravel by themselves. But one characteristic has remained constant – his ability to think out loud and change his mind frequently, sometimes through 180 degrees. This can be endearing or exasperating, funny or confusing, or sometimes all of them at once

But my main impression of him in 1981 was of a driven, highly motivated workaholic who took expeditioning very seriously indeed. I frequently wondered how much Chris actually enjoyed the expedition itself until I realised that he lived it through his planning and tactical awareness. His enjoyment actually comes largely from getting the organisation right, until, that is, he gets onto the mountain itself, when a switch is thrown and the simple thrill of climbing takes over.

On Kongur it seemed at one stage that Chris wouldn't get much satisfaction at all, for after an early foray to establish an Advance Base in a huge glacial basin below the South Ridge, he contracted pneumonia. He was incredibly lucky, first that the illness started on his return to Base Camp, not when he was on the mountain, and that Dr Charlie Clarke (who had been with him on Everest South-West Face) diagnosed it immediately and put him on a very powerful course of antibiotics. Chris made an astonishingly rapid recovery and within a couple of weeks was back in action.

The climb itself was a protracted affair, hampered by constant spells of bad weather with high winds and, being so much further north of the Karakoram/Himalayan ranges, bitter cold. The first attempt foundered on a knife-edged ridge leading to the summit pyramid, the difficulty of which had indeed been grossly under-estimated, even ignored, during the recce. When eventually success came it was only after spending four nights stormbound at the far end of the knife-edged ridge, bivouacked into tiny one-man slots that became known as the snow coffins. Running out of food and gas, most teams would have given up, but when the weather cleared they pushed on to the top, where they had yet another bivouac while they ensured that they really had reached the highest of three possible summits before a long and dangerous descent. Peter Board-man dislodged a rock abseiling down from the summit which hit him a glancing blow on the head and knocked him out. He was only saved from sliding off the end of the rope by his glove jamming the rope in the karabiner brake system he was using to abseil with.

Michael Ward and I had waited in support at Advance Base and had nearly given them up for lost before we spotted four minute dots on a snowline high above. On their return late that evening Mike and I were the first to hear their story. Chris thought that the climbing on the summit day was very reminiscent of the North Face of the Matterhorn, even of the Eiger in winter. I couldn't help but

be moved by the state of exhaustion they were all in. Chris's face
and beard were caked with icicles and frozen snot. Al's voice was
reduced to the merest whisper and Joe Tasker was alarmingly thin
and pinched. Only Pete, despite his blood-caked hair, seemed still
to be strong and have something left in reserve. He had obviously
been the strongest throughout the whole expedition and had done
a lot of the trail-breaking. Al, and to a lesser extent Joe, hadn't
performed very well: both had been on a winter expedition to the
West Ridge of Everest only a few months earlier and had returned
emaciated and very tired. Al had led this protracted and unsuccessful venture and I wondered if he had ever really recovered. Chris
himself, at forty-seven, had performed extremely well, conserving
his energy and pacing himself brilliantly. Considering that only a
few weeks earlier we were worried, not just that he wouldn't be
able to climb, but that his life itself could be in danger, it was an
astonishing performance, particularly to spend so much time above
7000 metres where physical deterioration is rapid.

The ascent of Kongur has never really had the acclaim it deserved,
partly for the reasons mentioned earlier but also because it was
perceived as being a large traditional expedition, which was actually
very unfair as the medical objectives were totally separate from the
climbing. In fact, very few peaks the height of Kongur have been
climbed alpine-style at the first attempt by such a small team; the
nearest comparison would be Broad Peak (8047 metres), climbed
by the Austrians Schmuck, Wintersteller, Diemberger and Buhl,
though even this outstanding ascent wasn't the first attempt. A
German team tried the year before, though they didn't get very high
before admitting defeat. Annapurna (8091 metres) in 1950 was
another major ascent but this was very much in the traditional
mould with nine climbing members and Sherpa support. Kongur
was, without splitting hairs, as genuine an alpine-style ascent as
one could wish for, even the route taken on the second attempt
was different, so there was very little ground covered twice.

The expedition had an unhappy aftermath, however, and again
this centred on Chris's team selection. In 1982 Chris was going to
Everest from Tibet to attempt the long unclimbed North-East Ridge.
The upper part of the ridge had, in fact, been climbed for it is joined
at around 8400 metres by the old North Col route, attempted so
often by the British between the wars and climbed by the Chinese,

possibly in 1960, and certainly in 1975. But the long pinnacled ridge running down to the Raphu La (a col at 6500 metres) was perhaps the most obvious line on the mountain that had never been attempted. Al Rouse had designs on the ridge and had applied for permission to the Chinese Mountaineering Association, but in the end suggested it made more sense for Chris to lead the expedition, as most of the administrative dealings with the CMA and Jardine Matheson would be a rerun of the Kongur expedition. Essentially, it would be the same team as on Kongur, but with no medical research programme. Throughout the Kongur expedition the four climbers made plans for 1982 and on their return to Base Camp they started organising gear to be sent to Lhasa the following year.

It was obvious on the return from Kongur that, despite the four's success on the mountain, some relationships were strained, particularly between Pete Boardman and Al Rouse. Pete found Al's incessant bullshitting irritating (though it has to be said that many people thought he raised it to an art form), and he was unimpressed with Al's high-altitude performance. Al seemed unaware of the tensions but, as an observer, I could see that something was afoot. Shortly after our return to the UK Chris drove down to Sheffield to tell Al he wasn't going on the expedition. Al was devastated, claiming with some justification, that he had actually been thrown off his own expedition! Chris was clearly upset and felt guilty about the way it had happened but justified his actions as pragmatic, saying, that if the chemistry of the team wasn't right there would be no chance of success. Experienced Bonington-watchers felt he had been manoeuvred by Pete and to some extent by Joe and that he could have solved the problem by strengthening his team by inviting two more climbers and making three pairs which would have been more flexible and, in case of illness, given more backup. Instead Dick Renshaw filled Al's place and the team remained as a foursome with Charlie Clarke as doctor and Adrian Gordon from Hong Kong as Base Camp manager.

What was particularly sad about Al's exclusion was that, unbeknown to Chris, Al, who prided himself on being one of the lads in the competitive rock climbing hothouse of Sheffield, had over the previous two years done much to promote Chris as a more accessible and popular figure. He had defended him from a lot of ill-founded criticism and had considered Chris a close friend. It was a mighty blow to his ego to be excluded in what did appear to be a rather callous manner but Al, who also suffered a relationship ending at much the same time, tried at least in public to put a brave face on it. Privately though, he was distraught and from then on his whole mountaineering life seemed devoted to proving that he could climb well at high-altitude. It was a dangerous game to play and one that he lost five years later on K2, having made the first British accent.

Perhaps the last word on the sorry saga should come from Don Whillans who, on a visit to Sheffield soon after the axe fell, greeted Al philosophically: 'Aye-aye, lad – welcome back to 'uman race!'

· 22 ·

'Big E' 1982

IT IS A tribute to Chris Bonington's flexibility of mind that only seven years after the ascent of the South-West Face of Everest, his whole philosophy of climbing had moved on from a huge siege-style oxygen-aided extravaganza to just a four-man oxygenless attempt on just about the longest route on the mountain, the North-East Ridge. It is interesting to speculate whether, in his heart of hearts, he ever thought he had any realistic chance of climbing Everest without oxygen himself. The crucial section of the ridge is a series of serrated pinnacles that look for all the world like the hardest sections of the Cuillin Ridge on Skye. Like the Rock Band on the South-West Face, the pinnacles start at around 8000 metres. Even allowing for Chris's rampant optimism and accepting that he had his private doubts, it does seem extraordinary that he was prepared at the age of almost forty-eight to be part of a very small team, which if it had succeeded would surely have brought off possibly the most astounding climb ever achieved in the Himalaya. I could not help feel right from the start that he had bitten off more than he could chew.

But there was no doubting the sheer romance of the project. Simply to go into Tibet in 1982 and retrace the approach to the mountain that was so steeped in the history of pre-war British expeditions was an opportunity few could ignore. Like Al Rouse, I was bitterly disappointed not to be asked to go to film, for I had

North Face of Everest from
Rongbuk Monastery

thought I had done enough on Kongur to justify my inclusion. Joe Tasker, who had shot some really stunning summit footage on Kongur, was keen to do the whole film this time. Once again I feared that he, too, was taking on too much.

As on Kongur, the team flew via Hong Kong to Beijing for negotiations with the Chinese, then flew on via Chengdu to Lhasa. As dawn lit up Eastern Tibet, they saw range upon range of mountains stretching away to the north, completely unexplored and virtually unheard of. It was a view that haunted Chris and one that sowed the seeds of an idea that took fifteen years to come to fruition.

In 1982 Lhasa was well on its way to becoming a large Chinese garrison city, but even so was considerably less than half the size it is today. Doing what would become the normal tourist route in 1997 was a revelation, and the team walked and filmed around the Potala Palace, the Jokhang Temple, Barkhor Square and the Norbulinka, the Summer Palace. However oppressive the Chinese presence, there was no doubt about the devotion of the pilgrims prostrating themselves around the Jokhang, some having travelled hundreds of miles to do so.

The expedition was far more gruelling than the year before. Kongur had been a cold mountain, but approaching Everest across the Tibetan Plateau from the north in early spring was even worse. On the Kongur expedition we had been accompanied by a trekking party from Jardine Matheson, including David and Carolyn Newbigging, who had both coped wonderfully well with the conditions. Once again they were to go to Base Camp and see for themselves the objective they were sponsoring. They must have left Base Camp under no doubt that this time they were staking very long odds on success. Even at Base Camp life was unbelievably harsh with blasting winds blowing down the Rongbuk valley. Compared with Base Camp on the Nepalese side of the mountain it is a grim spot, yet paradoxically one that you can drive to. The Chinese have built a road all the way and, unlike the Khumbu Glacier, Base Camp is actually on 'dry land' below the snout of the Rongbuk Glacier. The shock to the system of arriving virtually unacclimatised at 5200 metres is slowly offset by the long approach to Advance Base, which is a horizontal distance of twelve miles with only about 1200 metres of height gain. Here, on the same site as the pre-war expeditions' Camp 3, the long North-East Ridge is seen in its entirety. Not

surprisingly the early British attempts chose to climb to the North
Col and then up the North Ridge, thus bypassing most of the long
serrated North-East Ridge which rises in leaps and bounds from
the Raphu La, the col at 6,500 metres which commands a spectacular view of the East (Kangshung) Face of Everest, Lhotse and
Makalu.

The four climbers were not planning an alpine-style ascent as
such, but a series of forays up the ridge, establishing camps (mainly
snow holes) and occasionally fixing short stretches of fixed rope.
It was a colossal task for such a small team. From their arrival at
Base Camp on 16th March it took until the beginning of May to
reach the foot of the Pinnacles which barred the way to the junction
with the old North Ridge route.

At this point, at around 8000 metres, things started to go wrong.
Chris was obviously at or very near his limit and felt that Peter
Boardman in particular was much stronger and faster. He began
to doubt whether he himself could be anything other than an encumbrance on a summit bid. Then Dick Renshaw, the strong silent
single-minded survivor, who had made a brilliant ascent of Dunagiri
with Joe Tasker in 1975, felt a tingling sensation and numbness
down the left side of his body while climbing on the First Pinnacle
with Joe. The sensation soon wore off but they all decided to go
down for a rest. Back at Base Camp Charlie Clarke diagnosed the
problem as a slight stroke and strongly advised Dick against going
up again. The following day he went for a stroll down to the nearby
Rongbuk Monastery and had another mild stroke. Charlie realised
this was serious and that Dick would have to leave immediately
and that he, Charlie, would have to accompany him as far as
Chengdu where altitude would cease to be a problem. Chris meanwhile had told Pete and Joe that he was pulling out as well. He
was just too exhausted to attempt the ridge but thought he could
get to the North Col to support them if, having climbed the Pinnacles, or indeed made the summit, they decided to descend by the
far easier North Ridge.

Of the remaining two only Pete seemed fully fit. Joe was having
some sort of bowel trouble and losing blood. But he had a badly
ulcerated throat and Charlie thought that he had probably swal-
lowed a lot of blood, which might have been the problem. Looking
back now, Charlie feels:

We were all in a state of mind that was wholly unrealistic. You've got to do this to some extent on any expedition because you're taking risks that are way beyond any you take in normal daily life. In 1982 Chris wasn't the leader in the same way as he has been on most expeditions, we all knew each other too well. I think it was unfeasible for him, or for me as the doctor simply to say, 'Look, folks, this just isn't on.' But you do get into these very strange decision-making modes. I was in that mode and so was Chris.

And so Charlie left with Dick, promising to return as soon as he could, and Chris and Adrian Gordon, his non-climbing Base Camp manager, accompanied Pete and Joe back to Advance Base from where, after a rest day, the pair set out for the last time to the foot of the ridge.

For the next two days they kept radio contact with Chris and Adrian as they regained their high point on the ridge. On 17th May Chris could see them through a telephoto lens as they climbed new ground and their pace slowed to a crawl. As dusk fell he took a photograph of them on a tiny col between the First and Second Pinnacles. There was no radio contact later that evening, but this was almost certainly because they had now disappeared out of line of sight or had decided to save weight and leave the radio behind.

Chris and Adrian had spent the two days trying to reach the North Col and did so on the 19th May. Pete and Joe had still not made contact and by now Chris was worried. They spent two nights on the North Col, studying the Pinnacles and the upper reaches of the mountain through binoculars. There was no sign of Pete and Joe, though Adrian Gordon spotted a tent some way below the First Step, which gave them brief optimism. But it was the wrong colour and, by now seriously concerned, they descended to Advance Base where Charlie had just arrived from his dash to Chengdu and back. He came out to meet them. Chris, exhausted and in tears embraced Charlie:

'They've had it. I'm sure they've had it.'

'I know.'

It was impossible to mount a search party on the ridge; Chris was too tired and Charlie and Adrian too inexperienced, but Chris and Charlie went by jeep round to the Kharta valley and walked up to a point below the Kangshung Face where they might have spotted some sign of what had happened. There was also the freak chance that Pete and Joe might have survived a fall on the face and be trying to fight their way down. But there was still no clue as to what might have happened, and they returned to Rongbuk where Adrian had supervised packing the gear. Charlie carved a simple memorial stone, which they left on the top of a moraine with the unimpeded view of the North-East Ridge behind it.

Back home the expedition came in for some criticism, though it was ironic that whereas the South-West Face team was considered by some to be too big, the North-East Ridge team was now thought to be too small. John Hunt felt that just for once Chris had got it wrong. 'I thought he went insufficiently manned and there simply wasn't, at the critical time, enough backup. There was no one in close support. Somebody surely should have been able to get back onto the Ridge.' This is fair comment, but it is also worth remembering that in a far more famous but uncannily similar mystery in 1924, Mallory and Irvine had also disappeared high on the North-East Ridge. Only Noel Odell had been able to ascend to the top camp and a short way beyond. It was a large expedition but in the end it didn't make any difference. Neither, more recently had it when Mick Burke disappeared near the summit. Above 8000 metres you are on your own, however many climbers are below you, or even with you for, unless you can move under you own steam, a conventional rescue is virtually impossible. However, there was a good case to be made that the team should have been larger. My own feeling was that Chris was in awe of Pete and Joe's phenomenal performance and felt that if he couldn't match them, he couldn't tell them what, or what not to do. Pete and Joe had shown on Kongur just how driven they were and though they both had excellent mountaineering judgement they might have overestimated even their capacity to survive. For whatever happened, it was in perfect weather. Though the mystery of how they died is far from solved some clues have emerged.

At the time Chris guessed that the two had simply fallen. The Kangshung side of the ridge is often corniced; it is very steep and the Pinnacles themselves would give precarious and probably unprotected climbing. If one fell the other would probably be pulled off. But several years later a photograph taken by an American expedition showed a red patch in a hollow *beyond* the Pinnacles.

It could have been a rucksack, a collapsed tent, or possibly a body. Or it might have just been blown there from another expedition altogether. Some years after this a Kazakh expedition found Pete Boardman's body on the Pinnacles. He looked as though he was resting. It is still not at all clear what had happened but one theory is that Joe collapsed beyond the Pinnacles, and Peter had tried to retreat. In 1988, when Harry Taylor and Russell Brice climbed over the Pinnacles, they bivouacked in much the same spot as the red patch, though now it was covered in monsoon snow. From there it was an easy traverse to the North Ridge and, unable to make a summit bid themselves because of heavy snowfall, they descended to the North Col. If Pete and Joe *had* crossed the Pinnacles, Russell and Harry couldn't understand how Pete, knowing support was waiting at the North Col, could have chosen to return along the North-East Ridge, though snow conditions were very different. Perhaps when or if Joe's body is discovered it will shed more light on the mystery. Sadly, unlike the case of Mallory and Irvine, there seems no possibility that they could have climbed Everest, for Chris and Adrian would surely have spotted them from the Col.

Back at home Chris had once again the appalling task of consoling Joe's girlfriend Maria and Pete's wife Hilary. Both women wanted to visit Base Camp and even go as far as Advance Base to help come to terms with their loss. Both Chris and Jardine Matheson did everything possible to smooth their passage through China and Tibet, and Chris to this day has close friendships with them. Together with Pete's mother Dorothy, and the Tasker family, Chris was instrumental in setting up the Boardman Tasker Award for Mountain Literature, which over the years has come to be seen as the number one literary prize in the climbing world. The Award is held annually at the Alpine Club in London and Chris has only ever missed one ceremony. Friends of Pete and Joe, plus authors, publishers, critics and climbing world luminaries gather to celebrate and pay tribute to those two great climbers whose own books have inspired many of the subsequent winners of the Award.

After the expedition Chris promised Wendy he would never go back to Everest again. He couldn't give up climbing, it was not just a big part of his life – it *was* his life. But at least he would leave Everest alone. Wendy now admits she took the promise with a pinch of salt.

South West Summit of Shivling

· 23 ·

Having It on a Plate

ONE OF THE most sensible things about Chris's climbing career
has been that, having chosen to climb, he has been extremely shrewd
about who he has chosen to climb with. I must make it clear that
I am referring here to major projects, not days out in Britain where,
on the contrary, he will take anyone up a climb, regardless of their
ability and experience, if he thinks they can do it – even on occasion
when they can't. But from his early partnership with MacInnes,
Whillans and Clough, through Nick Estcourt, Dougal Haston, Peter
Boardman and Joe Tasker, he has had partners with a lot of ability
and a lot of common sense. In the early 1980s, after the death of
Pete and Joe, he needed a reliable partner, not just for climbing but
planning, discussing, and sparking off ideas. He found the ideal
person in Jim Fotheringham, a dentist working in Cumbria and a
member of Chris's local club, the Carlisle Mountaineering Club.
Jim had already had plenty of experience on Scottish winter routes,
the Alps, Kenya and Baffin Island. Together they planned their first
trip in 1983, a quick foray into the Indian Himalaya that happily
coincided with a conference Chris was attending in Delhi. This
meant that he got free flights and, as the conference was being
organised by the Indian Mountaineering Foundation, bureaucracy-
free access to the mountains with all the support of the Indian
Tourist Board. In short, he was handed the trip on a plate.

He had originally hoped to climb a new route on Bhagirathi 3, then changed to the East Face of Kedarnath Dome, a 3000-metre face very reminiscent of a Yosemite rock climb, but at high-altitude. Both objectives are in the Gangotri region, which is near the source of the Ganges, and is both spectacularly beautiful and reasonably accessible from Delhi. The pair envisaged a trip that would be not much more than an alpine holiday for both had urgent work commitments at home. When they arrived below Kedarnath Dome they were both impressed and slightly shocked at the scale of their project. Jim doubted they could do it before he was due back to work; Chris simply thought it was too big for a two-man attempt. They changed their objective again and settled for an attempt on the unclimbed South-West summit of Shivling. By doing this, the pair were embarking on a climb that few outside the élitist world of Himalayan exploration would have heard of, yet it was to provide Bonington with one of his very best first ascents and keep him, at the age of forty-nine, right up in the forefront of world climbing.

Shivling is a beautiful twin-headed peak whose main summit is 6543 metres and the South-West summit about 100 metres lower. Chris and Jim were soon committed after an early start when they ascended a dangerous couloir that was threatened from above by an icefall. At one point a car-sized block of ice hurtled down the couloir and bouncing from side to side off the gully walls, missed Chris by a couple of metres. They were relieved to reach a good, well protected ledge like a balcony, out of the firing range and, even though it was only midday, they decided to stop and wait for the cold of night to freeze the dangerous ground above them.

To their disgust the night was warm and, while carrying on would be dangerous, retreat was even less attractive. They decided to press on. When Chris got level with the icefall he realised it was even more horrifying than it had seemed from below – the whole lot looked ready to collapse. By some devious traversing, climbing over rotten rock and snowy scree-covered ledges, they reached a basin above the icefall. Again they bivouacked early and next morning, cramponned up good hard snow, racing the sun as it rose and the thawing cycle started. With huge relief they reached the foot of a great granite ridge split with cracks and looking as though it would give wonderful climbing. The rest of the day was a complete contrast, climbing under a cloudless sky up firm rock until they found a flat spot on top of a huge boulder. Time for their third bivouac.

Despite a strong wind and a big black cloud forming during the night, the next day dawned clear and sunny. They were away by 8 a.m. and immediately the climbing got somewhat steeper and a lot harder. The leader had to climb without his rucksack, but because it was still well below vertical, it was almost impossible to haul the sacks; there was too much friction. So at the end of each pitch the leader tied off the rope to belay and abseiled back down, then both men jumared back up the ropes with their sacks. Progress was naturally slower than the day before.

As the ridge they were following became harder and harder, patches of snow from which to make brews became scarcer. When they found some ice in a crack, they reckoned it might be the last for some time, so they decided to make a cramped bivouac on the crest of the ridge. Before they did so, Chris, then Jim led difficult pitches and abseiled back to build a precarious ledge on which to erect their tiny tent. It started to snow as darkness fell. The previous night Chris had dropped his head torch. Now Jim knocked his off the ledge. Still lit, it went flashing into the black void. Despite an inch or so of snow falling the weather held and the sun soon burnt it off. Above, the climbing was even harder, and Jim had to pull out all the stops to lead a fine overhanging corner perched over the huge drop.

As on the Ogre with Doug Scott years before, Chris was both envious that he had missed the crux pitch, and very impressed with Jim's lead, which brought them onto more broken ground. Technically it was not too difficult but increasingly alarming, as everything was loose and rickety. There was no point in bothering with runners as there was nothing solid enough to place them on. The consequences of a fall would almost certainly be fatal for both men.

Eventually Chris found himself at a knife-edge of snow leading to a fantastically steep and pointed summit. It was already late and another bivouac was inevitable. They had almost run out of food and the descent had to be faced. Early next morning Jim suggested they forget the last few feet and think about getting down, but Chris insisted that this finished it off. After two more pitches they stood just below the top. A perfect point, it was too small for more than one person to stand on. Chris posed for the obligatory ice axe-waving shot, feeling a momentary joy in the climb they had done, but already worried about getting down. To reverse their route seemed out of the question, so they started descending a horrendously steep snowslope to the col between the two summits of Shivling. It was so dangerous that Chris feared that in the event of one falling the other would be pulled off as well. So he suggested they climbed down unroped.

'Oh,' said Jim. 'It's like that, is it? OK.'

Chris led off down, heart in mouth, trying to distribute his weight evenly, facing in, kicking steps – don't look down . . . concentrate . . . concentrate. Behind him Jim was equally frightened and impressed with Chris's boldness. He thought it was the most dangerous bit of ground he'd ever been on, but they both made the comparative safety of the col. In the knowledge that so many accidents happen on the descent, Chris felt a nagging fear for the rest of the day as they down-climbed towards the valley. It appeared to go on forever until only a few hundred metres above the valley bottom they found some old fixed ropes leading from a different descent line and realised they had descended by a new route. All that remained was a long walk to Base Camp.

Only days later they were back in England. For Chris it was one of the best mountain experiences he had ever had: a genuine two-man alpine-style ascent of an unclimbed technically difficult peak. If anything was needed to prove that Chris was still a force to be reckoned with, this was it. It was a reaffirmation of what he himself enjoyed most. With Jim he had recaptured an enthusiasm for Himalayan climbing and seemed to be going through an Indian summer (literally!) in his career.

And it wasn't just in the Himalaya, for Chris had been invited to go to Antarctica to climb Mount Vinson, at 5140 metres the highest peak on the continent by Dick Bass and Frank Wells, two rich American businessmen whom Chris had met at Everest Base Camp in 1982. Their dream was to climb the 'Seven Summits', the highest points on each of the seven continents. They had failed on Everest but already bagged Aconcagua, McKinley (Denali), Elbrus and Kilimanjaro. Everest may be the hardest one for an inexperienced mountaineer, but in 1983 Vinson was by far the most difficult to attain, whatever their experience, simply because getting to Antarctica was such a logistical and financial obstacle. Today the Seven Summits have become a commercial proposition for trekking companies, so it just requires money.

Chris, at the time, wasn't particularly interested in bagging the set, but was fascinated by the prospect of climbing in Antarctica and accepted the invitation. As one of America's top climbers, Rick Ridgeway was also invited, for Dick Bass and Frank Wells needed them both, not exactly as guides, but to give their team the experience and strength to make their success more likely. They also took with them Steve Marts, a highly experienced mountain film-maker.

When the team met up in Santiago (for they were to fly to Vinson from Punta Arenas at the southernmost tip of South America), Chris realised what a huge amount of planning and money had gone into the venture. However, his and Ridgeway's planning was a shambles: they seemed to have forgotten about climbing gear! It took an anxious twenty-four hours to borrow ropes and ironmongery from some friendly Chilean climbers, before they left for the flight over the Southern Ocean. This was made in a converted Dakota DC3, specially adapted for Antarctic work, and piloted by Giles Kershaw, an Englishman acknowledged as being the most experienced Antarctic pilot alive.

Bonington found the flight down to the Vinson massif quite fascinating. 'There was an empty desolation and beauty, the like of which I'd never seen before. It went on for hour after hour – unclimbed, unnamed peaks, walls as challenging as the North Face of the Eiger...' The first view of Vinson was something of an anticlimax: 'It looked little more than a long walk.' Landing the DC3 on skis proved to be rather more exciting than Chris would have wished. Then suddenly they had arrived in the silent frozen wasteland. Their first job was to secure the plane against violent storms that could spring up by digging deep holes and burying anchors tethered to the wings. When Chris recce'd the approach to Vinson he realised that the scale of the mountain was much bigger than he had imagined. On the crest of a low ridge he absorbed the scene. 'I was alone for the first time for several days in this vast empty land. I revelled in its emptiness, the purity of the air, the absolute silence, the still grandeur of the mountain forms and the immense space of the polar ice cap.'

They needed to establish two camps before striking out for the top. Chris insisted on making an emergency snow hole at the first of these and found an almost ready-made one on a shelf in a crevasse. He felt that Dick and Frank thought he was being unnecess-

arily careful, referring to it as 'the Bonington Bolt Hole', but Chris
was all too aware of what could happen if they lost the tents. With
twenty-four hours of daylight it was important to get into a sleep
rhythm, even if it meant sleeping in sunlight, but as they approached
the upper slopes they went into the shade. The effect was instant
penetrating cold. 'Without the brightness of the sun the icy towers
and walls around us appeared grim and threatening. There was no
more laughter. We were like a band of hobbits entering the Misty
Mountains.'

On the summit day Chris found that Frank Wells, going slowly
against the wind, had a frostbitten nose which, if he carried on,
would be permanently damaged. Chris, hugely disappointed,
offered to take him down. Frank suggested Steve Marts accompany
him, letting Chris go to the top. Dick Bass objected – there would
be no film. Chris lost his temper, saying he didn't mind missing the
summit if it was a question of safety, 'But I'm not going to sacrifice
the top for a bloody film.' In the end Chris and Rick Ridgeway set
out for the top, in order to ensure that *someone* got there, but Rick
soon turned back with badly misted goggles. Chris climbed to the
summit on his own, full of conflicting emotions, feeling both
supreme elation and also guilt that he'd got his own way. Then,
rather curiously, he prayed to God 'to help me be less selfish, less
single-minded in my drive for my own gratification'. One can't help
feeling that the prayer was the spiritual equivalent of shutting the
stable door after the horse had bolted. St Augustine had once prayed
a similar prayer. Chris descended to the camp, worried both about
a band of high feathery cloud that could herald bad weather, and
the reception he would get. To his relief the others greeted him
warmly and congratulated him, but were less than happy when
Chris suggested quite forcibly that they retreat to the Bonington
Bolt Hole to sit out the threatened storm. Frank Wells was deeply
depressed at the idea of losing all the height they had gained and
having to re-ascend, but agreed to the plan, though he harboured
a dark suspicion that Bonington, having got his summit, didn't
want anyone else to get there. One can't help feeling that Chris
was, if anything, trying to make up for his selfishness by acting in
an ultra-responsible way. In fact the storm didn't materialise and
three days later the others climbed Vinson in perfectly calm conditions. Dick Bass went on to complete the Seven Summits the

following year when he climbed Everest, but Frank Wells stuck at six, not convinced that he could survive another attempt at 'Big E'.

So Chris had Mount Vinson, if not handed to him on a plate, then without too much time and trouble. It was the first of the Seven Summits for him and the idea of doing them all must have crossed his mind. For when he returned from Antarctica Chris broke a promise.

A Norwegian shipping magnate and a keen amateur climber, Arne Naess, was leading an expedition to Everest and had originally asked Chris for advice, then added an invitation. In the aftermath of Pete Boardman and Joe Tasker's deaths, Chris decided he had finished with the mountain. But after Shivling and Vinson his old enthusiasm was fired up and he asked Arne if the invitation still stood, for the Norwegians were going for the South-East Ridge with oxygen. It was a temptation he simply couldn't resist, even if it caused George Greenfield to observe that almost the entire population of Britain assumed that Chris Bonington had climbed Everest several times already, and the very few who knew he hadn't didn't care anyway. So when Chris announced that he was going back in 1985 at the age of fifty to climb 'the Yak Route' as the Sherpas cynically call the South-East Ridge, there were some raised eyebrows amongst the cognoscenti who couldn't quite understand why he wanted to. But Everest is, even today, a big prize, and when he had the chance to do it himself handed to him on a plate, Chris realised that, even if it didn't mean much in mountaineering terms, it still meant a lot to him. Wendy who, in the back of her mind, had never quite believed his promise in 1982, was instantly support-ive. By now Wendy knew and understood Chris's swings only too well. It was Daniel and Rupert who were surprised and indignant, and said so, but once the decision was made there was no stopping Chris.

I do not propose to describe this particular expedition in any great detail. The observant reader may have noticed that every single Himalayan expedition Chris had been on up until 1985 was to attempt either a first ascent or a new route, and the same is true of those after '85. In a way, to go to Everest by the South-East Ridge with oxygen and a big team was Chris's only retrogressive step, however understandable his personal ambition may have been. But it was a bold thing to attempt at the age of fifty, and if the climb

itself posed no questions, whether Chris could actually manage it
certainly did.

Chris worked hard on planning during 1984, but did take time
out to try another two-man ascent, this time in the Karakoram on
a remote mountain called Karun Koh. Pete Boardman had spotted
it on the southern horizon when they were high on Kongur and
thought it might have been K2, but it was on the wrong bearing.
Nothing much was known about it and Pete had wanted to try it.
Now Chris was keen to do it and, rather touchingly, invited Al
Rouse to go with him. This was undoubtedly a way of restoring
the damaged friendship after the Everest affair. Though the attempt
on Karun Koh failed in constant bad weather, Chris and Al came
back friends, but they were never to climb together again, for Al
was killed on K2 in 1986. There is a famous summit shot on Kongur
which was made into a poster. Now it is a poignant reminder that
Chris is the only one left.

Chris had formed good rapport with both Arne Naess and the
rest of the Norwegian team, and proposed Pertemba for his usual
role as sirdar. He, too, had made a promise to his wife not to climb
Everest again, though he agreed to go as far as Base Camp. On the
subject of wives, it is worth mentioning that Arne Naess was married to pop megastar Diana Ross, who definitely did not include
high-altitude climbing amongst her hobbies!

The Norwegian expedition went almost exactly according to
plan. A camp was established on the South Col, by which time
Bonington had made some acclimatisation forays, the highest one
being high on the Lhotse Face below the Col. With the knowledge
and cunning of so many expeditions Chris now wanted to drop
right down to the village of Pheriche. This lay a long day's walk
below Base Camp but he felt it important to have a decent rest at
a lower altitude before returning for his summit bid. Before he left
Base Camp Pertemba approached him and said he'd like to come
with Chris to the top – another broken promise, but one that pleased
Chris enormously. It would put the seal on years of friendship if
they could go together.

From Base Camp Chris, who is nothing if not conscientious in
writing postcards, sent me one to my college address in Bristol
where I was still working. Most of it was unintelligible, but it
finished with: 'Can't wait to get back to the Avon Gorge for some

real climbing!' Most people who saw the card assumed it was a slightly patronising little joke to a friend who wasn't about to climb Everest himself, but I knew that those words summed up the essential Bonington: even on the eve of achieving his ambition he still couldn't resist the idea of a warm afternoon in the Gorge, testing himself on something slightly too hard and ending up with just enough rope to reach the ice cream van on the grassy Downs above the cliffs. I would like to say that I wished him well, but of course by the time I got the card he had long since arrived home.

The first summit attempt, which was all-Norwegian, had failed. The second team consisted of two Norwegians, Bjørn Myrer-Lund, Odd Eliassen, Chris, Pertemba and two more Sherpas, Ang Lhakpa and Dawa Nuru. As they climbed the Lhotse Face they could see a great plume of cloud flying from the summit and soon the unsuccessful team joined them. They had reached the South Summit, tantalisingly close, before being beaten back by the wind. Next day the second team reached the Col and spent the afternoon brewing, dozing, and in Chris's case reading a Tom Sharpe book, *The Wilt Alternative*.

The team was ready to leave at 1.30 a.m. with Pertemba in the lead and Chris bringing up the rear. The others, younger and fitter, pulled ahead. Chris, tired and depressed, felt he would never make it and was also surprised to find the South-East Ridge was not exactly a walk. As they gained height the sun rose and Chris could see across to the North-East Ridge and the snow-plastered Pinnacles where he had last seen Pete and Joe. It seemed to Chris that they were never gaining any height and behind him the summit of Lhotse refused to drop down to their level, but at 8 a.m. they pulled out onto the South Summit – less than 100 metres of vertical height to gain and about 400 metres distance to the top.

It was a brilliant morning but the team had doubts about how much oxygen they had left. Chris was adamant. 'I was prepared to risk anything to get to the top.' Pertemba too backed him: 'We go on.' Now the only obstacle was the Hillary Step, twenty metres of steep unconsolidated snow leaning against a rock wall with an appalling drop down the Kangshung Face into Tibet on the right. Bjørn led it and tied off a rope at the top that the others used as a handrail. Chris again was going last. As he reached the top Dawa Nuru waved him through – his oxygen had run out. On the final slopes Chris was on the edge of hallucinating and felt the presence of Doug Scott and, curiously, Wendy's father urging him on. He had visions of Mick Burke, last seen just about where he was standing; of Pete and Joe now somewhere below on the North-East Ridge; of Nick on K2; of Dougal's big summit grin . . . suddenly he was there, kneeling in the snow racked with sobs . . . of exhaustion, of loss, and of fulfilment. At last Chris could see for himself the great 360-degree panorama across Tibet round to Kangchenjunga and Makalu, down into the Western Cwm. Below him, and on the other side of the Cwm, was the summit of Nuptse, the reverse view that he had had twenty-four years ago. Congratulations followed all round, photographs were taken, and to their surprise and pleasure Dawa Nuru slowly climbed up to them without oxygen, Then it was time to go.

Chris collected a few pebbles from the highest outcrop of rock below the summit and followed the others down. As usual the descent was nerve-racking as tiredness seeped through his body. The others had all drawn far ahead when Chris, descending the wide snowslope saw what looked like a tent, and approached it without thinking. Suddenly he realised it was the body of a woman sitting in the snow, 'fair hair blowing in the wind, teeth bared in a fixed grimace'. He looked away and carried on descending. It was Hannelore Schmatz, wife of the leader of a German expedition in 1971. She had reached the summit but died of exhaustion on the descent. Going more and more slowly, Chris ran out of oxygen above the South Col. Walking across to the tents he had one last short stretch of uphill that took him a quarter-of-an-hour. Then it was endless brews, dozing on and off and deep satisfaction, though he was still at 8000 metres.

The next day he and Pertemba descended into the Western Cwm. Chris ran down through the hazardous Khumbu Icefall, vowing it would be his last trip through it, and walked into Base Camp to congratulations and bottles of beer. For him, Everest was over. For the record Chris Bonington was the 173rd person to reach the summit and, until the fifty-five-year-old Dick Bass climbed it ten days later, Chris held the record for being the oldest summiteer.

Chris returned home to letters of congratulations from all over the world from friends and total strangers, all delighted that his quest was over. He was profoundly fulfilled but under no illusions that it meant much to anyone except himself. It was a focal point in a climbing life. However, he had absolutely no intention of giving up serious climbing and even on his way home he had started preparations for his next expedition to yet another beautiful twin-headed peak. This was Menlungtse which lay just over the Nepalese border into Tibet.

Even if Chris doesn't think that he has changed much many people have noticed that by finally climbing Everest a lot of his insecurity and obsessiveness has ebbed away. True, he is still deeply competitive, whether in a game of bridge, war games, or on a rock climb, and he can still have the odd temper tantrum, often with himself, but there is an inner calm in Chris that wasn't there before. The naked ambition that had been a significant part of his motivation has been largely satisfied and Chris now seems much happier to take life as it comes. The contrast between his leadership style on Kongur, which was my first experience of it, and on his most recent trips to Sepu Kangri in Tibet in 1997 and 1998 could hardly be greater. In 1981 he had been a driven man, almost desperate to succeed and very much into himself. On Sepu Kangri he was laid back and outgoing. Even though both expeditions failed he was a happy man, content to exist in one of the last great wildernesses of the world.

Menlungtse

· 24 ·

Menlungtse

Menlungtse was to dominate Chris's imagination for the next three years. In 1986 he contented himself with an alpine season with Jim Fotheringham and in 1987 he got permission for Menlungtse. This had not been easy. For a start Menlungtse was a name bestowed on the mountain by Eric Shipton, who had made an illegal foray over the Nepalese border into Tibet in 1951. Not unnaturally the Chinese Mountaineering Association had never heard of it, as its local name is Jobo Garu. It was not on the list of approved peaks and when he eventually got permission, Bonington had got himself another long sought-after plum.

It was to be a joint Norwegian/British expedition with Jim Fotheringham and Chris's Everest summit partners, Bjørn Myrer-Lund and Odd Eliassen. They attempted a spur on the south end of the West Face but had appalling weather and faced high technical difficulties. Retreating in a storm, Bonington, being the last down, was abseiling off a snowstake, which popped out as he put his full weight on the rope. He somersaulted backwards and managed to grab another piece of fixed rope that had been left hanging – miraculously he saved himself from a certain death fall. The 'luck of the Boningtons', or just a very quick reaction? Not for the first or last time Chris seemed to be leading a charmed life. But on this occasion the expedition failed.

At home Chris became involved in a minor but very enjoyable

adventure. St Kilda is the most westerly of the outer Hebrides. As a bird sanctuary and an army base, climbing was banned on its huge sea cliffs, but Pete Whillance, a leading rock climbing activist at the time who was completing a degree in outdoor education, managed to get permission to visit. Somehow Chris inveigled his way onto the trip and I was invited along to film news reports for ITN, a job I had done several times before in the Himalaya. Getting to St Kilda meant a long overnight voyage in a converted Scottish trawler. Several of us were horribly ill and I found filming from a pitching boat smelling of diesel fuel and fish oil particularly unpleasant.

Once on Hirta, the biggest of the islands that make up St Kilda, Chris's infectious enthusiasm was almost overwhelming. It was the first time I had been with him since his Everest ascent and I was actually astonished at the new, tolerant Bonington. This impression was briefly marred when I paused to be violently sick while filming from an inflatable dinghy as Pete Whillance jumped onto wave-washed rocks.

'Film, you bastard – film!' came the stentorian voice of our leader.

He was quite right and even though I completed the shot with my eyes closed and my anorak covered in, well, never mind, I was later bemused to see that bit of film as footage on 'News at Ten'.

Chris climbed several good new routes, but the main event was the first ascent of Conachair Cliff by Pete Whillance and his partner Ian McMullan. It was a long and technically desperate climb up one of the biggest sea cliffs in Britain. Chris accepted early on that it would be far too hard for him, which again he would have found a difficult admission to make a few years earlier, and contented himself by commentating and supporting me on the film side. On this, our second collaboration we began to understand each other, and my respect for his professionalism in front of the camera grew.

Pete and Ian completed the climb on the very last day of our three-week stay and we returned on the boat to Oban in a gale. I was secretly delighted to see that Chris went very pale and succumbed soon after we set sail, though his incorrigible optimism didn't stop him from fantasising about a return visit with Arne Naess in a hired helicopter. Perhaps Arne would bring his wife this time, I thought.

Chris re-applied for permission for Menlungtse for 1988. Jim Fotheringham couldn't return so Chris invited Andy Fanshawe, who was the National Officer of the British Mountaineering Council. Chris had just been Vice-President and was impressed with this dynamic young climber. Andy was surprised and flattered to be invited and obviously became very fond of Chris, even if he found the generation gap slightly daunting.

The Menlungtse region was where Eric Shipton had taken his famous pictures of 'yeti' footprints and Bonington, either with his eye on the main chance, or because he was genuinely intrigued, stirred up a mass of speculation over some unusual tracks Odd and Jim had photographed in 1987. The result was sponsorship for the expedition and an accompanying BBC crew to film a yeti search.

Andy commented, 'Most of the climbing world thought he had found a brilliant scam for raising money and admired how he readily made a fool of himself without embarrassment.' Andy could never decide whether Chris actually believed in the yeti's existence or not. And neither can I. But it certainly spawned several good cartoons in the daily press. A final word comes from the American climber John Roskelley, who wrote a book about his own attempt on Menlungtse. Every chapter starts with a definition from *Roskelley's First Climbers' Dictionary*, for example:

nomad/'no – mad/ n. 1. A member of a people free of stress and madness created by house payments, car expenses, charge cards and civilised life, 2. What I should have been.
Yak/'yak/n. a Tibetan way of life on the hoof.
Yeti/'yet – e/ n. (Tibetan 1951) 1. A source of funds for another free trip 2. A Tibetan bogeyman.

Chris's second expedition involved two American climbers, David Breashears, who is one of the best climbing cameramen in the world, and Steve Shea, plus a three-man BBC crew and Dr Charlie Clarke. Alan Hinkes, soon to make his name as an 8000-metre peak-bagger, was also there to ferry film and news reports to the outside world, for Chris had also got sponsorship from the *Mail on Sunday*.

The first major setback to the second expedition was a telegram arriving for the team when they had reached Kathmandu. It was from the Chinese Mountaineering Association, informing them that permission had been withdrawn for Menlungtse. This was almost certainly for some unfathomable internal political reason and Chris, instantly stung into action, pulled out all the stops to persuade the CMA to relent. He got on BBC's 'Breakfast Time' for an interview, and then rang David Wilson, our old friend from Kongur who was now Governor of Hong Kong, to lobby Beijing. Meanwhile the expedition was stuck in Kathmandu for over a week while telexes were exchanged. At last (and as usual) Chris got his own way and permission arrived to cross the Nepalese border into Tibet.

Andy Fanshawe spent a lot of the walk-in to Menlungtse being impressed by Chris's formidable drive to keep the momentum of the expedition going – walking double stages to hire yaks, negotiating at every checkpoint with the help of a dynamic liaison officer, and finding time to look after Andy himself, who initially suffered blinding headaches as they were driven in a matter of hours from the Nepalese border straight up onto the Tibetan Plateau at almost 5000 metres. He was also amused when Chris produced a Polaroid camera and took a couple of shots of Tibetan villagers. Within minutes the entire female population wanted to have their photos taken, and to achieve this were prepared to bestow their favours on Chris, often communicating this in unambiguously graphic ways. Andy couldn't hide his amusement:

' "Ladies, please!" said the debonair Bonington, "One at a time!"

' "What do they see in the old knacker?" I said to Hinkes' back. He was already walking towards Chris.

' "Let me have a go with that thing," he pleaded.'

Once at Base Camp the BBC started their search for the elusive yeti. However, by this time they were so far behind schedule that they only stayed a few days before returning to England, needless to say without finding anything other than a few piles of animal dung of unknown origin.

The climbing team of Chris, Andy Fanshawe, David Breashears and Steve Shea made a gallant attempt on the West Summit (7023 metres). The problem was that after three bivouacs and having climbed hard mixed ground, followed by a very steep, iron-hard icefield, they came up against a vertical headwall of compact granite. From below there seemed to be an obvious gully cutting through, but when Andy Fanshawe in the lead reached the upper end of the icefield, he could see no sign of it. Below him, Chris and David were muttering about retreat. Andy got angry.

'Oh, come on! Let's at least give it a try! We haven't got to the gully yet.'

Chris turned and exploded, 'Andy, just fuck off will you!' Andy was stunned. Chris jumared up to him.

'Andy, just cool it! Steve's knackered. David reckons we should go down.'

Andy suggested a compromise, to at least try and find the elusive gully. He traversed under the headwall where he was horrified to see only a thin ribbon of water ice that looked quite vertical. 'It's desperate! This is the gully and it's desperate!'

The four descended without incident and had three days' rest at Base Camp before setting out to have a look at the East Ridge. On the way Chris confessed that he still felt very tired and was contemplating giving up. Below the ridge they camped by a little lake and unpacked the sacks. David and Steve produced one pile of gear, Andy and Chris another. Something was missing, as Andy realised.

'"Have you got the rope?" Chris said to me.

'"No, I thought you packed it."

'"Oh dear me!" he whispered. "It's a balls up."'

In the event it didn't matter because the East Ridge looked horrendous and everyone agreed it would be too difficult and far too dangerous. So what next? Chris announced he was pulling out – he hadn't recovered after the first attempt. David Breashears also gave up and so in the end did Steve Shea. Which only left Andy, until he remembered that Alan Hinkes could still be at Base Camp, having returned from a mail run. The two of them joined up and went back to the original West Ridge with Chris's blessing, though he must have felt an echo of Pete and Joe's last departure for the North-East Ridge of Everest as they set out.

This time Andy found the only feasible route through the headwall which gave very hard climbing, with a final pitch comparable with the Ogre at a slightly lower altitude. The pair reached the lower West Summit as night fell and, with no bivouac gear, retreated in the dark to the top camp without traversing across to the higher main summit (7181 metres). (Two Slovenian climbers, Marco Prezelj and Andrej Stremfelj climbed this in 1992.) Andy and Alan made a safe descent to the foot of the ridge where Andy told Chris what they'd done:

'"Only the West Summit, I'm afraid," I said. I can't imagine what had got into me. What was I afraid of? What did I mean, "Only the West Summit"? I was overjoyed by our climb.

'"*Really* well done," said Chris spontaneously, suddenly back in Sandhurst voice.'

And so after two attempts Chris had to be satisfied with second prize. At last age seemed to be catching up with him, not so much in a lowering of standards, but by the length of time it took him to recover. It was a lesson he learnt quickly, for over the next ten years he became increasingly conscious that at high altitudes he would probably only have enough energy in him for one shot at the summit, and that he had to make it count. But even after Menlungtse, at the age of nearly fifty-four, Chris was not done yet, and his capacity to surprise his friends and rivals with impressive and committing ascents was far from over. His rock climbing standards have hardly slipped, if at all, and he still tries to lead an E2 every year, which requires a lot of trawling through Lake District guidebooks to find a suitably soft touch!

In 1988 Brummy Stokes led an expedition to the North-East Ridge of Everest during the monsoon, in which Harry Taylor and Russell Brice climbed over the Pinnacles and then descended to the North Col. It was a great effort, but shamelessly hyped by the media as 'Everest's last problem conquered' – which caused Sir Jack Longland, veteran of the 1933 expedition, to observe how curious it was that the recent expedition had succeeded at a point considerably lower than where his expedition had failed! Be that as it may, by succeeding in crossing the Pinnacles, Taylor and Brice deterred Chris from going ahead with a very big expedition he had planned for 1989, which would have included the Burgess twins, Mo Anthoine and Joe Brown.

'I think I felt a sense of relief when they did it,' he admitted in an interview in *Mountain* magazine. 'I was planning to be an Advance Base support leader and what's the point in that?' What indeed? It is hard to fathom why he considered it in the first place, apart from a feeling of unfinished business. But unlike the South-West Face of Everest, where cracking the Rock Band was a big step into the unknown, even without Taylor and Brice's effort over the Pinnacles there was very little if any new ground to be covered. What Wendy would have thought if he had gone ahead can hardly be imagined.

SUHAILI and Iceberg

And Now For
Something Completely Different

AFTER CHRIS'S INTRODUCTION to sailing with Robin Knox-Johnston, the two kept in touch in that loose and informal way that is very common amongst climbers, and presumably sailors as well. In 1991 Knox-Johnston approached Chris out of the blue and asked him if he fancied a trip to Greenland in his faithful old ketch *Suhaili* in which he had become the first person to sail single-handed non-stop around the world. The team would consist of two climbers and two crewmen, plus Knox-Johnston. Chris was instantly taken with the idea and started looking for an objective. His research led him to phone a young man called Jim Lowther who was only twenty-five, but had already been on ten Greenland expeditions. Jim is the third son of the Earl of Lowther, and manages the Lowther Estates, which own a huge chunk of Lakeland's eastern fells. (When he once enrolled on a beginners' hang-gliding course and was told it would be held on Blencathra and High Street, he is reputed to have responded, 'Ah, two of ours.') Jim has a tremendous zest for life, a natural curiosity and an enthusiasm for climbing and mountain exploration that almost rivals Chris's. His encyclopaedic knowledge of Greenland led him to quickly find an objective in the Lemon Range called the Cathedral. Needless to say, it was unclimbed. Chris took Jim climbing and was impressed with his performance and invited him on the expedition.

They sailed from Whitehaven into the North Atlantic, passing

close to Rockall. Unfortunately the sea was too rough to risk
making a new route on the house-sized rock, which frequently has
heavy seas breaking right over it. Chris was in the company of two
other sailing novices: Jim Lowther and BBC's Radio Two presenter
John Dunn, who would accompany the boat to Iceland sending
back reports to his evening programme. He quickly settled into the
new disciplines of sailing and living in a confined and generally wet
space that would never keep still. (I later received a postcard from
Iceland with the triumphant message scrawled across it: 'I WASN'T
SICK!') Chris found that learning to steer to a compass bearing was
both strenuous and surprisingly difficult until you develop a sort
of subconscious feeling for the combinations of wind and waves.
One invaluable lesson Chris learned from Robin Knox-Johnston
was the declaration of a Headland, a tradition Robin instigated on
a Round-Britain Race when, on rounding first a treacherous, then
any headland, the whisky is broached and a toast drunk. Chris
thought this an excellent idea and has transferred it to climbing
circles where it has been unreservedly welcomed. Robin found Chris
'very congenial; we got on with each other. Both of us were very
relaxed in the other's company.'

The voyage to their first port of call, Iceland, was uneventful,
except that while slicing onions in a rolling sea Chris cut his hand
deeply. Jim Lowther stitched it up very professionally and to everyone's relief it healed well. If it had become infected it could have
meant abandoning the climbing part of the adventure.

The voyage from Iceland to Greenland was broken by the appearance of a huge iceberg, which, as these are prone to rolling over as
they melt, are normally best avoided. But Robin couldn't resist the
thought of thousand-year old ice in his whisky and he launched a
small dinghy to manoeuvre close enough to hack a few lumps off.

Robin was impressed by Chris's two main reasons for sailing to
Greenland. The romantic one was that it was more satisfying and
pure to approach a mountain naturally, using just the power of the
wind to get you there, instead of a helicopter, bus or jeep. The
practical one was that once you *did* get there you had a ready-made
Base Camp that was far better stocked than any frame tent could
ever be. What's more you could move it around whenever you
needed to – at least in theory. However, in Greenland's summer
the condition and movement of the pack ice guarding the entrance

to the fjords that led into the mountains would be critical. Robin was naturally primarily concerned with the safety of *Suhaili* and it was decided to try and reach the Sidegletscher under power. This glacier was the nearest the boat could get to the Cathedral to drop off tents, food and gear before retreating to a safer berth. It was a gruelling slow passage weaving through gaps in the pack ice.

'I was not thrilled with the situation,' commented Robin. After taking six hours to cover four miles, Robin, Chris and Jim went ashore in a dinghy, Robin observing. 'He set his feet apart rather deliberately and then stamped them; the landsman was back in his element.' Robin also noticed that up until now he had been in charge but the second they reached shore, Chris took over. There was no problem whatsoever with their sudden role-change.

Their camp was all of thirty metres from the shoreline and all the stores, pulks (sledges), ropes and ironmongery were unloaded. Robin was worried that *Suhaili* could get into trouble if the wind sprang up and drove the pack ice into her, so he sailed the boat back to a safer mooring, taking a great deal of care to ensure she was anchored to rock pinnacles ashore as well as by her sea anchor. 'When we had finished *Suhaili* wasn't going anywhere in a hurry, but all the same I was well aware that I was incapable of not worrying about her.' He returned to the climbers with mixed feelings about leaving his boat and wondering why he wanted to go mountaineering anyway.

Meanwhile, Chris and Jim, plus a two-man film crew, Allen Jewhurst and Jan Fester, who had flown out before them, had carried loads over rough moraine to a point where it would be possible to put on skis and haul the pulks. Robin, when he did a carry the following day, was disappointed that the glacier was so dirty. There were a few crevasses on the way to the first camp, and Chris enjoyed telling him a macabre story about someone who had got jammed in one and took three days to die.

'Now I didn't tell him any nasty stories of people dying at sea. Why's he done this to me?'

The following day, 6th August, was Chris's fifty-seventh birthday, which apparently everyone had forgotten. Chris sat in his tent feeling homesick and lonely when there was a tuneless rendering of 'Happy Birthday to You' from outside, and he was presented with a tiny birthday cake and a miniature bottle of champagne that

Wendy had organised. She had made sure the candles were the joke ones that never go out however hard you blow – was this a not very subtle message to her beloved, if venerable husband?

Pulk-hauling was a gruelling introduction to mountaineering in Greenland for Robin Knox-Johnston. Once they put their skis on he fell back, and by the time he caught the others up at rest stops they would be setting off again; a situation that inevitably got worse as the day wore on. Chris and Jim decided that the most straightforward way up the Cathedral was by a long gully leading to an easy-looking ridge. The first thing to do was give Robin a climbing lesson for he had hardly had any time to prepare for this half of the expedition. He was given a very basic course in ice climbing and abseiling, barely adequate for what they were preparing to do. He is a burly, obviously strong man with a huge amount of heart; it would have to suffice. The following day they set off. By the time he had climbed the 300-metre gully, cramponing up 40° ice, he was moving quite confidently. However the ridge leading to the top was not the scramble it had appeared from below, but a series of rock walls and pinnacles making for complicated route-finding. The problems became more frequent and Robin lacked the experience to move easily and safely over this sort of terrain. He told Chris he was happy to wait for them to press on to the summit. Chris instantly rejected the idea; Robin tried to persuade him.

'I'll be all right. We've got to make it to the top.'

'You'll do as you're told.'

It was a brief burst of Bonington anger, ostensibly directed at Robin, but really at himself for allowing a beginner to get into a potentially serious situation. They pressed on to a huge pinnacle where Chris and Jim both led difficult pitches. Robin followed with great effort, but was visibly tiring. At 6.30 in the evening, with snowflakes in the air, it was time to retreat. Chris felt he had let the side down; Robin had sailed them to Greenland, Jim Lowther had got them to the foot of the Cathedral, but he, Chris, had failed to get them up the mountain. The three managed to descend in good order, shepherding Robin down the long gully, and regained their tents twenty-five hours after setting out.

Time was not on their side. They were all due back on board *Suhaili* soon and Robin was increasingly aware that the longer they delayed, the more vulnerable his boat became. So he and the film crew decided to return and Chris and Jim would have one more attempt. On their second attempt, Chris and Jim soloed the gully and reached the ridge seven hours faster than on their first attempt. They were going to bypass the large pinnacle by abseiling down a gully behind it and then traversing to regain the ridge beyond. It was a very ambitious thing to do. Like the Hinterstoisser Traverse on the Eiger, it represented a point of no return, except that in this case they would *have* to return, there was no easier way down. But once the rope was pulled down there simply had to be a way of climbing backup.

As usual, they had badly underestimated the difficulties of the ridge. Chris led all the way and was climbing near his limits. Time slipped by and pinnacle followed pinnacle, giving hard mixed climbing, and every pitch would have to be reversed. Climbing one pinnacle that Chris was sure would be the summit, he was appalled to find at least another four that were higher. They had been going for fourteen hours and had no bivouac gear. Common sense in the form of Jim Lowther prevailed, though even then a part of Chris wanted to go on. But he could see that even now, getting back would be a trial, and only some thirty metres below the final pinnacle (though it was still about 200 metres away horizontally) they turned round.

Reversing the abseil down the gully was desperate, and Chris had to pull out all the stops to get out of the trap. By the time they had regained the shoulder and comparative safety it was one in the morning and they were in deep twilight. They stopped for about an hour and Chris slept (and worried) fitfully. When he awoke he was racked with violent shivering and Jim, anxious that he was in the first stages of hypothermia, urged him to get up and get moving. Descending the long gully, Chris allowed himself to be lowered down each pitch to the end of the rope where he cut a large stance and made a belay. Then Jim climbed down facing in. Chris was impressed by Jim's speed and had difficulty taking the rope in quickly enough.

At last the angle eased enough to walk down facing out and after twenty-eight hours of almost continuous movement they regained the tent, too tired for anything except tea, and crashed into sleep. After a day's rest they had just two days to get back to the point where *Suhaili* would pick them up. The climbing part of the expedition was over and the landlubbers had to become sailors again. Chris, snuggled in a wet sleeping bag, was only too happy to let Robin take over.

The voyage home was not as easy as the outward leg. The weather deteriorated as they reached Iceland, and later Robin wrote that they were about to learn why Iceland was originally colonised – it is an easy place to sail to but can be all but impossible to leave. In fact, it took four attempts before they finally got away and made a speedy passage down to the Orkneys. Sailing down past Stromness they passed Hoy on the left with the huge red cliffs of St John's Head and the Old Man next to them. Chris was at the helm in a gusty following wind with waves coming from all over the place. Robin watched him carefully; in conditions like this it would be all too easy to damage the boat, but he was delighted and strangely moved to see that Chris had absorbed everything he had learnt and was now at one with the boat. He let Chris carry on and they swept past the Old Man and carried on down the Pentland Firth, and then the North Sea. On 12th September they chugged up the Thames and Robin produced a bottle of whisky he had saved for the moment. He proposed a Headland, the last of the trip, and they slid into St Katherine's Dock to berth *Suhaili*. The two-month adventure was over.

The voyage had cemented the friendship between Chris and Robin even though they are very different people. Robin is fairly bullish, very decisive, and much the same in public as in private. Chris is more complex, probably more prone to self-analysis, very conscious of his public image and as a leader more circumspect, but this is not surprising. On a boat you can only have one leader and decisions simply can't be taken by committee. The magic of their trip is that both men found the other's company so easy and each earned the respect of the other. So much so that Chris and Robin returned to Greenland in 1998 (though Chris flew each way and only used the boat as a mobile Base Camp). They would like to do another voyage further afield but each is, at present, noticeably reticent about where and when.

Chris actually returned to Greenland for a third time with Jim Lowther and Graham Little from Edinburgh, when they completed several hard technical climbs on the rock spires of the Lemon Mountains. He is returning yet again in 2000 with Jim, Graham and Jim

Fotheringham, his insatiable appetite for first ascents still unsatisfied.

Since his trip down to Mount Vinson and his own ascent of Everest, Chris Bonington has flirted on and off with the idea of doing all the Seven Summits. It has been typical Bonington dalliance – sometimes he seems quite excited by the idea, but for long periods he can't see much point in it as it has become, with the inception of trekking and adventure companies, not much more than a glorified series of package holidays. But having done the two hardest almost by accident, it wouldn't be too difficult to knock off the rest if he really wanted to. Having also done Kilimanjaro and Elbrus (the highest mountain in Europe and arguably the most boring), he has only three more to go – Aconcagua in South America, McKinley (Denali) in North America and Carstenz Pyramid in New Guinea. It is quite impossible to predict whether he will complete the series or not. Halfway through the Elbrus trip in 1993 he suddenly decided it wasn't worth it, and invited Jim Fotheringham and me to go with him and Harish Kapadia to climb in the Kinnaur region of the Indian Himalaya. I was delighted to put filming the Seven Summits on the back burner, where it still remains.

Walking up the Tirung Gad towards Rangrik Rang

· 26 ·

Joint Ventures

Harish kapadia from Bombay or Mumbai as we must now call it can lay claim to have visited the Indian Himalaya more often than anyone else. His depth of knowledge is awesome and his output of books on the various areas is equally impressive. He has the knack of ferreting out interesting unclimbed mountains in areas that are still unexplored. In 1992 Chris had accompanied him to the Panch Chuli mountains near the Western Nepalese border, along with Dick Renshaw, Stephen Venables, Graham Little, Victor Saunders and Steve Sustad.

It was quite an eventful trip including an ascent in good style of the South-West Ridge of Panch Chuli 2 by three Indian members, and the first ascent of Panch Chuli 5 by Renshaw, Venables and Sustad. A near tragedy occurred on the descent at night when an abseil anchor failed, and Venables fell seventy metres to be held in a tangle of ropes by Renshaw in his gloved hands. Venables broke an ankle, a leg, and had chest injuries. Chris, who had stayed behind at the top camp, saw the light from a head-torch falling through the darkness. Descending for help the following morning he too fell, this time 150 metres down a steep snowslope, cartwheeling out of control over the bergschrund at the bottom of the slope, and coming to rest with only a few bruises to show for it. Chris and Steve Sustad made it down to Base Camp and the next day Chris walked all the way back to the nearest village, where he could radio for a helicopter. Meanwhile, Victor Saunders and Dick Renshaw managed to lower Venables to a relatively safe spot and after two days an Indian Air Force helicopter picked him off the slope by landing on one skid. This was a dangerous manoeuvre that could have killed everyone, as Venables was bundled aboard with the blades rotating only inches from the surface of the snow. To this day Saunders swears that they actually cut a shallow groove above the tents!

It is not difficult to understand Chris's attraction to expeditioning with Harish. Not only do you get the pleasure of his company, and the friendship of the Indian members of the expedition, but the feeling that Harish can smooth away any obstacle that lies in his path and you will be transported on his magic carpet to Base Camp. (Harish is, after all, a cloth trader in Mumbai and spends most of his working hours sitting cross-legged on one!) Not only that, but on the way you will get the benefit of all Harish's knowledge and experience, giving you a unique insight into an area that would be in any case be inaccessible if you were on your own, since the presence of Europeans on a first ascent is still only tolerated if you are part of an Indian expedition.

Chris and I were in Mumbai once, he doing his work for LEPRA and I attempting to free expedition gear from the Indian Customs (a story in its own right). While we were there Harish's wife Geeta arranged a puja, or blessing, to celebrate Chris' sixtieth birthday which would be in a couple of months' time. Two Hindu priests came to the Kapadias' flat and began chanting, ringing bells and offering various items of fruit, flowers and incense. Chris had to sit cross-legged on the floor for about two hours and took the whole thing very seriously, though I can never understand whether his interest in religion, particularly Buddhism, is any more than skin deep. He confesses to being agnostic and doesn't, to my knowledge, do much in the way of worship of any kind unless he is in the mountains. It seems to me he is actually quite superstitious and only does it to ward off bad luck. Rather like the yeti, it is hard to fathom out what, if anything, he does believe, or even whether he knows himself. He often claims that he is not a man of ideas but of deeds, which would seem to preclude any profound spiritual insights. And yet, as with the puja, he is moved easily and when it finished he was almost in tears. Geeta had explained that at the age of sixty, Hindu men sometimes renounce all worldly goods and leave their family home to spend the rest of their lives relying on alms. They sometimes even renounce their clothes as well. Later on I told Graham Little that I couldn't see Chris wandering naked along the streets of Keswick armed with only a begging bowl, to which he retorted that, apart from the nudity, Chris had been doing something like it more or less all his life!

After the puja we had a fascinating journey to the mountains. Harish is a train lover and we were booked on the sleeper to Delhi, then on to Chandigarh where a rack railway climbed up a never-ending series of bends to Simla, the old summer residence of the British Raj. Today it has the sad air of a Home Counties suburb that has long fallen on hard times. From here a coach drive takes you up the Sutlej valley, once the setting for Kipling's *Kim*, but now as industrialised as the Rother Valley near Sheffield. This leads to the wonderful winding gorge leading into the Tarung Gad, a paradise of woods, high granite crags, Buddhist villages and a clear bubbling river. Chris was so taken with the great sweep of unclimbed rock that he toyed with the idea of a rock climbing holiday here without ever bothering to go up the valley to the big mountains. Nothing came of it, though he even managed to get Johnny Dawes, a dynamic and extraordinarily talented rock climber, enthused with the idea. It is possible that Chris might be possessed with great foresight. Perhaps our grandchildren will dismiss the snow peaks as boring and dangerous and just do the Himalayan equivalent of outcrop climbing, as has happened to some extent in the Alps. The possibilities in an area like Kinnaur are infinite, ranging from technical bouldering on perfect granite next to the river, to 1000-metre high walls of Yosemite-like splendour.

When we reached our mountain, Rangrik Rang, I was curious to see how Chris performed these days at altitude for, apart from one day on Elbrus the year before, I hadn't seen him on a big mountain since Kongur thirteen years earlier. As far as I could see there was really no difference at all, except perhaps that after a long day he was prepared to admit to being tired, but so was everyone else. Certainly when going uphill he seemed as strong as ever. He and Jim Fotheringham unlocked the key to the summit when they completed a route up a steep ice face that led to a traverse to a col from which the long summit ridge could be climbed. The effort meant a day's rest while the prospective Indian and British summit party left Advance Base for the top. Bonington and Fother-ingham caught up easily the following day, so there wasn't much wrong with Chris at sixty, and the eight members of the team who made the summit were rewarded with spectacular views of Kamet, the Gangotri Peaks and range upon range of mountains stretching away into Tibet.

In 1995 Chris returned to Nepal to an unclimbed peak to the west of Everest called Drangnag-Ri. Once again he went with a Norwegian team and in fact the expedition was to mark the tenth anniversary of their successful 1985 ascent of Everest. Chris had first seen the mountain from Menlungtse and suggested to Arne Naess that it looked a good objective and at 6801 metres not too high. He saw it again in 1983 when he and I made a quick trip to Everest Base Camp with Pertemba and a film crew to make a documentary to mark the fortieth anniversary of the first ascent. On the way back Chris had the idea of hiring a helicopter to have a close look at Drangnag-Ri and to take photos, and I accompanied him to get video footage. It was nearly a very close look indeed and was quite the most spectacular (i.e. terrifying) ride of my life. The Nepalese pilot pushed the helicopter to its limits to cross a high col which we seemed only to clear by a few metres before flying past a sensationally steep peak that made the distant view of Everest and Lhotse look quite tame.

In 1995 the walk-in over the 5750-metre high Tesi Lapcha Pass was, Chris thought, an expedition in its own right. The mountain was so steep it was decided to use fixed rope to give as many as possible a chance for the top. Chris did his fair share of the leading, noting that he was going better than he had done for years, reading the ground and attuned to his environment. 'This was why I was still climbing at the age of sixty.' On the hoped-for summit day, 30th April, exactly ten years since Chris took on the summit of Everest, no less than ten climbers started out from Camp 2, but progress was slow and there were far too many people getting in each other's way in deteriorating weather. In the end Chris, Bjørn Myrer-Lund, Ralph Høybrakk and two Sherpas, Perna Donge and Lhakpa Gyalu, pressed on with Chris leading. 'I hardly noticed the altitude, my concentration on the summit was so great. It was as if fifty years had dropped away from me. I felt as if I had regained all the drive and single-minded focus of my youth to take me up the steep ice of that soaring ridge.'

Suddenly Chris realised that he had nearly run out of mountain and let out a whoop of triumph. Lhakpa Gyalu was first to join him. A veteran of Everest '72, '75 and '85, Chris pushed him past to be first on the top. As he balanced on the knife-edged ridge Chris received an electric shock and there was the hissing sound of lightning about to discharge. Chris yelled at Lhakpa to get down. Bjørn and Ralph wanted to risk going to the summit but, with the atmosphere sizzling, Chris insisted everyone descend, himself going last and feeling very vulnerable as he sat in the gathering storm waiting to abseil off his own ice axe.

There were those at this point of his career who thought he should give up big mountains – to quit while he was still ahead. I must confess to feeling that way myself, particularly following the death of Paul Nunn, who had been killed with another friend, Geoff Tier, in 1995. But Chris still had one more major ambition to resolve. His 'mystery mountain' north-west of Lhasa, first seen in 1982, remained as elusive as ever. In 1996 Chris at last got permission for its ascent. It was too late to organise and find sponsorship for a full scale expedition, but he and Charlie Clarke took off at short notice to try and find the elusive mountain. They still had nagging doubts that on their arrival in Lhasa they might be told they could not go any nearer. But all seemed to be well, and they set off by way of four-wheel-drive Land Cruisers to explore the Nyenchen Tanglha range. It was more or less the equivalent of being let loose in the whole of the Swiss Alps in the early nineteenth-century – nothing had been climbed and nothing beyond the main river systems and major valleys had been travelled by Europeans.

It took three days to drive over the Tibetan Plateau via Nakchu, billed as the highest town in the world, which it may or may not be, but it must surely be the highest ugly town in this or any other universe. From Nakehu they carried on north-west before traversing several high passes and dropping down to cross the Salween River at Diru. From here a half day's drive led them to the start of a wonderful walk up the Khinda valley to an ancient Bon monastery at Samda the Sam Tso Taring, a sacred lake over which Chris's mountain, Sepu Kangri towers. With little time available Chris and

Charlie ascertained that there was at least the possibility of a couple of feasible routes to the summit plateau of the mountain. But the recce would not be complete without at least travelling round to the south side of the mountain, a much longer and more complex approach that finally revealed a far steeper and harder side. Satisfied that the original way would almost certainly unlock the key to Sepu Kangri, Chris and Charlie returned to Lhasa and then home. They had been away only a month, and had never even unpacked a rope, but Chris found it one of the most enjoyable trips he had ever had, 'doing a Shipton', travelling light over unknown country and covering large distances every day. Once home Chris started planning for 1997.

An Ambition Achieved

CHRIS BONINGTON HAD every reason to feel that his ambition to climb what had become known as 'Chris's Secret Mountain' – Sepu Kangri – was on the verge of fulfilment in 1997. He assembled the current team of stalwarts: Jim Fotheringham, Jim Lowther and Charlie Clarke, plus a new face, John Porter, a very experienced climber who now lived just down the road from him in Caldbeck. In his remorseless fascination with electronic gadgets, Chris also planned to have a website and satellite communications at Base Camp, and invited Duncan Sperry, climber and specialist in Internet communications to run it. I was drafted in late in the day as film-maker.

The previous year Chris had more or less decided that a very obvious ridge that led up to a subsidiary summit of Sepu Kangri called the Turquoise Flower, was the best route to follow. But Jim Fotheringham wasn't sure and thought that a long broken ridge leading to a complex area of snowfield, and crevasses could lead more easily to the top. The climbing team set out to recce this alternative but after two days climbing onto the ridge Chris dismissed it (in Jim's view rather hastily) as being too long and possibly too dangerous. So they chose the first option which we soon started to call the Frendo Spur after the climb on the Aiguille du Midi above Chamonix which has a similar pronounced snow and ice arête.

Neighbours at Sepu Kangri – Tsiri, Kharté and niece

The weather, which had started off cold and changeable soon became cold and unchangeable – it snowed for a lot of the time. Jim Fotheringham led a horrendously difficult mixed snow, ice and rock pitch that led up to a small col on the Frendo where a camp was made. There were never more than two or three days of fine weather and progress was slow. Because of this a lot of fixed rope was used and nobody ever felt brave (or stupid) enough to cut loose and go for the summit. After four weeks we began to accept that success was unlikely. The weather was getting warmer, the lake was melting slowly and the snowfalls were getting heavier. Confined to Base Camp, Chris was incredibly reluctant to admit defeat, which to the rest of us seemed inevitable. He would retire to his tent, only to re-appear two hours later with another far-fetched scenario that wasn't on without at least four days of perfect weather which we hadn't had, and weren't likely to. After one such attempt to persuade us, on the basis of twenty seconds of watery sunlight, that the good weather had arrived, Chris retreated to his tent again as it started snowing. Charlie took me by the arm and in his best confiding bedside manner, murmured, 'I wonder if I could be the first doctor to get someone sectioned via E-mail?'

This was the first time Chris had taken satellite communications to the mountains and he was very aware of their convenience but also their disadvantages. Our doctor, Charlie Clarke, made lifesaving use of the satellite phone when he consulted a colleague for a second opinion on the ectopic pregnancy of a neighbouring yak-herder's wife – gynaecology not being an area of medical expertise often called for on climbing expeditions. As for the drawbacks of our battery of communications, the immediately obvious one was knowing that disaster as well as triumph would be relayed via 'News at Ten' directly to our nearest and dearest. But, as Chris resolutely observed, 'You can't turn the clock back, you have to come to terms with technology and use it, not let it use you.' The real pay-off in his view was the number of schools and individuals using the website, identifying with the progress of the expedition and sharing its highs and lows.

Before he left Base Camp Chris announced that he would come back in 1998 for another attempt, and on his return to England he set about organising it. This time we arrived in Tibet at the end of some of the worst flooding ever recorded in China. Flying into

Lhasa airport we could see that the normally arid plateau looked more like the Norfolk Broads. Even the three-day drive to the road-head was problematic with large areas of road and many bridges washed away. The Frendo Spur seemed even less attractive than the year before and Chris resolved to give the Fotheringham Ridge another close look. This time, by changing the start of the route, the five climbers – Graham Little, Victor Saunders, Scott Muir, Elliot Robertson and Chris himself – cut out some of the ridge that had so discouraged Chris the year before, and after a short recce everyone decided that this line would give the best chance of success. The weather was only marginally better than in '97.

On the first attempt the team seemed to have success in the bag, climbing to a point they estimated was only a few hours from the top. But the Sepu Kangri weather closed in yet again and after sitting it out for two nights in increasingly dangerous snow conditions they decided they would have to retreat while they still could. Just one more day of fine weather would have seen the mountain climbed. Chris was obviously disappointed and already I wondered whether he would have enough drive left for a second attempt. He was muttering about needing at least a week's rest which, in fact he got, as it snowed on and off for the next few days. When the four left for the second attempt Chris still looked tired and on the second day, getting to the end of the Fotheringham Ridge, he fell further and further behind in the new deep soft snow. Eventually, with much emotion Chris decided he had to come down if he wasn't going to be an encumbrance on the others. Elliot Robertson nobly volunteered to accompany him while Graham, Victor and Scott, who used the three pairs of snowshoes the expedition had prudently bought in Kathmandu, ploughed on.

At Base Camp I filmed the sad sight of Chris and Elliot plodding the last yards into camp. With his voice breaking, Chris explained what had happened, and we both wept. He had wanted this mountain so much for so long. But typically he bounced back within minutes, saying that it was all part of the game, and if anyone got to the top he'd be pleased – so long as everyone got down safely.

The other three pressed on in very dubious snow conditions until below Camp 3 Graham Little decided he had had enough and settled for a solo ascent of the Turquoise Flower, the subsidiary summit. Standing on top of a snow dome he could see all the way down the Frendo Spur to the minute orange blobs of Base Camp. The next day he made a safe descent. Victor and Scott meanwhile climbed to the West Summit, within two hours of the top, in deteriorating weather. Convinced that a satellite weather forecast promising better weather would prove correct, they retreated to their top camp and sat it out in increasing cold and misery for two more nights before being forced to retreat, which they did with trepidation and great effort but, more importantly, safely. Once again the expedition had failed but only just. There would be no point in returning for what was essentially a couple of hours' high-altitude hill walking to the highest point.

Charlie had said to me in the middle of the expedition that this looked like the last big Bonington extravaganza and we were lucky to be part of it. I could see what he meant but I wasn't so sure, and am still not, for Chris will always have a trick or two up his sleeve. However, I'm sure Charlie is correct in that big mountains (Sepu Kangri is only just under 7000 metres) are losing their attraction for Chris. He could never adopt a leadership role like the notorious Dr Karl Herrligkoffer, who never went higher than Base Camp, and Chris knows that all over Tibet, Nepal, India and Pakistan there are mountains of around 6000 metres that will give magnificent challenges for many years to come.

I felt as we returned once more over the Tibetan Plateau to Lhasa, that Chris had found, even in failure, a peace and tranquillity that had eluded him even on his successful expeditions. At sixty-four he was happy just to be part of this remote and inhospitable but stunningly beautiful environment. What you *did* in it, how well you performed were comparatively unimportant. He talked with Charlie about future explorations in the vastness of Northern Tibet. Despite the Internet, the satellite calls and 'News at Ten', Chris was indeed becoming a latter day Eric Shipton. Perhaps he will eventually even feel able to dispense with his electronic toys.

· 28 ·

What Next?

As CHRIS IN his sixties is still clocking up endless expeditions, the question could well be asked – where does he get the money? Book royalties, as the majority of authors will tell you, are more like unexpected surprises once the initial sales have dwindled; the slide library that he set up just about pays its way; so his main source of income is from lecturing, which has changed radically over the years. From the Eiger to Everest period, the Bonington lecture was relatively simple – he turned up with a projector and a tray of slides and that was more or less it. But after Everest '75, the presentation became ever more sophisticated, and from 1985 Chris employed Richard Haszko, a climber from Sheffield, as his roadie for the punishing annual lecture tour. For many years this consisted of a show almost every night, a drive next day to either the next venue or, more likely, the nearest available crag, where a climb would, as usual, take longer than planned, and then involve a panic-stricken drive to the next lecture hall – on one occasion this involved a police escort into Hull!

Richard remembers Chris being quite hard to work for in the early years, finding him highly strung and unable to relax. Since Chris climbed Everest, however, Richard, like so many others, has seen him become laid back and philosophical – an essential quality to possess in an activity like lecturing, where if anything can go wrong it will. Richard knows that every lecture venue will present different problems. The estate car that they travel around in is crammed with magic boxes that can cope with virtually any scenario. Spares of everything are carried but, as the technology has become more complex, cock-ups are harder to sort out. If, when using three projectors, the slides go out of synch, it can be a nightmare re-setting them, particularly if there is a large audience murmuring discontent. Richard's worst experiences were in Ireland, when he crashed the car in a dramatic collision with a lorry, and when he had set up a lecture in Mold, North Wales, for which Chris was held up by a motorway pile-up. Richard was forced to go on stage himself and tell Bonington stories to an ever more hostile audience until Chris turned up just before a riot broke out.

But the days of the large public lecture seem to be numbered. Rival attractions like satellite TV have meant that there is more adventure shown on the box than ever before. This, combined with the fact that Chris's expeditions are now to remote, unknown areas rather than to crowd-pulling names like K2 or the Eiger, has meant an inevitable decline in interest. In fact the winter of 1999 will see Chris's swan song as far as the public lecture tour is concerned, though doubtless he will continue to do the odd one. What has grown dramatically in the last ten years is the business presentation. This is a far more demanding activity but, it has to be said, can be extremely lucrative. It also involves a lot of travel to virtually anywhere in the world for a single show.

Bonington normally uses the 1975 Everest expedition as a metaphor for the running of a successful business. Essentially, he proposes that if everyone has the same goal, understands the problems, knows their own role (and their limitations), then the company will stand a much higher chance of success. He makes the point that in an expedition, as in business, you can have too many chiefs and not enough Indians, and he learnt that it was important to have people who were perfectly happy to act in a support role and (in business terms) didn't want to run the company.

His presentations fall roughly into two categories. The motivational one is where Chris will interact with his audience and set up question and answer sessions and use role-play as a way of getting people to understand how decisions can be made. The other type is the more straightforward after-dinner occasion. In either scenario he understands that, however serious his message, most audiences still want to be entertained and impressed and, as a change from staring at endless diagrams and pie-charts on overhead projectors, his shows provide a breath of fresh air to jaded middle-managers waiting for the bar to open. Certainly, he has never been so busy or had such varied assignments and, as ever, he is keen to ensure he is giving value for money.

By the time these words have appeared in print, Chris Bonington will be receiving his old age pension; a sentence that is hard to believe. He will, in all probability, have led his annual E2, preferably on his birthday, and he will be as busy or busier than ever. Of course, climbing, the pure simple joy of scaling a piece of rock, a snowslope, or iced-up gully is still what makes Bonington tick.

While this book was being written Chris had a salutary reminder of what climbing can involve. He took his half-brother Gerald to Lochnagar to climb Parallel Gully B, a classic Scottish Grade 5 ice climb. Chris had led the crux pitch, placed a good nut runner in a horizontal crack and run the rope out to the top of a steep snows-lope. He had taken what, in hindsight, he admits was a totally inadequate belay on both the picks of his axes inserted into hard snow. Gerald, following, almost got up the crux, which was only a few metres above the start of the pitch, when both his axes ripped out of the ice. He fell into soft snow but to his alarm he didn't stop and fell about another fifteen metres before he was suddenly jerked to a halt by the rope. Only ten metres above was Chris, 'thrashing about in the snow'. Where had he come from?

When Gerald fell off, the jerk had instantly pulled Chris off his stance and his belaying axes pulled straight out. Suddenly Chris was plunging headfirst through the air.

'I had a snap shot of the snowslope funnelling into the top of the tight chimney of Parallel Gully B – I had 200 metres to go – I'm going to die. I wondered if it was going to hurt when I smashed into rock on the way down. And then I stopped, still facing down-wards on the snowslope above Gerald. We were both suspended on either end of the rope from the one runner I had placed . . . I had flown about forty metres.'

Amazingly, Chris had only broken a couple of ribs and was bruised and shocked. Another party came to their rescue and they were able to finish the climb in the dark. I heard about the accident a few days later and rang Chris.

'I hear I was within a whisker of writing a bestseller.'

He *did* laugh, but with broken ribs it hurt him. He was still shocked and contrite at how nearly he had killed them both, with all the grief and misery it would bring to their families and friends.

It is now forty-eight years since the tall, rather earnest schoolboy in flapping plimsolls did his first climb at Harrisons Rocks; now the hair is grey and thinning, the beard white, but the almost child-like raw enthusiasm is as fresh as ever. In 2000 he is planning his 'Family Millennium' expedition to, one hopes, an easy mountain in Eastern Nepal with Gerald, Daniel and Rupert, their wives and the family doctor. I reminded him that there is a golf course right outside Kathmandu airport – perhaps he could persuade Wendy to go as well?

I don't think for a moment that Chris's serious climbing days are anywhere near over. He will plan expeditions for as long as he is able to put one foot in front of another. Whatever the project, whether Greenland, Antarctica or Tibet, one thing will be certain, that Chris Bonington will be doing something new. In an age where media-obsessed poseurs can be decorated for stringing a few pack-age holidays together, Bonington is a true explorer. On his last visit to England, Reinhold Messner observed that British climbers still persistently under-rate their most successful mountaineer ever who, paradoxically, still commands immense respect throughout the world. If any doubting young climber needs persuading, go and climb Malbogies in the Avon Gorge in plimsolls, or Coronation Street on a snowy winter's day, or the Medlar on Raven Crag of Thirlmere, or the Central Pillar of Frêney, armed only with pebbles for the crux or . . . The list of achievements, like the man who made it, just goes on and on . . .

Climbing Record

(updated from *Mountaineer* by Chris Bonington, Diadem Books)

Symbols: * *first ascent*, *w *first winter ascent*, † *first British ascent*.

1951 Ash Tree Gully *Dinas Bach* (Tom Blackburn) – first climb; Hope *Idwal Slabs* (Charles Verender) – first lead.

1952 Chimney Route *Clogwyn Du'r Arddu* (Dave Pullin); Rana Temporia *Quinag* * (Tony) – first new route, a VS.

1953 Agag's Groove *Buachaille Etive Mor* *W (Hamish MacInnes, Kerr McPhaill, John Hammond, G. McIntosh) – first winter climb; Crowberry Ridge Direct *w and Raven's Gully *Buachaille Etive Mor* *w (Hamish MacInnes); Hangover *Clogwyn y Grochan* (Geoff Francis) – first 'Brown' route.

1954 Surplomb *Clogwyn y Grochan* (Steve Lane) – second ascent.

1955 Macavity *Avon Gorge* * (Geoff Francis) – first new route on Avon's Main Wall.

1957 First alpine season: South-East Face of Aig. du Tacul * (Hamish MacInnes). Steger Route *Cattinacio* and Yellow Edge and Demuth Route *Tre Cime* (Jim Swallow); North Wall Direct of Cima Una † (German climber). Malbogies *Avon Gorge* * (Geoff Francis, Henry Rogers).

1958 Bonatti Pillar of Petit Dru † (Hamish MacInnes, Don Whillans and Paul Ross, with Walter Phillip and Richard Blach); West Face of Petites Jorasses † (Ronnie Wathen).

1959 Comici/Dimai, Brandler/Hasse † and Cassin/Ratti routes *Tre*

Cime (Gunn Clark); Woubits (Jim O'Neill) and Mostest (Jim Swallow) *Clogwyn Du'r Arddu* – second ascents.

1960 Annapurna 2 * by West Ridge *Nepal* (Dick Grant and Ang Nyima) – expedition led by Col. James Roberts; King Cobra *Skye* * (Tom Patey).

1961 Nuptse * by South Face *Nepal* (part of second summit team with Jim Swallow, Ang Pemba and Les Brown – first pair: Dennis Davis and Tashi) – expedition led by Joe Walmsley; Central Pillar of Frêney, Mt. Blanc * (Don Whillans, Ian Clough and Jan Djuglosz).

1962 Trango *Castell Cidwm* * (Joe Brown); Ichabod *Scafell* (Mike Thompson) – second ascent; Schmid/Krebs Route *Karwendal* † (Don Whillans); Walker Spur of Grandes Jorasses (Ian Clough); North Wall of the Eiger † (Ian Clough).

1963 Central Tower of Paine * by West Face *Chile* (Don Whillans) – expedition led by Barrie Page.

1964 North Face of Pointe Migot * and West Ridge of Aig. de Lepiney * (Tom Patey, Joe Brown and Robin Ford); Andrich/ Fae Route on Civetta (Jim McCarthy); Medlar * (Martin Boysen) and Totalitarian * (Mike Thompson) *Raven Crag, Thirlmere.*

1965 Coronation Street *Cheddar* * (Tony Greenbank); The Holy Ghost *Scafell* * (Mike Thompson); West Face of the Cardinal * (Tom Patey and another); West Face Direct of Aig. du Plan * (Lito Tejada Flores); North-East Ridge of Dent du Midi * (Rusty Baillie and John Harlin); Right-Hand Pillar of Brouillard, Mt. Blanc * (Rusty Baillie, John Harlin and Brian Robertson).

1966 North Face Direct of the Eiger * – in supporting role; Old Man of Hoy *Orkneys* * (Tom Patey and Rusty Baillie).

1968 North Face of Aig. d'Argentière (Dougal Haston) – in winter.

1969 March Hare's Gully *Applecross* *w (Tom Patey); Great Gully of Garbh Bheinn *w (Tom Patey and Don Whillans).

1970 South Face of Annapurna *Nepal* * – leader of expedition – summit reached by Dougal Haston and Don Whillans.

1971 East Face of Moose's Tooth *Alaska* – attempt with Jim McCarthy, Tom Frost and Sandy Bill curtailed by bad weather; White Wizard *Scafell* * (Nick Estcourt).

1972 South-West Face of Everest *Nepal* – leader of expedition curtailed by cold and high wind; Great Gully of Grandes Jorasses

(Dougal Haston with Mick Burke and Bev Clarke in support) – attempt in winter.

1973 Brammah * by the South Ridge *India* (Nick Escourt) – joint leader of expedition with Balwant Sandhu.

1974 Changabang * by East Ridge *India* (Martin Boysen, Doug Scott, Dougal Haston, Tashi and Balwant Sandhu) – joint leader of expedition with Sandhu.

1975 North Face Direct of Aig. du Triolet *w (Dougal Haston); South-West Face of Everest *Nepal* * – leader of expedition – summit reached by Dougal Haston and Doug Scott, Pete Boardman, Pertemba and Mick Burke(?).

1976 North Face of Pt.20,309 *Kishtwar, India* (Ronnie Richards) – attempt gaining two-thirds height; East Ridge of Mt. Cook and Symes Ridge of Mt. Tasman *New Zealand* (Nick Banks, Keith Woodford and Bob Cunningham).

1977 The Ogre * by the South Face *Pakistan* (Nick Escourt) and the West Ridge (Doug Scott) – the South Face climb ended at the West Summit. Clive Rowland and Mo Anthoine took part in the West Ridge ascent to the foot of the summit tower.

1978 West Ridge of K2 *Pakistan* – leader of expedition curtailed after death of Nick Escourt in an avalanche below Camp 2.

1980 Pts 6200m * and 5400 * *Kongur Group, China* (Al Rouse and Mike Ward) – climbed during a reconnaissance expedition.

1981 Kongur * by the West Ridge *China* (Al Rouse, Pete Boardman and Joe Tasker) – expedition led by Mike Ward.

1982 North-East Ridge of Everest *Tibet* – leader of expedition curtailed after disappearance of Pete Boardman and Joe Tasker.

1983 Orion Face of Ben Nevis (Stuart Fife); South-West Summit of Shivling * by the South-East Ridge *India* (Jim Fotheringham); Mt. Vinson *Antarctica* † (Dick Bass, Tae Maeda, Yuichior Miura, Steve Marts, Rick Ridgeway and Frank Wells) – soloed final section prior to ascent by the others. Expedition led jointly by Bass and Wells.

1984 West Ridge of Karun Koh *Pakistan* (Ikram Khan, Maqsood Ahmed and Al Rouse) – leader of expedition curtailed by bad weater; Cruel Sister *Pavey Ark* (Jim Loxham) – first E3 lead.

1985 South-East Ridge of Everest *Nepal* (Odd Eliassen, Bjorn Myrer-Lund, Pertemba, Ang Lhakpa and Dawa Nuru) – expedition led by Arne Naess.

1986 North-East Pillar of Norliga Skagastozstind *Norway* (Odd Eilassen); Athanor *Goat Crag* (Dave Absalom) – first 6a lead. Yellow Edge *Avon Gorge* (Steve Berry); South Pillar of Grosse Drusenturm *Rätikon* and North-East Diedre of Brenta Alta (Jim Fotheringham).

1987 South-West Buttress of Menlungtse West *Tibet* – leader of expedition curtailed by bad weather.

1988 Menlungste West * by the West Ridge and Face *Tibet* – leader of expedition – summit reached by Andy Fanshawe and Alan Hinkes.

1991 Lemon Mountains *Greenland* – as climbing leader with Robin Knox-Johnston.

1992 Panch Chuli II * *Kumaon, India* West Ridge, with Graham Little on Indian/British Kumaon expedition – joint leader with Harish Kapadia.

1993 Chisel *, Ivory Tower *, Needle * *Lemon Mountains, Greenland* (Lowther, Little, Ferguson).

1993 Elbrus and North-East Ridge of Ushba *Caucasus*.

1994 Rangrik Rang * *Kinnaur, India* – Indian/British expedition with Harish Kapadia.

1995 Drangnag-Ri * *Rolwaling, India* (Hoibakk, Myrer-Lund, Pema Dorge, Lhakpu Gyalu).

1996 Sepu Kangri *Tibet* – reconnaissance with Charles Clarke.

1997 Sepu Kangri *Tibet* – expedition defeated by heavy snowfall.

1998 Sepu Kangri *Tibet* – Muir and Saunders reach West Shoulder; Seamo Uylmitok * Little.

A Select Bibliography

Al Alvarez, *Feeding the Rat, Profile of a Climber*. (Bloomsbury, 1988). A biography of Mo Anthoine with an account of the Ogre epic.

Geoff Birtles, *Alan Rouse, A Mountaineer's Life*. (Unwin Hyman, 1987). Contains a chapter by Chris Bonington on Kongur exploration and Karun Koh expedition.

Chris Bonington, *The Next Horizon*. (Victor Gollancz, 1973). Second volume of CB's autobiography.

Chris Bonington, *Everest, South-West Face*. (Hodder and Stoughton, 1973). Account of unsuccessful 1972 expedition.

Chris Bonington, *Everest the Hard Way*. (Hodder and Stoughton, 1976). Successful ascent of the South-West Face.

Chris Bonington, *Quest for Adventure*. (Hodder and Stoughton, 1981). A history of adventure since the Second World War.

Chris Bonington, *Kongur, China's Elusive Summit*. (Hodder and Stoughton, 1982). Exploration and first ascent of a major peak in Sinkiang.

Chris Bonington and Charles Clarke. *Everest, the Unclimbed Ridge*. (Hodder and Stoughton, 1983). Account of tragic disappearance of Peter Boardman and Joe Tasker.

Chris Bonington, *The Everest Years, a Climber's Life*. (Hodder and Stoughton, 1986). Third volume of CB's autobiography.

Chris Bonington, *Mountaineer*. (Diadem Books, 1989). A coffee table photographic autobiography.

Chris Bonington, *The Climbers, a History of Mountaineering*. (BBC Books/Hodder and Stoughton, 1992).

Chris Bonington and Robin Knox-Johnston, *Sea, Ice and Rock*. (Hodder and Stoughton, 1992). Account of sailing to and climbing in Greenland.

Chris Bonington and Charles Clarke, *Tibet's Secret Mountain, the Triumph of Sepu Kangri*. (Weidenfeld & Nicolson, 1999).

Jim Curran, *Suspended Sentences*. (Hodder and Stoughton, 1991). Chapters on Kongur, St Kilda and filming 'The Climbers' at Nanga Parbat Base Camp.

Andy Fanshawe, *Coming Through*. (Hodder and Stoughton, 1990). Account of second Menlungtse expedition.

Peter Gillman and Dougal Haston, *Eiger Direct*. (Collins, 1996).

Peter Gillman, *In Balance*. (Hodder and Stoughton, 1989). Contains extended article about CB and several chapters about Everest, Old Man of Hoy, etc.

Alan Hankinson, *Changabang*. (Heinemann, 1975). A joint effort by six authors but put together by Hankinson.

Dougal Haston, *In High Places*. (Cassell, 1972). Haston's autobiography.

Tom Patey, *One Man's Mountains*. (Victor Gollancz, 1971). Several articles and songs about CB.

John Roskelley, *Last Days*. (Hodder and Stoughton, 1992). Account of a Menlungtse expedition and reference to Yeti hunts.

Victor Saunders, *No Place to Fall*. (Hodder and Stoughton, 1994). Contains account of Panch Chuli expedition.

Doug Scott, *Himalayan Climber*. (Diadem Books, 1992). A coffee table photographic autobiography with chapters on Everest, Ogre, Changabang, etc.

Joe Tasker, *Savage Arena*. (Methuen, 1982). Autobiography with chapter on 1978 K2 Expedition.

Walt Unsworth, *Everest*. (Allen Lane, 1981). Standard reference book to history of Everest.

Ken Wilson, *Hard Rock*. (Granada, 1974). Description by CB of Old Man of Hoy.

INDEX